WITHDRAWN

Woodrow Wilson's China Policy

1913-1917

TO

TU-HUA AND P'IN-WEN

WOODROW WILSON'S
CHINA POLICY
1913-1917

By Tien-yi Li

1969
OCTAGON BOOKS
New York

Reprinted 1969

by special arrangement with Twayne Publishers

OCTAGON BOOKS

A DIVISION OF FARRAR, STRAUS & GIROUX, INC.

19 Union Square West

New York, N. Y. 10003

AM

LIBRARY OF CONGRESS CATALOG CARD NUMBER: 79-96186

Printed in U.S.A. by

TAYLOR PUBLISHING COMPANY

DALLAS, TEXAS

Preface

This volume begins with the academic career of Woodrow Wilson who, no deep student of the Far East, only casually touched upon this area in his writings. His knowledge of China was chiefly acquired through his contact with American missionaries and friends working in that country. With a sense of pride and superiority he thought that the United States as a leading Pacific power should help to implant the basic principles of Christianity and democracy in Chinese soil. Out of a profound sympathy for the weak, oppressed and underdeveloped peoples, he became benevolently inclined toward China as an independent nation.

President Woodrow Wilson's approach to Chinese problems was tactically different from that of his predecessor, although both of them basically championed traditional American policy. Wilson boldly reversed the practice of international cooperation, the basis of Taft's diplomacy. Taft had favored the cooperation of American bankers, with the blessing of the department of state, in an international financial consortium so as to chaperon the bankers of the European imperialistic powers lest they impose on China's integrity contrary to the Hay policy. Wilson favored the Hay policy but would not lend the countenance of the United States government to selected or favored American bankers. To the surprise of the world, Wilson impulsively announced his disapproval of continued participation of the American banking group in the Six-Power Consortium. Soon after, he accorded *de jure* recognition to the Republic of China independently of other powers.

For the sake of China, Woodrow Wilson encouraged President Yüan Shih-k'ai against the more democratic impulses of the opposing Kuomintang. He did this to strengthen China's internal unity and order without which true democracy would be unable later to take root. In spite of his personal aversion to Yüan's imperialistic and dictatorial leanings, he never failed to give Yüan diplomatic and moral support. His recognition of the Peking government and his favorable attitude toward the monarchical movement bore witness to his fervent hope for a united China under Yüan's leadership—democracy could come later. To Wilson's disappointment, Yüan finally proved a complete failure in leading the new republic into unity and solidarity.

After the outbreak of the First World War, Japan took advantage of the situation to advance her long-cherished designs upon China. By her seizure of Shantung and her presentation of the Twenty-One Demands she intended to place China under her virtual protection and control. The threat to China's integrity was a vexing problem for Woodrow Wilson. Increasingly occupied with other difficulties confronting the United States, he found it hard effectively to check Japanese aggression. All he could do was to lodge protests and caveats on paper; but these at least kept the Japanese out of Fukien and thus helped somewhat to temper the Twenty-One Demands to something short of a complete Japanese protectorate over China.

During his first term of office as President of the United States, Woodrow Wilson, more idealistic, inexperienced and unsophisticated than his predecessor, did not fully grasp the hard realities of international politics. Both economically and politically his China policy failed to come up to his own expectations. His good intentions and moral encouragement, however, won him China's gratitude.

A continuation of the present study would lead to such problems as the Lansing-Ishii Agreement, the organization of

6

a new consortium, China's participation in the war, the Shantung question at the Peace Conference of Paris, the League of Nations, and other Chinese problems left unsettled in the First World War. But these topics are beyond the scope of this book, a study of the China policy of Woodrow Wilson from 1913 to 1917. I hope to examine the later phases of his China policy in a subsequent volume.

Chinese personal names and book titles have been Romanized according to the Wade-Giles system. The Chinese characters for them are given in the appendices at the end of this book. Some personal names which have not been spelt strictly according to this system, but the spelling of which has been generally accepted in the West, are not changed, while their correct Romanized forms are given in parentheses when first introduced. In the case of Chinese place names, the forms which have acquired an accepted Western spelling are used.

Words are certainly inadequate to express my indebtedness to Professor Samuel Flagg Bemis under whose tutelage and guidance I developed a keen interest in the history of Sino-American relations and did my research work on the present subject and without whose inspiring and persistent encouragement this volume could not have been completed. In its original form, this study was a dissertation presented for the degree of Doctor of Philosophy in Yale University. My thanks are also due to the staffs of the Sterling Memorial Library of Yale University, of the Division of Manuscripts of the Library of Congress, and of the National Archives. In the preparation of this book, they aided me by granting access to their extensive collections of papers and documents relating to my field of study. I am particularly obliged to Professors Hajo Holborn, Leonard W. Labaree, Kenneth S. Latourette, and Harry R. Rudin who read my thesis and offered valuable criticisms and corrections; and to Professors George A. Kennedy and Wu-chi Liu and Mr. Joseph J. Burgess who made indispensable suggestions for improvements in style. I should like also to acknowledge my appreciation to Professor Richard L. Walker who found time to read the manuscript critically in his busiest hours; to Mrs. Alice Yü who checked the typescript; and to Mrs. Linda Ong who helped me with the proofreading.

Grateful acknowledgment is made to the publishers for permission to reprint from the following copyrighted material: Woodrow Wilson, "Democracy and Efficiency," in the *Atlantic Monthly,* vol. 87 (Boston, the Atlantic Monthly Company, 1901); Willard Straight, "China's Loan Negotiations," in George H. Blakeslee, ed., *Recent developments in China* (New York, the Hafner Publishing Company, Inc., 1913); and William Jennings Bryan and Mary Baird Bryan, *The Memoirs of William Jennings Bryan* (Philadelphia, the John C. Winston Company, 1925). Finally let me express my thanks to Mrs. Ruth Bryan Rohde for permission to quote from the papers of William Jennings Bryan deposited in the Library of Congress, and to Mrs. Woodrow Wilson for permission to quote from the papers of President Woodrow Wilson also deposited in the Library of Congress.

TIEN-YI LI

Yale University
Sept. 15, 1952

Contents

CHAPTER ONE

Academic Backgrounds

Woodrow Wilson's interest in the Far East dates back to his academic years, to the turn of the last century. As a moralist and a preacher of international peace and justice Wilson seems to have disapproved of American territorial expansion abroad. The Spanish-American War, according to him, was simply a repetition of the experience of the United States in the war with Mexico. But what had been done could not be undone. Once a physical foothold had been established in the far Pacific, it was difficult to step back, and the United States was bound to stay there.[1] In a real sense the acquisition of the Philippines was but a natural point in the development of the American nation. It ushered in a new era, presented a new frontage toward the Orient, and placed the United States in the presence of new forces which were destined to make the politics of the twentieth century different from those of the past.[2] It clearly pointed out and added weight to the fact that America as a newly grown-up power in an interdependent world was sure to play a role, and a most important role, too, on the stage of politics in a part of the world where it had heretofore maintained a largely commercial and missionary interest.

Wilson had always been inclined to read surpassing merit into British and American political ideals and moral principles. He was no deep student of the Orient. It was Western political thought which had engrossed his attention. He does not appear ever to have made any attempt at a critical comparison between

Western and Eastern scales of values. He took it for granted that the culture of the West was superior to that of the East. It was the dictate of history that Western standards should be spread among and inculcated in the less advanced peoples. American annexation of the Philippine Islands was not the cause, but rather an indication of the major role America was in duty bound to play in the indoctrination and transformation of the Oriental peoples. With a sense of pride and superiority he remarked in 1901:

We might not have seen our duty, had the Philippines not fallen to us by the willful fortune of war; but it would have been our duty, nevertheless, to play the part we now see ourselves obliged to play. The East is to be opened and transformed, whether we will or no; the standards of the West are to be imposed upon it; nations and peoples which have stood still the centuries through are to be quickened, and made part of the universal world of commerce and ideas which has so steadily been a-making by the advance of European power from age to age.[3]

It was America's responsibility, thought Professor Wilson, to impart her principles of self-help, order and self-control, and her drill and habit of law and obedience to those undeveloped nations which in the course of their political development needed America's character and good principles more urgently than her political methods and institutions. By sympathy and example, rather than by force and coercion, America should make her influence felt, and thus enable those peoples to stand on an equal footing with the other nations of the world. The American part in fulfilling this obligation should be direct in the Philippines as an American possession; it should be indirect in China as an independent state.[4]

It was also Wilson's idea that the implantation of Western principles was not the only justification of what America had attempted in the Orient. In his thought altruism and self-interest often operated hand in hand.[5] The prosperity of the

American nation through expansion of trade should be taken into account equally, and trade was an effective means by which the spread of ideas could be realized. Wilson thought that people who traded in goods also traded in ideas.[6] He perspicaciously realized the importance of the great Far Eastern market which all the world coveted—"the market for which statesmen as well as merchants must plan and play their game of competition, the market to which diplomacy, and if need be power, must make an open way."[7] It would be ideal if America, in carrying out her policy in the Far East, particularly in China, could serve both purposes at the same time: the instillation of moral standards and the protection of rightful interests.

The remarkable success with which America exerted her influence and played her "indirect" part in the Chinese Boxer Rebellion of 1900 measured up to Wilson's ideal. It was in this great upheaval that the American voice "told for peace, conciliation, justice, and yet for a firm vindication of sovereign rights, at every turn of the difficult business."[8] When he mentioned the American troops as having been among the first to evacuate China, and spoke of John Hay as having "a calm poise of judgment," and "a steady confidence,"[9] he implied approval of the open door policy together with its corollary of the preservation of China's territorial and administrative integrity.

In his scholastic years Wilson held liberal views with regard to immigration. When he wrote of the Chinese exclusion bill which Congress had passed in 1879 but President Hayes had vetoed,[10] he showed sympathy and admiration for the thrifty and skilful Chinese immigrants on the Pacific coast, who could "live upon a handful of rice" and "work for a pittance," and whom the Caucasian laborers, being unable to compete with them, had murdered on a large scale in "wanton attacks upon the Chinese quarters of the towns."[11] His sympathy was even more conspicuous when he discussed the Chinese exclusion act

13

of 1892, which had been passed as a result of a popular clamor against the entrance of Chinese immigrants into the United States. The Chinese laborers, he asserted, had been feared, hated, and excluded from America not because of their alien habits or their disposition to stand aloof from other people around them, but because of "their skill, their intelligence, their hardy power of labor, their knack at succeeding and driving duller rivals out." [12]

Later as a candidate for the presidency he still kept his liberal views about immigration in general,[13] but his opinions on Oriental immigration in particular changed in the discretion and expediency of the presidential campaign. He came forward in open support of the exclusion of the Chinese and the Japanese on the ground that they were incapable of being assimilated into a homogeneous race.[14] Apparently presidential aspirations made him change his mind on this issue. His sympathy for and attitude toward China as a nation, however, remained unchanged.

Wilson, who valued Christian principles above the material advantages of modern times, naturally took a keen interest in American missionary activities in China. Through his cousin, S. I. Woodbridge, a lifelong missionary and editor in China,[15] he kept in close touch with the spread of the Gospel in that country. He had known Woodbridge since boyhood and had always been on intimate terms with him. Corresponding as he did with his cousin from time to time, he was acquainted not only with the missionary work in the vast Chinese empire but with Chinese political and social trends and events as well. After his election as President of the United States he heard even more often from Woodbridge who was at all times ready to speak for the Chinese people and to supply valuable information.

Woodbridge was not the only American evangelistic worker in China who was in contact with Wilson at times. Charles

E. Scott, who had studied at Princeton and for many years engaged in missionary work in the Chinese Province of Shantung, also kept his old teacher informed about general situations in China. Being earnest, energetic, sympathetic with the Chinese struggle for freedom, and suspicious of Japan's aggressive designs, he often informally wrote long reports on China, which seem to have influenced or enlightened Wilson as much as the letters from Woodbridge. Another occasional correspondent was Bishop J. W. Bashford, one of the most influential and prominent men in the American community in Peking. When the Chinese Revolution broke out in 1911, Governor Wilson asked him to write "about Chinese matters of interest to the United States." [16] After that, Bashford, well known as lecturer, educator, and church leader in America, seldom failed to make his voice heard in Washington on matters regarding China. President Wilson had a high respect for his opinions.

From the very beginning Woodrow Wilson had taken a profound interest in the Princeton work in Peking, that is, the Y. M. C. A. of Peking manned and financed by Princeton in connection with the International Committee of Young Men's Christian Associations. He had been generous in his subscription to the work and had recognized its importance and helpfullness to China. When Professor Lucius Hopkins Miller of Princeton University asked him to write a letter voicing his interest and faith in the work, "couched in such terms as you would be willing to have appear publicly," [17] the President responded with heartfelt sympathy and commended the "statesmanlike scope and consequence" with which the work had been carried on. [18]

Between Wilson's election and his inauguration as President of the United States, the Chinese problem came to the fore. Negotiations for an international loan to China and the question of the recognition of the Chinese Republic were being widely discussed in newspapers and pressed for solution. Under such circumstances the President-elect could not but give attention to the Chinese situation. In a letter to John S. Thomson he professed that he was studying it and added that he had a profound and lasting interest in China's fortunes.[19] In response to Sun Yat-sen's congratulations he told the Chinese leader that he had "watched with the keenest interest the recent course of events in China" and had "felt the strongest sympathy with every movement which looks towards giving the people of the great empire of China the liberty for which they have so long been yearning and preparing themselves." [20]

The selection of a competent diplomatic representative to the Chinese post invited Wilson's immediate attention. He agreed with William Jennings Bryan that the United States should send to that country a man of marked Christian character, because he thought certain remarkable services could be rendered there through such a man.[21] He remarked: "The thing most prominent in my mind is that the men now most active in establishing a new government and a new regime for China are many of them members of the Y. M. C. A., and many of them also men trained in American universities. The Christian influence, direct or indirect, is very prominently at the front and I need not say, ought to be kept there." [22] Bryan himself would have been the right man to represent the United States in China from the Christian point of view. Bishop Bashford had started a movement to raise the American legation at Peking to an embassy and to urge Bryan to take up the ambassadorship.[23] President Wilson's political mentor, Colonel Edward M. House, promised to try Bryan out on the idea, if Wilson granted permission.[24] Bashford made a personal appeal to Bryan, believing that by taking up the post of ambassador to China the latter, with his "tact and unselfish statesmanship," could gain influence with the leaders of China and above all "could render a service which God would greatly bless and which the whole world would recognize." [25] But Wilson's decision to appoint Bryan as secretary of state ended the movement altogether.

Wilson then turned his consideration to the ex-president of Harvard University, Charles W. Eliot. Wilson told House that he was profoundly sympathetic with the Chinese people and wished to do everything possible to assist them. To his mind Eliot would be an ideal choice to help uplift the Chinese in their common struggle for self-help. House suggested that Jesse Grant, a son of President Ulysses S. Grant and a loyal Democratic supporter of Wilson, desired the Chinese post, but Wilson did not consider that suggestion.[26] The President-elect wrote to Eliot: "I am very much concerned that our representatives in China and Japan should be of the best quality the country affords. I believe that there is probably nothing [that] more nearly touches the future development of the world than what will happen in the East and it ought to happen, so far as our influence extends, under the best possible guidance." And he expressed his wish to have a conference with Eliot about that very matter.[27] Accordingly he saw Eliot and offered the Chinese post in such a complimentary way that the latter consented to take it into serious consideration. After the interview he intimated to House the hope that he could enhance the American foreign service by selections as comparable to Eliot as possible.[28]

Bryan, on the contrary, thought that Eliot had better be sent to any country other than China.[29] He told House that Wilson's selection for the Chinese post was the poorest one that could be made because "Eliot was a Unitarian and did not believe in the divinity of Christ, and the new Chinese civilization was founded upon the Christian movement there."[30] After consultation with his family Eliot declined the offer because it met with their disapproval.[31] Wilson was thus saved from a conflict of opinions with his future secretary of state. But he felt very much distressed about the matter, and his disappoint-

17

ment was naturally proportionate to the enthusiasm with which he had urged the Chinese mission upon Eliot.[32]

After Eliot's rejection of the post President Wilson continued to give his thought and concern to the problem. He decided to sound out the Y. M. C. A. leader John R. Mott, and wrote to Bryan asking for comment on his suggestion of Mott. In keeping with Bryan's thoughts he laid emphasis on the Christian influence in China and the importance of maintaining that influence there. He knew Mott very well and depicted him as gifted with statesmanlike qualities, sufficiently acquainted with the Chinese situation, and amply trusted all over the Christian world. Mott was at that time travelling in China and, in case of acceptance of the tender, could remain there to assume duties as American minister.[33] In another letter to Bryan, Wilson reiterated his determination to find "exceptional men" for all the chief diplomatic posts. By exceptional men he meant "men who will see and think"—Mott was certainly one of such men.[34] Bryan heartily endorsed Mott.[35] Wilson formally tendered the post to Mott on February 24, adding that the Chinese mission seemed to him of great importance both for China and for the world. To his disappointment he again met with a courteous but explicit refusal. In spite of Wilson's request for reconsideration and the appeal from many others Mott remained resolute and declined for the second time.[36] Thus the question of appointment of an American minister to China was postponed and remained unsolved until Paul S. Reinsch was recommended.

Before his inauguration as President of the United States, Wilson, with a sense of superiority, had visualized the role that America should play in China in spreading democratic ideals, imposing Christian morals, and helping the Chinese people toward order and self-help; had spontaneously cultivated a warm and sympathetic feeling for the Chinese in their struggle for liberty and self-government; had indirectly but sensibly

18

acquired a knowledge of the Chinese Christian influence and political situation; and above all had unmistakably realized the importance of the development of American trade as well as of the protection of American legitimate interests within the Chinese borders. His anxiety to choose one of the most competent men for the Chinese post bore witness to his eager interest in friendly and tutelary relations between China and the United States. In short, before he actually took the reins of government, Woodrow Wilson was predisposed to a benevolent China policy. Buoyed up by his own moral attitude, it rested on American Protestant missionary influence and national idealism tinctured by the exigencies of presidential politics.

From this background the new President approached the problems of China and the Far East, amidst the hard realities of international politics on the eve of the First World War. First pressing for decision was the relation of the United States Government to the international banking consortium and its loan to China.

NOTES:

1 Woodrow Wilson, *A History of the American People* (5 vols., New York and London, 1902), V, 296. Hereafter cited as W. Wilson, *History*.

2 Woodrow Wilson, "Democracy and Efficiency," *Atlantic Monthly*, vol. 87 (1901), 292. Hereafter cited as W. Wilson, "Democracy and Efficiency."

3 *Ibid.*, p. 297.

4 *Ibid.*, pp. 297-298.

5 William Diamond, *The Economic Thought of Woodrow Wilson* (Baltimore, 1943), p. 133. Hereafter cited as W. Diamond, *Economic Thought.*

6 *Ibid.*, pp. 136-137.

7 W. Wilson, *History,* V, 296.

8 *Ibid.*, V, 299.

9 *Ibid.*, V, 299.

10   Wilson must have referred to the so-called Fifteen Passenger Bill of 1879 passed by Congress but vetoed by Hayes. For information about this bill, see Tyler Dennett, *Americans in Eastern Asia* (New York, reprint ed., 1941), pp. 541-542. Hereafter cited as T. Dennett, *Eastern Asia.*

11   W. Wilson, History, V, 185-186.

12   *Ibid.,* V, 213-214.

13   On many occasions Wilson as a presidential candidate expressed liberal views on immigration in general. In a letter to L. E. Miller of the Jewish newspaper *Warheit,* for example, he said: "I, like other Democrats, have always held liberal views with regard to immigration. I feel that it would be inconsistent with our historical character as a nation if we did not offer a very hearty welcome to every honest man and woman who comes to this country to seek a permanent home and a new opportunity." See Wilson to L. E. Miller, August 23, 1912, Library of Congress, Papers of Woodrow Wilson, series II, box 26. Hereafter cited as Wilson Papers, followed by the series number and the box number. For an unfavorable interpretation of Wilson's views as expressed in that letter, see the president of the American Association of Foreign Newspapers to President Taft, August 29, 1912, Library of Congress, Papers of William Howard Taft, presidential series No. 2, box 75. Hereafter cited as Taft Papers, followed by the series number and the box number. Here Wilson was blamed for having held liberal views in regard to Chinese immigration only and for having been unfriendly to immigrants from Europe.

14   In a letter (quoted in the *Independent* for October 10, 1912) to the ex-mayor of San Francisco, James D. Phelan, Wilson said: "In the matter of Chinese and Japanese coolie immigration I stand for the national policy of exclusion. The whole question is one of assimilation of diverse races. We cannot make a homogeneous population out of people who do not blend with the Caucasian race. Their lower standards of living as laborers will crowd out the white agriculturists and will in other fields prove a most serious industrial menace. . . . Oriental coolieism will give us another race problem to solve, and surely we have had our lessons." Wilson to James D. Phelan, date not given by the editor, requoted from *Independent,* vol. 73 (1912), p. 863.

15   S. I. Woodbridge finished his studies at Princeton and went to China in 1882. Two years later in Japan he married Jeanie

Woodrow, Wilson's cousin on the maternal side and also the companion of Wilson's first wife since childhood. After their marriage he and his wife lived at Chinkiang in China for almost twenty years, energetically and enthusiastically engaged in evangelistic and literary work. In 1902 they moved to Shanghai at the call of the China Pan-Presbyterian Conference. There they started the *Chinese Christian Intelligencer,* a weekly newspaper in Chinese which was built from nothing but was soon widely circulated both in China and abroad. In 1909 Woodbridge also became the editor of the *Bi-Monthly Bulletin,* a paper printed in the English language. See John W. Davis, "In Memoriam—Mrs. Jeanie Woodrow Woodbridge, Southern Presbyterian Mission", *Chinese Recorder,* July, 1913. This article is attached to a letter from Wilson to Woodbridge, August 23, 1913, Wilson Papers, II, 38.

16   J. W. Bashford to Wilson, March 12, 1915, Wilson Papers, II, 77.

17   Lucius Hopkins Miller to Wilson, May 1, 1913, *ibid.,* II, 35.

18   Wilson to Lucius Hopkins Miller, May 5, 1913, *ibid.,* II, 35.

19   Harley Notter, *The Origins of the Foreign Policy of Woodrow Wilson* (Baltimore, 1937), p. 202. Hereafter cited as H. Notter, *Origins.*

20   Requoted from R. S. Baker, *Woodrow Wilson: Life and Letters* (8 vols., Garden City, N. Y., 1927-1939), III, 417-418. Hereafter cited as R. S. Baker, *Wilson.* Also see H. Notter, *Origins,* p. 202.

21   Wilson to Bryan, January 16, 1913, Library of Congress, Papers of William Jennings Bryan, A, box 55. Hereafter cited as Bryan Papers. For Bryan's idea about the selection of an American representative to the Chinese post, also see James Kerney, *The Political Education of Woodrow Wilson* (New York and London, 1926), pp. 291-292. Hereafter cited as J. Kerney, *Political Education.*

22   Wilson to William Jennings Bryan, February 51 (*sic*) 5th or 11th, 1913, Papers of Ray Stannard Baker, series I, A, box 3. Hereafter cited as Baker Papers, followed by the series number and the box number. Also see H. Notter, *Origins,* p. 207; and R. S. Baker, *Wilson,* IV, 31.

23   J. Kerney, *Political Education,* pp. 288-289.

24   Edward M. House to Wilson, February 1, 1913, Yale University Library, the House Collection. Hereafter cited as House Collection.

25   J. W. Bashford to Bryan, March 20, 1913, State Department archives in the National Archives, Washington, D. C., file 893.00/634. Hereafter cited as SD, followed by the file number.

26   Entry of January 17, 1913, Diary of Edward M. House, MS. in the House Collection of the Yale University Library. Hereafter cited as House Diary. Later in a letter to House, Jesse R. Grant (Jesse Grant's complete name) mentioned that the China mission had been offered to Charles W. Eliot. See Jesse R. Grant to House, March 24, 1913, House Collection.

27   Wilson to Charles W. Eliot, January 20, 1913, Baker Papers, I, A, 5.

28   Entry of January 24, 1913, House Diary. Also see H. Notter, *Origins,* p. 206.

29   Entry of January 29, 1913, House Diary.

30   Entry of January 31, 1913, *ibid.*

31   Charles W. Eliot to Wilson, January 27, 1913, Wilson Papers, VI, 238. Also see the same letter in Baker Papers, I, A, 5; and Henry James, *Charles W. Eliot: President of Harvard University, 1869-1909* (2 vols., Boston and New York, 1930), II, 228-229. Henry James's statement that Wilson offered Eliot the post of ambassador to Japan instead of that of minister to China is apparently mistaken.

32   Wilson to Charles W. Eliot, January 30, 1913, Baker Papers, I, A, 5.

33·   Wilson to Bryan, February 51 (*sic*) 5th or 11th, 1913, *ibid.,* I, A, 3. Another copy of this letter is in Bryan Papers, A, box 55, and is dated February 21, 1913. This date is obviously a typographical error, because on February 14 Wilson mentioned to Bryan that he had written of Mott, and by February 17 Bryan had endorsed Wilson's selection of Mott. See Wilson to Bryan, February 14, 1913 and February 17, 1913 respectively, Bryan Papers, A, box 55.

34   Wilson to Bryan, February 14, 1913, *ibid.,* A, box 55.

35   Wilson to Bryan, February 17, 1913, *ibid.,* A, box 55.

36   Basil Mathews, *John Mott: World Citizen* (New York and London, 1934), pp. 436-438; R. S. Baker, *Wilson,* IV, 31-32; and H. Notter, *Origins,* pp. 234-235.

CHAPTER TWO

American Withdrawal from
the Consortium

The United States under the leadership of Presidents Taft and Wilson strove by all peaceful means to maintain the principle of equal opportunity for the commerce of all nations in China and to preserve that nation's administrative and territorial integrity as laid down by John Hay at the turn of the century. Both Presidents were staunch exponents of the traditional American open door policy. But their methods of carrying it out were often at wide variance. Their respective approaches to the problem of the international consortium illustrate this difference.

President Taft, well versed in the Far Eastern situation through his administrative experience in the Philippines and by his personal visit to China, found it good policy to counterbalance the unscrupulous actions of other powers by participating actively in international financial assistance to China. It was his idea that the United States, on the basis of concerted action, could exercise a restraining influence on political intervention of the other lending powers.

President Wilson, on the other hand, had no direct personal experience with the Far East. He was motivated by a benevolent sympathy for weak nations rather than by a practical knowledge of the interplay of international politics. He favored aloofness from all collective endeavors that might interfere with the free development of China as a nation. He thought that the United

States independently could exercise a moral influence to the best advantage of China.

Taft's approach was initiated from the practical point of view, whereas Wilson's was based on ethical grounds. It is important that we should bear this point in mind when we discuss Wilson's reversal of Taft's "dollar diplomacy," [1] and American withdrawal from the international consortium.

1.

To understand the complicated problem, diplomatic as well as fiscal, of China's foreign loans that elicited the first expression of President Woodrow Wilson's China policy, we shall have to describe the international loans which were threatening to extend and deepen the shadow of European imperialism over that distracted country. This must involve some account of President William Howard Taft's efforts to substitute "dollars for bullets" to neutralize the political effect of such loans. It was at a time when the European powers had temporarily abandoned the scramble for territorial acquisitions at China's expense to indulge in a rivalry for economic concessions and, through economic concessions, political control. To temper that rivalry, to hold it in check, to see that no one imperialist power used these loans as an instrument to extract political concessions, the Taft administration had lent the sanction of the United States government to the international consortium of private bankers.

The international consortium arose out of the Hukuang loan negotiations[2] initiated by England and France and soon joined by Germany, into which President Taft, by direct communication with the Chinese regent, Prince Ch'un, forced the admission of an American banking group[3] with a view to using American capital ostensibly as an instrument for the promotion of China's welfare and prosperity and for the maintenance of her political independence and territorial integrity.[4] It was known as the Four-Power Consortium before admission of Russia and Japan.

In the summer of 1908 when T'ang Shao-yi, governor of Fengtien Province, came to the United States as a special envoy to express thanks for the American decision to return to China a portion of the Boxer Indemnity for educational purposes, he suggested a loan of $300,000,000 in which all powers should take part but America should take the lead.[5] But the political situation in China was rather chaotic at that time, and the American government was not particularly interested in T'ang's plan. The suggestion was thus shelved. When the Taft administration came to power, it re-opened the question and tried to press the matter of currency reform upon the Chinese government. Later in 1910 the Peking government informed the American minister at Peking that it would give the American bankers preference if they were willing to undertake a loan of 50,000,000 Chinese taels.[6] To this proposal the American government answered promptly in the affirmative. Thereupon the Chinese government and the American banking group signed a preliminary agreement on October 27, 1910, for the proposed loan to "facilitate certain changes in the administration of Imperial and Manchurian Finance and to undertake certain Industrial Enterprises in Manchuria."[7] But now the American government favored international cooperation rather than individual control, and of its own accord extended an invitation to the other powers to share the loan equally. Upon the solicitation of the United States, the Peking government also gave its consent to the idea of internationalizing the loan. Then the American banking group and its consortium associates, the British, French, and German groups, entered into negotiations with China, and as a consequence, signed an agreement on April 15, 1911, calling for a loan of £10,000,000 to be utilized for the reform of the Chinese currency systems and for the promotion of such enterprises as immigration, reclamation, pasture, forestry, agriculture, and mining.[8] Before both parties had completed arrangements for the flotation of this loan, a revolution broke out in Wuchang, soon spread to other parts of China, and finally brought about the overthrow of the Manchu Dynasty and the establishment of the Chinese Republic. Under these altered conditions, this loan project was naturally postponed. In fact the loan was never issued, although the Four-Power Consortium had advanced to the Chinese government £400,000 as a first installment to meet the Manchurian requirements provided for in the loan agreement.[9] This advance and its interest were repaid out of the proceeds of the reorganization loan of April 26, 1913.[10]

The Hukuang loan, which gave rise to the international consortium, was meant for the construction of the so-called Hukuang railways in the Yangtze Valley in which the powers had taken a vital interest.[11] Under the guidance of the Taft administration, the American group actively negotiated with its associates and entered into an agreement with them by which the railway loan was to amount to £6,000,000 and to be divided equally among the four member groups.[12] The final agreement with the Chinese government was not signed until 1911,[13] the year in which the outbreak of the Chinese Revolution made any kind of railroad construction practically impossible. Suffice it to say that although the authorized loan was actually issued in 1911 and the real work of construction began two years later, the four banking groups never fully carried out their plan as shown in their loan agreement with China.

The Hukuang Railway loan was not the only proposal in which Taft's policy of international cooperation through the medium of finance and investment found expression. In 1909 Philander C. Knox, secretary of state, had unsuccessfully proposed to the powers the neutralization of the Japanese and Russian railways in Manchuria.[14] Had the proposal been accepted, America would have been able to share with other powers a large international loan for China to redeem control of the Manchurian railways. The Taft administration, however, was by no means discouraged by this failure and soon redoubled its efforts to bring about another international transaction, the above-mentioned currency reform and Manchurian industrial development loan.

After the establishment of the Republic of China in 1912, the Chinese government was confronted with almost insuperable difficulties. Its treasury was empty, and its resources were drained. Many government liabilities were awaiting liquidation before it could set its administrative machinery in full motion. In order to save this situation it had to resort to foreign loans. In the middle of February the Chinese acting minister of finance, Chou Tzu-ch'i, approached the representatives of the Four-Power Consortium for advances to meet the monthly needs of the government. Some days later, T'ang Shao-yi, who had arrived at Peking to arrange a coalition government on behalf of the Republican authorities at Nanking, discussed with those representatives the question of the immediate loan proposed by Chou and, in addition, suggested a large loan to reorganize the Chinese administration.[15] In response to the Chinese request, the consortium advanced to the Peking government 2,000,000 taels on February 28, and 1,100,000 taels on March 9. In a letter to the representatives of the consortium, Yüan Shih-k'ai, President of the Peking administration, confirmed the terms offered for the two advances and proposed

That in consideration of the assistance rendered by the groups to China in the present emergency, and of their services in supporting her credit on the foreign markets, the Chinese Government assures to the groups (provided that their terms are equally advantageous with those otherwise obtainable) the firm option of undertaking the comprehensive loan for general reorganization purposes already proposed to them, to be floated as soon as possible, and to be applied in the first instance to the redemption of the sterling treasury bills aforesaid.[16]

27

Only five days after he had made this pledge Yüan, under the pressure of immediate needs, concluded an agreement with a Belgian syndicate for a loan of £1,000,000 designed to consolidate the central and local governments and relieve the distresses prevailing among the people and in commercial circles.[17] The consortium powers, considering the conclusion of this loan as a breach of contract and good faith, entered a protest.[18] Then the Chinese government was forced to cancel the Belgian loan lest it should lose the support of the consortium. Thereupon negotiations were soon resumed with the consortium representatives.

During the months of May and June the consortium made three more advances to the Chinese government: 3,000,000 taels on May 17, another 3,000,000 taels on June 12 and still another 3,000,000 taels on June 18.[19] At the same time the four banking groups were enlarged into a Six-Power (or Sextuple) Consortium through the entrance of Russia and Japan who hitherto had blocked American plans for international investment in Manchuria, and without whose cooperation the consortium policy of America would be incomplete.[20] At Paris the banking groups of the six powers concluded a formal agreement for equal participation in the loan under discussion.

The reorganization loan negotiations[21] henceforth began to be almost wholly occupied with the discussion of the terms of supervision or control between China and the six banking groups. The latter decided to undertake the loan only on certain conditions, which were summarized by Willard Straight, the representative of the American group, as follows:

1. That the groups should have the right to satisfy themselves as to purposes for which funds were required.

2. That China should herself create a system of audit in which foreigners should be employed with powers not merely advisory, but also executive so as to ensure the effective expenditure of loan funds borrowed for the purposes specified.

28

3. That the salt taxes to be hypothecated for the service of this loan should be administered either by the existing Maritime Customs organization or by a separate Chinese service like the customs, however, under foreign direction, thus safeguarding the proper administration of the security despite the possible continuation or recurrence of unsettled conditions in China.

4. That the groups should take the first series of the loan of £60,000,000, at a fixed price, and be assured an option on the subsequent series at a price to be based on the market quotation of the first issue, thus giving China the benefit of any improvement in her credit.

5. That to protect the quotation of bonds issued and to assure a successful marketing of subsequent series China should not borrow through other groups until the entire loan of £60,000,000 had been issued.

6. That for a period of five years China should appoint the groups' financial agents to assist the administration in its work of reorganization.[22]

The reorganization loan was different from the previous loans, because it was to be used not for a definite program, but rather for general administrative purposes. Too much control by foreign creditors over the reorganization work of the Chinese government would certainly lead to infringement upon administrative integrity. It was natural that the Chinese government found it hard to accept the aforesaid terms, even at the hands of an international consortium. Strong internal opposition made the Peking authorities shrink from accepting them. As a result the negotiations came to a deadlock.

During the period of impasse the Chinese government, which was then in urgent need of financial support from abroad, on August 30, 1912, concluded with an independent British syndicate, G. Birch Crisp and Company, an agreement for a loan of £10,000,000.[23] The Crisp syndicate floated one half of the loan on the London market in September. The ministers of the six consortium powers, before long, strongly protested to China

29

against this loan agreement. Under such a pressure the Chinese government soon agreed to cancel the Crisp loan, thus breaking the deadlock in its discussions with the consortium.[24]

The negotiations went on during the winter of 1912-1913. In the course of time, disagreement arose among the consortium powers themselves. France, above all, took a very aggressive stand. During the later phase the discussions were attended with much strain among both the bankers and their diplomatic representatives. For example, the French minister at Peking served notice on his colleagues that the powers should insert a provision in the loan contract whereby the Chinese government admitted its liability for damages done to foreigners during the Revolution, and that it should be required to pay for the damages out of the proceeds of the pending loan.[25] This proposition gave rise to heated argument with the Chinese government and constituted a great stumbling-block in the way of negotiations. France was also strongly opposed to the internationalization of the reorganization loan in spite of the fact the United States, Great Britain, and Germany were all in favor of it.[26]

The greatest dispute among the powers concerned appointment of auditors and financial supervisors for the Peking government under the proposed loan. In pursuance of her uncompromising attitude France insisted upon the employment of her own nationals. She suggested that "the nationality of the appointees should be proportionate in number to the issue of bonds made in their respective countries." [27] Her ally, Russia, supported this suggestion, but the other powers did not seem to agree. In view of the lack of agreement among the consortium powers the Chinese minister of finance sent a note to the consortium, saying that he would break off the negotiations and borrow money elsewhere.

At this juncture Great Britain and Germany intimated that they were ready to accept the contract as it then stood, independently of the other powers.[28] It appeared probable that

Secretary Knox let it be known that any sudden change of attitude on the part of the American group would end in embarrassment to the government, and that the bankers should not decide upon any necessary change until the next administration had declared its policy regarding the matter.[37] He also formally told Henry P. Davison that it might be a serious mistake if the American group took any definite action at its meeting, and that its withdrawal from the loan negotiations would further delay rather than quicken a solution.[38] He advised the American group to stay in and await results patiently, because, as he informed the bankers as well as the American chargé d'affaires at Peking, E. T. Williams, the suggestion of ulterior motives and deliberate attempts to block the negotiations did not seem to be borne out in fact.[39]

It was obvious that the state department did not want to overturn its Chinese loan policy lest prestige be lost, and that if an early settlement proved impossible it would prefer to hand over the thorny problem to the incoming administration. Knox did succeed in being saved from embarrassment. The American group formally decided that before the end of the outgoing administration it would not alter its position.[40] The important thing to remember is that the European members of the consortium, impelled by imperialistic political considerations, were laying down conditions so exasperating to the American bankers and so onerous to the Chinese government that at the end of the Taft administration the American group was preparing to pull out.

Such was the position of the proposed six-power loan when the administration of President Taft gave way to the incoming government of Woodrow Wilson.

2.

Neither Wilson nor Bryan had given sufficient thought to the Chinese loan before it confronted them for immediate

33

decision. As men of anti-imperialistic mind they naturally disliked any form of exploitation by the European powers in underdeveloped countries. Being Christian friends of China as well as exponents of traditional American policy, they objected to the placing of China under foreign control, whether political, military, or economic. It was not to their liking to advance American political interests by encouraging a few financiers to participate in an international competition for special profits and rights. For this reason they favored American withdrawal from the international loan negotiations with the Chinese government. By no means did they thoroughly understand the crossplay of international politics in China.

The day after Woodrow Wilson's inauguration, Willard Straight, on behalf of the American group, requested Secretary of State Bryan's early advice on the future conduct of the Chinese loan negotiations.[41] The American ambassador to France, Myron T. Herrick, sent a telegram to Bryan on March eighth, also pressing for early decision. Herrick had become disappointed at the procrastination and selfishness of the other consortium powers, particularly Russia and Japan.[42] He felt that as long as the six powers held together China would be excluded from making loans in the financial markets of the world. In order to maintain the policy to preserve the integrity of China and to further her reconstruction, America would find it proper to relieve China from such financial exclusion. Therefore the United States government would perform an act of great service to China, if it could announce its intention to conclude the reorganization loan immediately or to withdraw from the consortium.[43] It now became clear that the policy of the international banking group in China had proved very disappointing, and it was urgent for the Wilson administration to consider the matter and make a quick decision as to whether or not it should continue the policy of its predecessor.

In reply to Willard Straight, Bryan indicated his willingness to have a personal interview with the American group. By talking face to face with the bankers, he hoped to have a better understanding of the loan matter which he described as being completely new to the President and himself.[44] After some further correspondence a date was finally set for the proposed interview.[45] On the afternoon of March tenth, Bryan had a long conference with the representatives of the American group, Willard Straight, Henry P. Davison, and Paul M. Warburg. Although he, like Woodrow Wilson, had long had a warm Christian sympathy for China,[46] he was practically ignorant of the facts or details regarding the loan negotiations.[47] On some vital points of policy he was at variance with his associates, Assistant Secretary of State Huntington Wilson and Counselor Chandler Anderson, who also participated in the discussions.[48] The latter two, thoroughly conversant with the loan situation, strongly opposed any reversal of dollar diplomacy. Both the President and Bryan disapproved.[49]

The conference also touched upon the general relations between China and the United States, including the problem of the recognition of the Chinese Republic, the question of the appointment of a competent minister to Peking, and the impending disruption of the Chinese army.[50] But the discussion was concentrated mainly upon the reorganization loan and the attitude of the new administration toward the protection of American interests in China. The representatives of the American group fully presented their views and took a perfectly clear position throughout the meeting. They said that they had participated in the loan negotiations upon the solicitation of the state department, had spent much time and money in acting as an instrument of the American Far Eastern policy, and would not continue their efforts unless the government renewed its request. To be brief, they would like to receive, at an early date, a decision from the state department as to its policy toward the international banking consortium so that they could decide what to do accordingly.

In accordance with the statement which Bryan dictated to his wife, Mary Baird Bryan, there were brought out during the interview four important facts in connection with the Chinese loan:

First, that no American financiers, except those in this group, could participate in the loan. Second, that the financiers interested in this loan expected to control future loans. Third, that the loan was to be secured by control of revenues. Fourth, that the six groups of financiers expected their governments to furnish such support as might be necessary, even to the use of force, to compel China to live up to the stipulations of the loan contract.[51]

No definite decision was made after nearly three hours of discussion.[52] Bryan stated candidly that he could not give an immediate answer to the demand of the American group, but would take action in due time. Davison further requested that should the state department decide upon a change of policy the American bankers be informed beforehand in order that they, in turn, could early communicate the fact to the other members of the consortium.[53]

Bryan soon brought up the matter at a cabinet meeting.[54] He reported the recent visit from the delegates of the New York banking houses and at the same time explained his own views. He found the loan objectionable because it constituted a monopoly of Chinese financial matters for the international consortium in general and a few American bankers in particular, because the contemplated security might injure China's independence, and because the United States, being tied with other countries and deprived of independent action, could not control matters in connection with the collection and enforcement of the loan.[55] Wilson agreed with him on the essential points of his report,[56] but no final conclusion seems to have been reached at the meeting. Several days later, Bryan went on a lecturing tour to the West, leaving Huntington Wilson as acting secretary of state for the period of his absence. Prior to his departure he had discussed the loan problem with the President again.[57]

At the next cabinet meeting of March eighteenth,[58] which Bryan did not attend because of his personal trip through the West, the Chinese question was again brought up for discussion. The President and almost all his associates present voiced their disapproval of continued participation in an enterprise which they thought would establish a monopoly of loans for a small group of bankers to the exclusion of many others and, above all, would interfere with China's freedom and independence.[59] They also considered a statement which the President had prepared in advance for use. Some moderate cabinet members toned down some of the President's harsh and critical phraseology. Finally it became satisfactory and acceptable to all.[60] Their original intention was to withhold publication until one or two days later, but when an inkling of the cabinet decision soon leaked out, Wilson found it necessary to release the document immediately to the press instead of conveying it to foreign governments through the state department.[61] The statement thus issued on March eighteenth marked so radical a change in American foreign policy and occupied so significant a page in the annals of Sino-American relations that it deserves to be quoted in full:

We are informed that at the request of the last administration a certain group of American bankers undertook to participate in the loan now desired by the Government of China (approximately $125,000,000). Our Government wished American bankers to participate along with the bankers of other nations, because it desired that the good will of the United States toward China should be exhibited in this practical way, that American capital should have access to that great country, and that the United States should be

37

in a position to share with the other powers any political responsibilities that might be associated with the development of the foreign relations of China in connection with her industrial and commercial enterprises. The present administration has been asked by this group of bankers whether it would also request them to participate in the loan. The representatives of the bankers through whom the administration was approached declared that they would continue to seek their share of the loan under the proposed agreements only if expressly requested to do so by the Government. The administration has declined to make such request, because it did not approve the conditions of the loan or the implications of responsibility on its own part which it was plainly told would be involved in the request.

The conditions of the loan seem to us to touch very nearly the administrative independence of China itself, and this administration does not feel that it ought, even by implication, to be a party to those conditions. The responsibility on its part which would be implied in requesting the bankers to undertake the loan might conceivably go the length in some unhappy contingency of forcible interference in the financial, and even the political, affairs of that great oriental State, just now awakening to a consciousness of its power and of its obligations to its people. The conditions include not only the pledging of particular taxes, some of them antiquated and burdensome, to secure the loan, but also the administration of those taxes by foreign agents. The responsibility on the part of our Government implied in the encouragement of a loan thus secured and administered is plain enough and is obnoxious to the principles upon which the government of our people rests.

The Government of the United States is not only willing, but earnestly desirous, of aiding the great Chinese people in every way that is consistent with their untrammeled development and its own immemorial principles. The awakening of the people of China to a consciousness of their responsibilities under free government is the most significant, if not the most momentous, event of our generation. With this movement and aspiration the American people are in profound sympathy. They certainly wish to participate, and participate very generously, in the opening to the Chinese and to the use of the world the almost untouched and perhaps unrivaled resources of China.

The Government of the United States is earnestly desirous of promoting the most extended and intimate trade relationship between this country and the Chinese Republic. The present administration will urge and support the legislative measures necessary to give American merchants, manufacturers, contractors, and engineers the banking and other financial facilities which they now lack and without which they are at a serious disadvantage as compared with their industrial and commercial rivals. This is its duty. This is the main material interest of its citizens in the development of China. Our interests are those of the open door—a door of friendship and mutual advantage. This is the only door we care to enter.[62]

Courtesy would seem to have required that the foreign governments associated with the United States in the consortium should have been notified in advance of the action to be taken. The New York *Times* characterized it as a rather rude departure from international and diplomatic usage for Wilson to have the other powers learn from the newspapers of the sudden change in American policy.[63] At the cabinet meeting of March twenty-fifth, Wilson referred to the matter and admitted that it was a mistake to have released the statement to the press before informing the foreign governments.[64]

It was perhaps also a mistake that Huntington Wilson, the acting secretary of state who had been actively concerned with the policy in question, had not been apprised of its abandonment. The issuance of the statement without his previous knowledge immediately made him indignant. Before long he tendered his resignation.[65] He outspokenly expressed his distaste for the radical reversal of a policy, the motive of which, he argued, was first and primarily to protect China's integrity and sovereignty, to elevate the Chinese people, to develop Chinese natural resources, and to maintain the traditional American principle of the equality of commercial opportunity.

The only practical way of American participation in the reconstruction of China's finances, he argued in support of the dollar diplomacy, was to enlist the cooperation of dependable American bankers. He deplored the fact that the President had not consulted the state department temporarily under his charge, had failed to give adequate consideration to all facts and theories involved, and had determined the fate of the loan negotiations "with such quite unnecessary haste and in so unusual a manner." [66]

The President was likewise hurt and accepted the immediate resignation of his acting secretary of state in an exceptionally curt letter.[67] In the meantime he telegraphed Bryan that he found it impossible to retain Huntington Wilson, and that things would go perfectly well without the latter.[68] Bryan felt pleased to learn that the course of business was not disturbed at the state department, and he acquiesced in the President's action without complaint.[69]

In a telephone conversation with the state department the representatives of the American group were told to consider Wilson's statement as the government's reply to their request for a decision as to their future conduct in the loan negotiations. Thereupon they held an all-day conference on March nineteenth to discuss what measures were necessary to take. Henry P. Davison, unable to attend because of illness, kept up with developments over the telephone.[70] Finally they agreed to withdraw from the consortium and formally notified the secretary of state of their decision. They especially called the attention of the state department to the fact that they were already committed to some transactions with the Chinese government—namely, the Hukuang Railway loan agreement, their one-fourth share in the £400,000 advance under the currency loan agreement, and their one-sixth share in the reorganization loan advances made to China in 1912. Two of the latter advances had been due to the consortium on February 28 and March 9,

1913, respectively, but the Peking government had been unable to pay because of the non-conclusion of the reorganization loan. The Chinese minister of finance, in reply to a letter from the six banking groups pressing for payment, had requested an extension of six months or one year at seven and a half per cent interest *per annum*. But the consortium representatives at Peking regarded the Chinese answer as a failure to inform them of any definite arrangements for repayment and so requested their legations to give notice to China that she had defaulted her obligations. For this reason the American group asked the state department to instruct its minister at the Chinese capital to help adjust the matter in cooperation with his colleagues.[71] It is to be noted here that soon Wilson suggested an extension of six months in view of the reasonableness of the Chinese proposal,[72] and the American group consented to grant it in deference to his wishes.[73] After the conclusion of the reorganization loan between China and the remaining five powers the advances together with accrued interest were fully repaid.[74]

At the same time the American group dispatched a telegram to its representative at Peking for communication to his colleagues and the Chinese government, declaring its decision to withdraw from the present loan negotiations and to notify its retirement in the following June from the four-group agreement of November 10, 1910, in conformity with the provisions of the fourteenth article thereof.[75] It also issued a statement to the press, on the one hand defending its entrance into the consortium and its participation in the Chinese loan and on the other showing its disposition to serve the purpose of the Wilson administration.[76] With regard to such commitments as the Hukuang agreement and the currency reform loan, which they had already undertaken, it delegated the International Banking Corporation to act for it in China.[77]

Willard Straight, chief spokesman of the American group, preferred to make no comment on Wilson's announcement.[78]

But it was an open secret that he was opposed to the abandonment of the principle of international financial cooperation. He prophetically wrote to Frank McKnight on March twenty-fifth: "I believe the policy we have pursued has been so essentially sound that not only will it be justified by future events but it will assert itself to such a degree that even this administration will be forced to adopt more or less the methods of its predecessor." [79] He was right in view of the fact that a few years later circumstances compelled Wilson to reverse his own stand and return to a policy that the Taft government had once advocated.

Like Willard Straight, Philander C. Knox, the ex-secretary of state, did not care to make any public remark upon the repudiation of his favorite dollar diplomacy. Privately he too expressed the conviction that he could give definite facts to prove the inopportune character of Wilson's China policy.[80] More than a year passed before he openly denounced Wilson's withdrawal from the consortium as a puerile action which ran counter to the duty and interests of the United States and violated good faith with China and the other powers concerned.[81]

From a purely commercial point of view the bankers were quite disposed to drop out of the consortium, because the disorder and instability then prevailing in China made it impossible to have bonds satisfactorily secured. Certain members of the American group asserted that, even if the proposed loan could succeed, the costly delays would have largely consumed the banking profits. In this sense they felt happy to have been freed of an expensive burden. The bickerings of the other national groups in the consortium for special controls over Chinese sovereignty had also made participation a most uncomfortable business. But insomuch as the United States as a restraining factor in Chinese affairs was removed, Wilson's new stand, some leading bankers feared, might soon revive aggressive designs on the part of other powers and finally lead to the disruption and partition of the Chinese Republic.[82] In

42

such an event the United States would be deprived of the opportunity to trade with China on equal terms with other countries.

On this score certain influential newspapers took a most gloomy view of the political implications of American withdrawal from the consortium. The New York *Journal of Commerce,* for example, wrote that Wilson was helping to close the door of China's trade rather than keeping it open.[83] The Boston *Transcript,* the Detroit *Free Press,* and the New York *Sun, Globe, Evening Mail,* and *Herald* all made remarks in the same vein. What remained of the open door policy first proclaimed by John Hay was now, to quote the New York *Sun,* "no more than a grinning skeleton without vital organs or muscles." [84]

But a greater number of editors, particularly those of Democratic affiliations and anti-imperialistic inclinations, repudiated the idea that Wilson was facilitating the closure of the Chinese door to American merchants. They believed that the new administration was really intending to promote large and intimate trade relations with China naturally, but not by force. A unanimous approval could be seen in journals representing such a variety of sectional and political devotion as the Chicago *Record-Herald,* and *News,* the Philadelphia *Record,* the New York *Daily People,* the Baltimore *News,* the Milwaukee *Free Press,* the Louisville *Herald,* and the Houston *Post.* In Wilson's pronouncement they saw a gratifying resumption of the traditional wariness toward entangling alliance, a vigorous encouragement of American industrial and commercial activities on a broad basis, and a beneficial moral support of China through refusal to scramble for Chinese rights.[85] The Wall Street *Journal* felt pleased with the disposal of the dollar diplomacy which was "one of the least desirable legacies of the last administration at Washington," and was "about as un-American as the wit of man could devise." [86] The New York *Times* observed that the bankers would welcome their release from aid in a policy which should never have been entered upon at all, and which had thus far produced "nothing but trouble and vexation." [87]

Numerous messages of congratulation pouring into the President's office from various quarters gave further evidence of the popularity of the loan decision. They eulogized Wilson with one accord, and considered his new policy as something which embodied a clear vision, a broad statesmanship, and a high moral tone, won the confidence of the people in the new administration, helped to liberate the Chinese nation from the domination of the military powers of the old world, restored American influence and prestige in the Far East, and secured for the United States independence and leadership in the world's economic developments.[88] It was not unreasonable that in an atmosphere of felicitation Bryan wrote to Wilson: "I have yet to find the first man who dissents from your position on the Chinese loan." [89]

The foreign representatives at Washington were reported to have a kind of subdued complaint on their part because Wilson had ignored them in the Chinese matter. In London the American decision came as a complete surprise. Only on March eighteenth, the British foreign secretary, Edward Grey, told the House of Commons that the six consortium powers had unanimously agreed on the terms of the Chinese loan. No sooner was his remark in print than the news came of the American intention to withdraw. Naturally Wilson's announcement did not make pleasant reading for the British government. In Berlin it created consternation among the leaders of the German group. They felt hurt because they had received no previous intimation of withdrawal from their American partners.[90] It is to be recalled here that in the loan negotiations the United States had been the only power which Germany might lean upon should occasion demand it, for Russia and France on the one hand, and Great Britain and Japan on the other, had been acting together, and Germany had been feeling very much isolated. Now with the American retirement, Germany would be left without a friendly associate in the international concert. In Japan most newspapers expressed satisfaction at Wilson's action while some distrusted his sincerity.[91] But Japan never overlooked selfish motives. As it was customary, she wished the United States to be dissociated from Europe in the matter of Far Eastern policy and to confine its activities to the Western Hemisphere, so that she could deal with China with little American interference. In fact she desired to be China's chief creditor and was looking forward to a time when she could have a predominant voice in all Chinese loan matters. Wilson's new move, therefore, could possibly serve this ulterior purpose of hers.[92]

In order to know the true mind of the Wilson government the Japanese ambassador called at the state department and left for the acting secretary of state, Alvey A. Adee, a memorandum requesting an official exposition of the American disavowal of the policy of international concert in China.[93] Upon learning of the Japanese intention Wilson directed Adee to say on his behalf that the problem under discussion would be taken up with foreign embassies as soon as Secretary Bryan returned to Washington.[94] On April first, Bryan officially communicated American withdrawal from the consortium to the ambassadors of the five interested powers for the information of their respective governments.[95]

In China the press sounded a note of joy and applause, although a few journals cast some doubt on Wilson's action or even indulged in veiled sneers. Most editors laid emphasis on the moral value of the American announcement which, as the Shanghai *China Republic* put it, had come "not as another millstone round our necks, but as the balm of Gilead to hungering souls," and which was to be welcomed "as the harbinger of freedom from molestation, freedom from spoliation, freedom from an intolerable foreign yoke, and freedom from interference in the stupendous task of working out our own salvation in our own way." [96] The Chinese official circles also credited Wilson with justice and wisdom in declining participation in the imposition of stringent loan terms upon China. In a conversation with the American chargé d'affaires, E. T. Williams, Yüan Shih-k'ai expressed his personal gratitude for the American action and thought it would be of great assistance to his country.[97] Under Yüan's instructions the Chinese minister at Washington, who had earlier expressed his own appreciation to the state department,[98] made formal presentation of the thanks of the Chinese people for Wilson's "just and magnanimous attitude." [99]

As we have seen, the American statement with respect to the Chinese loan was largely a doctrinaire utterance. It did not result from a thorough understanding of the Chinese situation or a full grasp of all complications on the part of Wilson. It was prompted chiefly by his sense of justice, his sympathy for the Chinese people, his respect for the independence and administrative integrity of a weak nation, his disapproval of the terms of the loan arrangement, and, above all, his distaste for the use of finance as a tool of diplomacy. Naive and impulsive as it appeared, its moral value was really remarkable. The favorable reaction of both the American and the Chinese people proved that Wilson was right on ethical grounds, and that his good principles had been successfully applied to diplomacy for the moment. By adopting a new policy he had won China's profound gratitude. If America had lost any material advantage of cooperation with other powers, she was more than compensated by a growing confidence of the Chinese nation in her moral support.

It was true that Wilson meant to reverse the trend of dollar diplomacy. But it was untrue that he intended also to abandon the open door policy. As he had announced, the

interests of the United States were those of the open door—
the door of friendship and mutual benefit. According to him
this was the only door that his country cared to enter. This
again sounded like a virtuous principle, and he took it seriously.
By no means did he give up the idea of encouraging American
investments in China by ordering the withdrawal of a few
privileged banking houses from the international loan. He desired to give legitimate support not to one special group of
financiers but to all interested capitalists in the development
of Chinese resources. He would rather assist the bankers in
carrying on economic transactions upon their own initiative and
responsibility than use them as an instrument to advance
American political interests in a remote and under-developed
region. He refused to join with other governments in placing
the fetters of foreign financial control upon the new republic,
but he did not mean to be indifferent to the whole Chinese
situation. He thought he might exercise more restraining influence from without than from within in case certain consortium
powers contemplated indiscreet intervention in Chinese internal
affairs.

In this respect President Wilson was manifestly mistaken.
In the first place the five-power group soon brought the protracted and tortuous loan negotiations to a successful conclusion
in spite of American non-cooperation, and the Chinese government, compelled by bare necessity at home and great pressure from abroad, finally agreed to most of the projected
terms which Wilson had candidly condemned. Later, during
World War I, the international situation in China became such
that he found it necessary to reverse his own position by initiating
the formation of a new consortium.

In the final analysis Wilson's stand on the Chinese loan
was chiefly moral. Its success was more apparent than real.
Its importance, however, should not be overlooked, because it
marked the beginning of a new policy of independent action

and paved the way for another equally important act—the recognition of the Chinese Republic.

NOTES:

1 President Taft's policy in China is commonly described as "dollar diplomacy." It is a policy designed to serve benevolent political ends through the instrumentality of dollars. Willard Straight, the representative of the American banking group, significantly describes it as "the alliance of diplomacy with industry, commerce and finance." See Willard Straight, "China's Loan Negotiations", in George H. Blakeslee, ed., *Recent Developments in China* (New York, 1913), p. 122. Hereafter cited as W. Straight, "Loan Negotiations." Huntington Wilson, a staunch advocate of dollar diplomacy under the Taft administration, professes that the American government was then "using Wall Street to serve our national interest and to benefit other countries." See F. M. Huntington Wilson, *Memoirs of an Ex-Diplomat* (Boston, 1945), p. 216. Hereafter cited as F. M. H. Wilson, *Ex-Diplomat*.

2 For more information about the history of the loan, see Arthur G. Coons, *The Foreign Public Debt of China* (Philadelphia, 1930), pp. 34-38. Hereafter cited as A. G. Coons, *Foreign Public Debt*. Also see Frederick V. Field, *American Participation in the China Consortiums* (Chicago, 1931), ch. II *passim*. Hereafter cited as F. V. Field, *China Consortiums*.

3 The American banking group came into existence in June, 1909, at the instigation of the state department for the purpose of participation in the Hukuang loan. It consisted of four banking houses: J. P. Morgan and Company; Kuhn Loeb and Company; the First National Bank of the City of New York; and the National City Bank of New York. See *ibid.*, p. 35.

4 President Taft to Prince Ch'un, July 15, 1909, *Papers Relating to the Foreign Relations of the United States, 1909* (Washington, 1914), p. 178. Hereafter cited as *For. Rels.*

5 W. Straight, "Loan Negotiations," pp. 126-127.

6 F. V. Field, *China Consortiums,* p. 57.

7 John V. A. MacMurray, *Treaties and Agreements With and Concerning China, 1894-1919* (New York, 1921), I, 851. Hereafter cited as J. V. A. MacMurray, *Treaties and Agreements.*

8   For the text of the agreement, see *ibid.*, I, 841-849. For a brief history of the loan, see F. V. Field, *China consortiums,* ch. V *passim.*

9   *For. Rels., 1913* (Washington, 1920), p. 192.

10   J. V. A. MacMurray, *Treaties and Agreements,* II, 1018.

11   The Hukuang railways included the Hupei-Hunan section of the Canton-Hankow railway and the Hupei section of the Szechwan-Hankow railway. "Hukuang" is a geographical name for the two provinces of Hupei and Hunan. The proposed railways would run through these two provinces; hence the name of Hukuang railways. Before the entrance of the United States into the consortium, England, France and Germany had reached an agreement with China for the building of these railway lines. For the text of this agreement, see J. V. A. MacMurray, *Treaties and Agreements,* I, 880-885.

12   For the text of the agreement, see *ibid.*, I, 886-887.

13   For the text of the agreement, see *ibid.*, I, 866-877.

14   *For. Rels., 1910* (Washington, 1915), p. 231.

15   W. Straight, "Loan Negotiations", p. 137.

16   Yüan Shih-k'ai to the representatives of the consortium, March 9, 1912. See *For. Rels., 1912* (Washington, 1919), p. 120.

17   For the text of the agreement, see J. V. A. MacMurray, *Treaties and Agreements,* II, 947-950.

18   *For. Rels., 1912,* pp. 122-123.

19   F. V. Field, *China Consortiums,* pp. 80-82.

20   For a brief account of the admission of Russia and Japan into the consortium, see *ibid.*, pp. 101-109.

21   For details of the reorganization loan negotiations, see *For. Rels., 1912,* pp. 112-150; *For. Rels., 1913,* pp. 143-192; *Die grosse Politik der europäischen Kabinette, 1871-1914* (Berlin, 1921-1927), XXXII, 293-417; *Documents diplomatiques francais, 1871-1914* (Paris, 1929-1937) series 3, vol. II, nos. 31, 32, 49, 59, 85, 138, 164, 169, and 264; B. von Siebert, ed., *Graf Benckendorffs diplomatischer Schriftwechsel* (3 vols., Berlin, 1928), vols., II and III *passim;* W. Straight, "Loan Negotiations", pp. 137-161; F. V. Field, *China Consortiums,* chs. VI and VII *passim;* A. G. Coons, *Foreign Public Debt,* pp. 54-61; and C. F. Remer, *Foreign Investments in China* (New York, 1933), pp. 125-131, hereafter cited as C. F. Remer, *Foreign Investments.*

22   W. Straight, "Loan Negotiations," pp. 143-144.

23 J. V. A. MacMurray, *Treaties and Agreements,* II, 967-972.

24 On December 23, 1912 the Chinese government and the Crisp syndicate agreed to cancel the second half of the £ 10,000,000 loan. See *ibid.,* II, 1034-1035.

25 The American minister at Peking (William J. Calhoun) to the secretary of state, February 11, 1913, SD, 893.51/1344.

26 *For. Rels., 1913,* pp. 147-150.

27 *Ibid.,* p. 147.

28 *Ibid.,* p. 147.

29 *For. Rels., 1913,* p. 151.

30 F. V. Field, *China Consortiums,* p. 92.

31 Herbert Feis, *Europe: the World's Banker, 1870-1914* (New Haven, 1930), pp. 434-435. Hereafter cited as H. Feis, *World's Banker.*

32 The French, German, Japanese and Russian banking interests had direct official connections with their governments. No official tie bound the British banking interests, but they were in close touch with the British government. See *ibid.,* p. 455. For the services of governments to the interests of private investors, see Eugene Staley, *War and the Private Investor* (Garden City, N. Y., 1935), ch. VI *passim.*

33 F. H. McKnight to J. P. Morgan & Co., February 18, 1913, SD, 893.51/1351.

34 Memorandum by R. S. Miller, February 20, 1913, SD, 893.51/1342.

35 *For. Rels., 1913,* p. 164.

36 Huntington Wilson to President Taft, October 5, 1912, SD, 893.51/1083.

37 Memorandum by R. S. Miller, February 21, 1913, *ibid.,* 893.51/1341.

38 Philander C. Knox to Henry P. Davison, February 20, 1913, *ibid.,* 893.51/1342.

39 Knox to the American group, February 26, 1913, *ibid.,* 893.51/1317; and Knox to E. T. Williams, February 27, 1913, *For. Rels., 1913,* pp. 166-167.

40 Willard Straight to the secretary of state, February 27, 1913, SD, 893.51/1325.

41 Straight to the secretary of state, March 5, 1913, *For. Rels., 1913,* pp. 167-168.

42 Herrick thought that the consortium had been first formed in good faith but the introduction of Russia and Japan resulted in forcing such conditions into the loan convention as to cause it to "partake of the nature of a pawnbroker's loan." He made this remark in a letter to President Taft, dated October 24, 1912, and repeated it later to Woodrow Wilson. See Myron T. Herrick to Wilson, April 15, 1913, Wilson Papers, VI, 227.

43 *For. Rels., 1913,* p. 168.

44 Bryan to Straight, March 7, 1913, SD, 893.51/1336.

45 The time that they finally set for the meeting was four o'clock on the afternoon of March 10. See Straight to Bryan, March 7, 1913, SD, 893.51/1337; Bryan to Straight, March 8, 1913, SD, 893.51/1337; and Straight to Bryan, March 8, 1913, SD, 893.-51/1338. Bryan did meet the representatives of the American group according to schedule. See New York *Times,* March 11, 1913. But R. S. Baker says that Willard Straight and Henry P. Davison came to Washington on March 9, to call on Bryan. See R. S. Baker, *Wilson,* IV, 70. Josephus Daniels also states that "members of the big Morgan banking house" called upon Bryan on March 9. See Josephus Daniels, *The Wilson Era: Years of Peace—1910-1917* (New York, 1944), p. 158. Hereafter cited as J. Daniels, *Wilson Era.* In the light of the actual correspondence between Bryan and Straight and the newspaper reports, Baker and Daniels are most probably mistaken.

46 Bryan had visited China during his trip around the world from 1905 to 1906 and had been deeply impressed by the awakening of that nation "from the sleep of twenty centuries" as well as by the abandonment of "the old order of examinations for rank in scholarship." See William Jennings Bryan and Mary Baird Bryan, *The Memoirs of William Jennings Bryan* (Chicago, Philadelphia and Toronto, 1925), pp. 312-313. Hereafter cited as W. J. Bryan, *Memoirs.* As a pious Christian, Bryan had never failed to appreciate the development of the Christian influence in China. In his *Letters to a Chinese Official* he remarked: "As a fountain of water issuing from a hillside clothes a barren plain with verdure, so Christianity has scattered oases throughout China, and is today exerting an influence far greater than the actual church membership would indicate." Like Wilson his interest in China was based largely upon his belief in Christianity. See William Jennings Bryan, *Letters to a Chinese Official* (New York, 1906), p. 94.

47   See above, note 44; and R. S. Baker, *Wilson*, IV, 70. Bryan even frankly confessed to Henry P. Davison that he was entirely ignorant of Far Eastern affairs. "He had heard dimly of John Hay's 'Open Door' for China, but whether he wanted to keep it open was not quite clear." See Thomas W. Lamont, *Henry P. Davison: the Record of a Useful Life* (New York and London, 1933), p. 161. Hereafter cited as T. W. Lamont, *Davison*.

48   New York *Times,* March 11, 1913. Ransford Miller, chief of the division of Far Eastern affairs, was also present at the meeting.

49   By that time Huntington Wilson or Chandler Anderson or both had sent to the President a memorandum advocating continued participation in the Chinese loan. See R. S. Baker, *Wilson,* IV, 70.

50   New York *Times,* March 11, 1913.

51   W. J. Bryan, *Memoirs,* p. 362.

52   The conference began at four o'clock in the afternoon and continued until nearly seven o'clock in the evening. See New York *Times,* March 11, 1913.

53   T. W. Lamont, *Davison,* p. 162.

54   Later Bryan recollected that he had reported the conference to the President at a cabinet meeting, but did not specify when the cabinet meeting had been held. See W. J. Bryan, *Memoirs,* p. 362. According to David F. Houston, Bryan brought up the loan question at the cabinet meeting of March 14 and again presented the matter at the following meeting of March 18. See David F. Houston, *Eight Years with Wilson's Cabinet, 1913 to 1920: with a Personal Estimate of the President* (2 vols., Garden City, N. Y., 1926), I, 44. Hereafter cited as D. F. Houston, *Wilson's Cabinet.* R. S. Baker repeated Houston's account, saying Biyan raised the question on March 14 and made a further report on March 18. See R. S. Baker, *Wilson,* IV, 70. H. Notter also stated that Bryan first reported to the cabinet on March 14. See H. Notter, *Origins,* p. 232. According to Josephus Daniels, Bryan himself opened the discussion of the Chinese loan problem at a special cabinet meeting of March 18. See J. Daniels, *Wilson Era,* p. 158. As a matter of fact Bryan did not attend the cabinet meeting of March 18. This can be proved by the newspaper reports of the period in question. A report coming from Washington on March 15 said that Bryan was leaving for Chicago on the next day (March 16). See

New York *Times,* March 16, 1913. He was actually in the West on March 18 when the cabinet meeting was held and Wilson's statement about the Chinese loan was issued. See New York *Times,* March 19, 1913 and New York *Tribune* for the same date. Also see F. M. H. Wilson, *Ex-Diplomat,* pp. 248-249. Furthermore a cabinet meeting was actually held on March 12, two days after Bryan's interview with the American group. See entry of March 12, 1913, the Executive Office Diary for 1913, Wilson Papers, I, 21. It is also possible that Bryan made his report to the cabinet on March 12 instead of on March 14. At any rate, we can be sure that if Bryan did report to the cabinet he must have done it at a meeting held between his conference with the bankers and his departure for the West.

55   W. J. Bryan, *Memoirs,* pp. 362-363.

56   H. Notter, *Origins,* p. 232.

57   New York *Times,* March 19, 1913.

58   Entry of March 18, 1913, the Executive Office Diary for 1913, Wilson Papers, I, 21.

59   In contrast to the attitude of other cabinet members William C. Redfield, secretary of commerce, expressed the fear that if the loan should be disapproved, other countries would still make it, and the United States would fail to build up a large trade in China. See J. Daniels, *Wilson Era,* p. 158.

60   D. F. Houston, *Wilson's Cabinet,* I, 45.

61   New York *Times,* March 19, 1913.

62   *For. Rels., 1913,* pp. 170-171.

63   New York *Times,* March 21, 1913.

64   D. F. Houston, *Wilson's Cabinet,* I, 45.

65   For an account of the resignation of Huntington Wilson, see F. M. H. Wilson, *Ex-Diplomat,* ch. XXXIV *passim.*

66   Huntington Wilson to the President, March 19, 1913, Wilson Papers, VI, 234.

67   The President to Huntington Wilson, March 20, 1913, *ibid.,* VII, 1. Also see R. S. Baker, *Wilson,* IV, 72-73.

68   The President to Bryan, March 20, 1913, Wilson Papers, VII, 1.

69   Bryan to the President, March 20, 1913, *ibid.,* VI, 234.

70   New York *Times,* March 20, 1913.

71   The American group to the secretary of state, March 19, 1913, *For. Rels., 1913,* pp. 171-172.

72   The secretary of state to the American group, March 28, 1913, *ibid.*, pp. 175-176.

73   The American group to the secretary of state, March 31, 1913, *ibid.*, pp. 176-177.

74   F. V. Field, *China Consortiums,* p. 117.

75   *For. Rels., 1913,* pp. 172-173.   The fourteenth article of the four-group agreement reads: "Save as herein provided and as provided in an agreement between the Hongkong and Shanghai Banking Corporation, the Deutsch-Asiatische Bank, the Banque de l'Indo-Chine and the American group proposed to be entered into immediately after this agreement, no business of the kind falling within the scope of this agreement shall be concluded or entered into either directly or indirectly by any of the parties hereto or by any of those whom they respectively represent without the consent of the others." See J. V. A. MacMurray, *Treaties and Agreements,* I, 831.   In June, 1913, the American group actually gave notification of its withdrawal from the four-group agreement.   See Willard Straight to the secretary of state, June 27, 1913, SD, 893.51/1445.

76   For the text of the statement, see *Commercial and Financial Chronicle,* vol. 96 (1913), 825.

77   *For. Rels., 1913,* p. 173.

78   New York *Times,* March 19, 1913.

79   Herbert Croly, *Willard Straight* (New York, 1924), p. 453.

80   In reply to a request from John A. Sleicher, editor of *Leslie's Weekly,* for comment on or information about Wilson's statement, Knox made such a remark which is undated and placed at the end of the editor's letter.   See John A. Sleicher to Knox, March 21, 1913, Library of Congress, Correspondence of Philander C. Knox, vol. 20.   Hereafter cited as Knox Correspondence.

81   F. M. H. Wilson, *Ex-Diplomat,* pp. 220-221.

82   New York *Times,* March 23, 1913.

83   See "Effect of the Chinese Loan Veto," *Literary Digest,* vol. 46 (1913), 758.

84   See "Rescuing China from the Cross of Gold," *ibid.,* vol. 46 (1913), 692.

85   See above, footnote 83.

86   Wall Street *Journal,* March 21, 1913.

87   New York *Times,* March 20, 1913.

88   See Erving Winslow to Wilson, March 19, 1913; E. B. Biggar to Joseph P. Tumulty, March 19, 1913; Guy M. Walker to

Wilson, March 20, 1913; Austin J. Brown to Wilson, March 20, 1913; Charles R. Crane to Wilson, March 21, 1913; Frank J. Loesch to Wilson, March 23, 1913; William J. Bryan to Joseph P. Tumulty (with an enclosed communication from the Brotherhood League to Wilson), April 8, 1913, and many other messages of congratulation, Wilson Papers, VI, 227. Also see the congratulatory messages, SD, 893.51/1356.

89   Requoted from R. S. Baker, *Wilson,* IV, 76.

90   New York *Times,* March 20, 1913.

91   See English translations from the Japanese press of editorial comments on Wilson's statement, SD, 893.51/1403.

92   Thomas Sammons (American consul-general at Yokohama) to Franklin K. Lane, March 23, 1913, Wilson Papers, II, 35.

93   See Alvey A. Adee's memorandum of his conversation with the Japanese ambassador on March 24, 1913. The memorandum is attached to a letter from Alvey A. Adee to Wilson, March 24, 1913, Wilson Papers, VI, 227. For the Japanese memorandum, see *For. Rels., 1913,* pp. 173-174.

94   Alvey A. Adee to Sutemi Chinda (the Japanese ambassador), March 25, 1913, SD, 893.51/1361.

95   *For Rels., 1913,* pp. 177-178.

96   The Shanghai *China Republic,* March 21, 1913. See clippings from Shanghai newspapers, which are enclosed in a letter from Amos P. Wilder (American consul-general at Shanghai) to Bryan, March 24, 1913, SD, 893.51/1392.

97   *For. Rels., 1913,* p. 175.

98   See Alvey A. Adee's memorandum of his conversation with the Chinese minister on March 20, 1913. The memorandum is attached to a letter from Adee to Wilson, March 20, 1913, SD, 893.51/1355.

99   *For. Rels., 1913,* p. 175.

CHAPTER THREE

American Recognition of the Chinese Republic

The problem of recognizing the Chinese Republic arose in the latter part of the Taft administration and did not come to a solution until after the inauguration of Woodrow Wilson. As in the matter of the consortium, both Taft and Wilson strove to support the traditional American policy of the open door and the administrative and territorial integrity of China, but again they approached this problem in different ways. The basic difference between the method of Taft and that of Wilson, as already shown in the case of American loans to China, lay in the fact that the essence of the former was the concert of the powers while the substance of the latter was independent action. On the surface both methods were quite flexible. At no time did Taft abandon freedom to recognize the Chinese Republic independently if he saw fit, but this caution was intended more to appease public opinion and prevent undue delay than to displace the fundamental principle of international concert. In the matter of recognition, Wilson also welcomed the cooperation of the powers, but the lack of such cooperation did not in the least affect his decision to take independent action.

1.

As it had often been the case with a long dynasty in Chinese history, the Manchu regime, after a period of stability, peace, and prosperity, gradually became corrupt, decentralized, and poverty-stricken, and finally was confronted with a widespread revolution. Tottering toward its end, it tried everything in its power to amend the situation, but nothing proved of avail. Under such circumstances the Chinese revolutionaries felt so confident of their ultimate victory and were so desirous of the early establishment of an internationally recognized republic that they began to appeal for recognition even before the actual overthrow of the Manchu government. Only about five weeks after the outbreak of the revolution at Wuchang, their director of foreign affairs, Wu T'ing-fang, made such an appeal to the world, on November 15, 1911, through William R. Hearst in New York. His argument was that the Republic was already a fact and that fourteen of the eighteen provinces had declared independence of the Manchu Emperor and had pledged allegiance to the revolutionary government.[1] On November eighteenth, Wang Cheng-t'ing, then vice-president of the Wuchang revolutionary board of foreign affairs, called upon the American consul-general at Hankow, Roger S. Greene, and talked with him about the prospects for a recognition of the revolutionists as belligerents and for a recognition later of their republican organization as the government of China. He expressed the hope that the United States would be the first power to grant such recognition. Greene pointed out that his government could only recognize facts, and that, as the leaders of the revolutionary movement had yet to form a really responsible and authoritative central organization, at this time he could see no basis for the consideration of Wang's request.[2]

The first reaction of the American public to the Chinese Revolution was generally unfavorable. Some journals were of the opinion that the revolution would result principally in intensifying the old danger of the partition of China among the European powers. Others went as far as to say that the revolution was simply absurd and the Chinese people were utterly incapable of self-government.[3]

The American government did not show any special favor to the revolutionary party. Its cooperation with other powers in assisting the negotiations between the Manchu government and the revolutionaries and in thus bringing pressure to bear upon China to end the conflict seems to have given the impression that it was on the side of the Manchu Emperor.[4] In fact the American minister at Peking, W. J. Calhoun, did suggest to Washington that Yüan Shih-k'ai, commander-in-chief of the imperial forces, should be supported. He believed that if the powers had supported Yüan from the beginning the latter already would have put an end to the revolution.[5] But the government at Washington maintained an attitude of strict neutrality.[6] Its cooperation with other governments in aiding the negotiations between the opposing parties was actually more a step to prevent any individual action of intervention on the part of the powers like Russia, Japan, and England than a measure to support one party against the other. The United States, unless foreign interests in China were seriously threatened, advised that the powers concert on neutrality rather than intervention.

Before the above-mentioned negotiations between the two contending Chinese factions were brought to a conclusion, representatives from the rebellious provinces had convoked an assembly at Nanking and had taken up the direction of the revolution. They unanimously elected Sun Yat-sen Provisional President of the Republic of China, and soon set a republican government in motion. In order to enter into formal intercourse with foreign countries Wang Ch'ung-hui, the foreign minister at Nanking, directed an identical note to Washington, Tokyo, London, Paris, Berlin, and St. Petersburg, fervently requesting recognition.[7] No action on this request was taken by the powers because they awaited the final outcome of the negotiations. A peace settlement was reached between the negotiators on February 12, 1912; as a result the Manchu Emperor abdicated

in favor of a republican form of government to be organized by
Yüan Shih-k'ai. Upon the advice of Sun Yat-sen, who seems to
have valued the interests of the nation above personal honors
as was evidenced by the fact that he offered his resignation as
Provisional President, the Nanking Assembly three days later
elected Yüan in his stead. Thus was China reunited. The
Republic had become a fact.

As the Nanking government began to gather up wide support
of the Chinese people, American public opinion gradually
turned in favor of the republican movement. William Sulzer,
congressman from New York, had introduced a resolution early
in January, 1912, expressing sympathy with the Chinese people
in their efforts toward republicanism and favoring recognition
at the earliest possible date.[8] He again introduced a joint
resolution late in February for sending congratulations to China.[9]
In speaking for his proposal he more than once voiced the
hope that the United States would be the first country to accord
recognition. The enthusiasm with which the House of Representatives welcomed the establishment of another sister republic
was attested by passage of the Sulzer resolution without discussion. Later the Senate amended the resolution by changing
it into a concurrent one and omitting the preamble; this by no
means altered its essence or general tone.[10] Many individuals
and organizations also began to urge the American government
to take immediate action on recognition. Most noticeable of
all was the China Society of America which, composed of
Chinese residents in the United States and of distinguished
American citizens, passed a resolution on February 15, 1912,
requesting the President of the United States to be first among
the representatives of foreign countries to accord recognition.
It delegated its chairman, Louis Livingston Seaman, to make
a personal appeal to President Taft to such an effect.[11]

The Taft administration was not indifferent. As soon as
the abdication of the Manchu Emperor became known, it was

ready to find a solution for carrying on diplomatic relations with the republican government with Yüan Shih-k'ai as its head. Such an opportunity came when it was officially informed that China had entered upon a formative period and that the Chinese minister accredited to the United States would continue in the discharge of his functions under the designation of "provisional diplomatic agent." [12] In the matter of recognizing the change of form of government in a foreign country the American policy, according to Huntington Wilson, had for more than a century been to apply the *de facto* test and to enter into only informal relations with the new government of a state which had yet to win the consent of the governed and discharge its international obligations. In agreement with this established policy the Taft government promptly granted the Chinese request and at the same time ordered W. J. Calhoun to continue in the exercise of his office as its representative at Peking. The United States was therefore in full *de facto* relations with the Chinese Republic during the formative period. [13]

The United States had cooperated with other powers in helping the Chinese peace negotiations. It also desired to act in concert with them in the problem of recognition. Concerted action had at least three advantages: (1) to add strength to that principle which it held so indispensable for the execution of its China policy; (2) to remove the danger of being forestalled by other governments; and (3) to remind China of her international obligations. [14] But in order to avoid being too far involved in international complications in China the Taft government agreed to apply the policy of cooperation only as far as this course *would entail no undue delay.* It explicitly laid down this condition to both Japan and Great Britain when they inquired about the American attitude toward the principle of concert and the guaranties to be secured from China at the time of formal recognition. [15]

Here was a qualification that left the American government free to recognize the Chinese Republic independently in case concerted action caused unnecessary delay, and gave rise to trouble in Congress as well as international rivalry in China. Thus it was that during the first half of the year 1912 the Taft administration, suspicious of other powers' intentional delay and sensitive to public opinion at home, felt compelled to adopt an elastic policy of international cooperation if possible and independent action if necessary.

In spite of the American warning against inappropriate delay, the other powers would not consent to grant recognition without specific prior conditions. Japan proposed that at the time of recognition the countries concerned should secure from the new government a formal confirmation of all the rights, privileges, and immunities which foreigners had been enjoying in China. To this proposal Great Britain promptly agreed in principle. In considering this problem, the United States was more cautious and refrained from expressing definite views until the nature and conditions of those foreign rights, privileges, and immunities were more clearly explained. Russia specifically pointed out in a note to the United States that she would reserve her rights and special interests in North Manchuria, Mongolia, and West China. Japan made reservations with reference to South Manchuria and its bordering territory, eastern Inner Mongolia. To all these terms the United States assented only on condition that they had been previously covered by treaties and conventions.[16]

The bargaining of the powers about terms of recognition was certainly entailing delay. Repeated appeals from home and abroad were urging the American government to take prompt action. Under such circumstances the state department found it advisable to instruct its minister at Peking to make a report as to how far the existing Chinese government could meet the requirements for recognition in accordance with international law. News from the Chinese capital was fairly disappointing: the North and the South were only superficially united; the National Council was far from representing the popular will; and the coalition government was established by the political manipulations of only a small group of people. In spite of this discouraging situation the American minister suggested that recognition, especially if accorded by the powers acting in concert, would strengthen the influence of the only possible central government then in sight over the entire country.[17] In all probability the state department must have given careful consideration to that suggestion.

Two months had elapsed and the Taft administration had not reached any definite decision. At this juncture the newly appointed president of the council of ministers, Lou Tseng-tsiang (Lu Cheng-hsiang), renewed China's appeal to the United States for recognition.[18] In a new move, Knox addressed the following circular telegram to France, Germany, Great Britain, Italy, Japan, Russia, and Austria:

Confidential memorandum. The powers are in full accord, the American Government believes, in the view that a stable central government is the first desideratum in China and that formal recognition by the powers, when granted, would go far to confirm the stability of the established government.

The Provisional Government appears now to be generally in possession of the administrative machinery, to be maintaining order, and to be exercising its functions with the acquiescence of the people. The situation accordingly seems to resolve itself to the question whether there are any substantial reasons why recognition should longer be withheld.

Would the Government of (insert name of country) now be disposed to consider whether the present Chinese Government may not be regarded as so far substantially conforming to the accepted standards of international law as to merit formal recognition?

Knox intimated that in response to public opinion at home Congress would probably make "a strong demand for early recognition" if the Executive remained inactive.[19]

The powers were unanimous in rejecting Knox's overture. Conditions, they professed, were not such as to warrant formal recognition until a permanent constitution should have been adopted by a national assembly and the provisional government should have been succeeded by a permanent one duly invested with authority to express the popular will.[20] The Japanese minister at Peking even stated that recognition at this time would "serve to influence the ambition, increase the arrogance and add to the excitement of the young fledglings now in the Government and in the National Assembly." [21]

The powers' flat refusal of the Knox suggestion placed the United States in a very unpleasant position. If it took individual action to recognize the Chinese Republic, that would certainly mean the breakdown of the principle of concert which was the gist of Taft's China policy; it probably would also mean the collapse of the international consortium in which Taft himself had so strongly advised the American banking group to participate.

The caution of the powers seemed to be justified by the occurrence of a cabinet crisis, precipitated in July by the sudden resignation of Premier T'ang Shao-yi. Yüan Shih-k'ai publicly proclaimed that as the Chinese Republic had yet to make its foundations secure it could scarcely weather any political storm. Only by a show of military force did Yüan succeed in getting a new cabinet formed.[22] The cabinet crisis impelled the Taft administration to yield in principle to the new formula that recognition would not be granted until an ultimate republican form of government had been installed. It acquiesced in further delay in order to maintain the principle of international cooperation.

An open announcement of abandoning the idea of individual action altogether would have lost the sympathy of the Chinese people and have provoked American public opinion. The safest course for Washington out of the awkward dilemma would naturally be to cling as long as possible to the principle of concert and the new formula of recognition with the constitutional test as a prior condition, but to keep the door still open for independent recognition if concerted action proved impracticable.[23]

During the four months from August through November, 1912, the Chinese situation gradually became better. Elections took place for the members of the National Assembly scheduled to convene at the beginning of 1913. Should this elected body convene, the American government would have to face the question of whether it should recognize China as soon as the Assembly definitively proclaimed the adoption of a republican form of government, or whether it should withhold recognition until the full establishment of a new government in accordance with a permanent constitution formally adopted.

In the history of America's recognition of foreign governments precedents for both alternatives could be found. The case of the recognition of the Portuguese Republic in June, 1911, supported the first alternative, and other cases generally supported the second.[24] In his annual message of 1912 to Congress, President Taft said:

A constituent assembly, composed of representatives duly chosen by the people of China in the elections that are now being held, has been called to meet in January next to adopt a permanent constitution and organize the Government of the nascent Republic. During the formative constitutional stage and pending definitive action by the assembly, as expressive of the popular will, and the hoped-for establishment of a stable republican form of government, capable of fulfilling its international obligations, the United States is, according to precedent, maintaining full and friendly *de facto* relations with the provisional Government.[25]

The stand taken in this message with regard to the recognition of China was interpreted as comprehensive enough to cover both alternatives. But in analyzing the attitudes of the other powers the American government felt sure that no one, with the possible exception of Germany, would be willing to co-operate in recognizing the Chinese Republic before the formal organization of a constitutional government.[26] So far as the maintenance of the policy of concerted action was concerned, the second course, therefore, would serve the purpose of the United States better than the first. In essence the position which Taft took in his message to Congress did indicate a preference for the second course.

As a matter of fact the National Assembly of China did not meet according to schedule, and the Taft administration soon came to its constitutional end. Before he left the White House, President Taft did not have the chance to consider either the question of taking cognizance of any preliminary declaration on the part of the Chinese elective body or the question of waiting until China had fulfilled all the requirements as demanded by the powers. He simply adhered to a broad position and watched for further developments. Thus he succeeded in maintaining the policy of international concert until the expiration of his term of office, and allowed the complicated problem of the recognition of China to go over to the next administration.

2.

Before the Wilson regime began, the movement for an early recognition of the Chinese Republic had been daily gaining strength in America. The avoidance of protracted civil war in China in 1912 and the strengthening of the power of Yüan Shih-k'ai had swept away the doubts of many people as to the ability of the Chinese to establish a stable government. A new hope for immediate recognition had been raised in a great number of letters addressed both to the President-elect and to the outgoing President by American missionaries, church organizations, newspapers, chambers of commerce, and various clubs and societies.

In response to this demand of the American public, Senator Augustus Octavius Bacon introduced a joint resolution on January 2, 1913, providing for instant recognition on the assumption that the Chinese government then constituted represented the people and evinced permanency and stability.[27] But the Taft government which, as we have shown, had finally adopted the formula of the constitutional test resented Bacon's supposition and refuted it by saying that the new government at Peking was neither representative nor permanent nor stable. Lest Congress attempt to take over the ultimate power of decision as to recognition, Knox made it specifically explicit that the question of recognizing a new government should be determined by the Executive, not by the law-making power embracing, to use the words of Senator Bacon, "the joint action of both the legislative and the executive branches of the Government—the Congress and the President—acting in a legislative capacity." [28] Reports had it that if the resolution should pass Congress the President would veto it.

The delay of the Taft administration aroused much dissatisfaction. Woodrow Wilson's friend Bishop J. W. Bashford, who had time and again urged immediate recognition, wrote to Huntington Wilson on January 20, 1913: "I have not met a single American in China, save officials whose lips are sealed, without hearing complaints of the delay of our government in the recognition of the Republic. . . . Our attitude toward China is far more critical than the attitude of the French government in recognizing the United States in 1778 when we were in the midst of our Revolutionary War and the Continental Congress was even driven from the capital, and when recognition possibly turned the tide of war in favor of our republic." [29] John Stuart Thomson, who was the head of the Clark University movement for the recognition of China and whose work *China Revolutionized* in behalf of recognition had deeply impressed both the United States and China, laid all the blame for delay on Secretary Knox, whose chief interest in international matters, he said, seemed to be promoting loans on the part of certain bankers in exchange for control over the debtor countries.[30] The China Society of America under the chairmanship of Louis Livingston Seaman complained that their efforts to gain some kind of a definite reply from the state department with regard to the recognition of China had been answered with evasive statements.[31] Seaman himself openly asserted that if the state department had followed John Hay's open door policy in the preceding year China would have been recognized long ago.[32] Austin P. Brown, a real estate, railroad, and corporate financier well known for his surpassing interest in the cause of the Chinese Revolution, accused Taft of having taken a wrong position in regard to his treatment of the more than four hundred million people of China.[33] J. N. Butler of Peoria, Illinois, even remarked unreservedly that since the death of Secretary John Hay the course of action taken by the American government had been shameful and that seemingly the United States was withholding recognition for the purpose of continuing to cooperate with other powers in a policy of exploitation and robbery.[34]

With the inauguration of Woodrow Wilson the recognition movement gained still greater strength. The Chicago *Tribune* editorially stated that the American people would like to know why their government had abstained from recognizing the Chinese Republic.[35] Many other influential journals shared the same concern. Austin P. Brown again urged upon Bryan the imperative necessity of taking prompt action.[36] Following him hundreds of Americans, representing lawyers, doctors, merchants, bankers, manufacturers, importers, exporters, and every other branch of commercial enterprise, sent a petition to the President for immediate recognition.[37] William Sulzer, who was then governor of the State of New York and who, while in Congress, had done all he could to advance the cause of recognition, personally expressed to Wilson the hope that recognition would not be further delayed.[38] The Chamber of Commerce of the United States, on March twenty-fourth, formally transmitted to the secretary of state a resolution which it had earlier passed in favor of speedy recognition.[39] There were numerous other letters and telegrams directed either to the President or to the secretary of state for the same purpose.[40]

In answering all these petitions the new American administration did not mention the principle of concerted action or the formula of recognition with the constitutional test as a prior condition, but simply pointed out that it was giving careful attention to the problem and would dispose of it soon after full consideration. It was generally felt that Wilson, who had reversed the consortium policy of his predecessor, would also put an end to the disappointing apparent delay in welcoming a new sister republic into the family of nations.

The American legation at Peking now strongly favored recognizing China without delay. The day that Wilson's statement withdrawing from the consortium was given to the press at Washington, E. T. Williams, the chargé d'affaires at Peking, wrote a favorable report on the recognition question. He observed that general conditions in China had recently improved a great deal. The Chinese people were offering no resistance to the change of the form of government and, although politically ignorant and indifferent, would in due time give evidence of their ability to govern themselves. With the improvement of education and communications, localism or provincialism was giving way to a truly stable central government under the leadership of Yüan Shih-k'ai, who had exhibited a remarkable skill in strengthening unity and maintaining order throughout the country. In the light of such facts it seemed to Williams that "even the most discouraging features of the situation in China are not of a sort to recommend delay in recognizing the new government." Furthermore prompt recognition would do much to keep China from a return to monarchism, to deepen China's friendly feelings toward the United States, and, above all, to check the aggressive designs of other powers.[41] Although we cannot tell just how much influence Williams's report had on the course of action of the new administration at Washington, it was obviously in perfect harmony with the thinking of Woodrow Wilson, who also desired to recognize China at the earliest possible date.

The Chinese provisional government at once sensed the principle of a new American policy as manifested in the consortium announcement. Taking advantage of the opportunity to congratulate Bryan on his assumption of the office of secretary of state, the Chinese minister of foreign affairs, Lou Tseng-tsiang, presented a new appeal.[42] He also requested E. T. Williams to communicate by telegram the desire of Yüan Shih-k'ai for immediate recognition. In terms of Chinese internal politics such a recognition on the part of the United States would enormously strengthen Yüan's government in the eyes of the people and the National Assembly which would soon convene. In transmitting the Chinese message Williams added his own support of the request of Yüan out of a desire to assist the latter in removing a political tension apparently resulting from the assassination of the famous Kuomintang leader, Sung Chiao-jen, which reflected the irreconcilable conflict of authority between the Southern and Northern factions.[43] In reply Bryan instructed the American chargé d'affaires to inform Lou Tseng-tsiang that the question of recognition was receiving careful and sympathetic attention in Washington.[44]

As Bryan was not well acquainted with the legal or technical aspect of the recognition problem, he meanwhile requested Alvey A. Adee, the second assistant secretary of state, to formulate views and make suggestions. Adee, who had supported the China policy of the preceding administration, more or less stuck to the old formula of the constitutional test. In his opinion the Chinese government was still in a transitional period and could not be expected to take a permanent form until the convening of the National Assembly and the adoption of a permanent constitution. In such a case the American government was confronted with two possible courses of action. First, if it meant to recognize more explicitly Yüan Shih-k'ai as the head of the existing central government, that could be immediately effected by President Wilson's granting an audience to the Chinese minister at Washington. Second, if it intended to recognize the form of government in China as being that of a republic, that could be effected by a formal announcement of recognition to be made by the American legation at Peking only upon the proclamation and organization of a republican form of government by the National Assembly.

Adee seemed to recommend the first course in preference to the second, because he thought that Yüan's recent request appeared to be not a desire for the recognition of China as a republic, but a wish to have his status as President recognized in a more emphatic way.[45]

Neither Wilson nor Bryan seemed to agree with Adee on merely giving a more explicit confirmation of Yüan Shih-k'ai as the responsible head of the Chinese administration. On the contrary they preferred formal recognition of the Chinese Republic as a republic. At the cabinet meeting of April 1, 1913, the Chinese problem was brought up for discussion. It was pointed out that the meeting of the Chinese National Assembly was going to take place on April eighth and would be an appropriate occasion for recognition. Wilson desired to take prompt action, "because he wished to see China establish a stable government and he was afraid that certain great powers were trying to prevent her from doing so." David F. Houston, who was more cautious, proposed to wait until the intention of the Assembly was known. Some one doubted if China could really set up and conduct a republic. Wilson dismissed the doubt merely by remarking that the same kind of government, he had become convinced after many years of study, was not applicable to all nations.[46]

Here we can detect the basic motive back of Wilson's recognition policy. In weighing the Chinese situation he placed internal stability and freedom from foreign aggression above the republican form of government.

After the cabinet meeting of April first, Wilson had apparently made up his mind to have his administration take the lead in recognizing China. But before resorting to independent action he decided first to sound out other countries as to the possibility of their granting recognition simultaneously with the United States. Thus he instructed Bryan to send the following aide-mémoire on April 2, 1913 to the representatives in Washington of countries having treaty relations with China:

> The President wishes me to announce to you, and through you to your Government, that it is his purpose to recognize the Government of China on the 8th of April upon the meeting of its Constituent Assembly. He wishes me to say that he very earnestly desires and invites the cooperation of your Government and its action to the same effect at the same time.[47]

The next day E. T. Williams sent a telegram to Washington, reporting the political situation in China and again urging immediate recognition. The effect of the assassination of Sung Chiao-jen had been to aggravate sectional and partisan sentiments. The National Assembly which was scheduled to convene on April eighth, might delay its opening, because some representatives were remaining at Shanghai as a consequence of Sung's death. Nevertheless even if the delay of the National Assembly meeting should ensue, he believed that recognition on the proposed date "would check disintegrating tendencies and quiet existing unrest." [48] In an earlier report he had discredited the charge that Yüan Shih-k'ai had plotted to murder Sung, for Yüan was too astute a politician to have made such a blunder. As he saw it, the only hope for the preservation of order throughout the country lay in the person of Yüan, and the sooner the latter's government was recognized the better it would be for China and American interests there.[49] Obviously his support of the provisional government at Peking was both consistent and unflinching. To some extent he was taking sides with the Chinese President against the opposing faction headed by Sun Yat-sen.

Although Wilson was equally anxious to help stabilize Yüan's hold, he did not accept Williams's proposition that recognition should be accorded on the proposed date (April eighth) even if the convention of the National Assembly was postponed. At the cabinet meeting of April fourth, the Chinese problem was again discussed. The President and his colleagues agreed to wait for further developments in China.[50] It seemed to be a reasonable decision in view of Chinese internal dissension which was threatening the renewal of civil war and the total collapse of the hoped-for meeting of the elected representatives. However, the convocation of the Assembly might take place according to schedule and with success. Then the American government must be fully prepared to act as soon as further developments concerned with that constituent body warranted recognition. For this reason Bryan telegraphed to Williams a message to the President of China as coming from the President of the United States, which was to be communicated to the Chinese government *"when the Assembly shall have convened with a quorum and is organized for business by the elec-*

tion of its officers." [51] Here was a condition precedent to the recognition of China, if the Wilson administration had laid down any condition at all.

The other powers had been watching closely the policy of the Wilson administration. Soon after the announcement of American withdrawal from the international banking group they had begun to fear that Wilson might also take independent action in the matter of recognition. Both Great Britain and Germany had officially reminded the state department of the necessity of maintaining the principle of concerted action. But when Wilson announced his wish to recognize China on April eighth and invited the cooperation of the foreign governments, the other great powers unanimously rejected the proposal.[52] Their rejection was chiefly due to the fact that they had not yet been able to procure a definite guarantee of their rights and interests from the Chinese government. The attitudes of Japan and Great Britain particularly bore witness to this. Ostensibly the Japanese government declined Wilson's offer on the ground that a premature recognition would practically amount to an interference in favor of Yüan Shih-k'ai against the southern party.[53] But in a circular telegram communicated to Austria-Hungary it disclosed its real intention of securing the fulfillment of international obligations on the part of China.[54] In reply to the American note the British government attached renewed importance to a formal confirmation of the rights, privileges, and immunities enjoyed by its citizens in Chinese territory.[55] Among all the nations which had treaty relations with China, only four minor countries—Brazil, Mexico, Peru and Cuba—gave their whole-hearted consent to Wilson's suggestion.[56]

The Chinese Assembly opened duly on April eighth, but recognition was delayed by the United States. Curiosity was felt throughout the world as to why America did not take action on the promised day. One theory was that the Wilson administration had been disheartened by the flat refusal of the other great powers. But no evidence has been yet discovered fully to confirm this speculation. The United States seems to have decided to recognize China, when Bryan gave his instructions of April sixth as to the circumstances under which the prepared message of recognition was to be communicated to the President of China. Though the Assembly convened with a quorum on April eighth, it was still far from being organized for business—the opening meeting was merely a joint session to celebrate by proper ceremonies this initiation of representative government in China.[57] The Wilson administration might have felt unhappy about the lukewarm reception given by the powers to its proposal, but it had not been so discouraged as to reverse its course in favor of a policy of indefinite delay. The question was: Could the Assembly *start* at all to work on the ultimate establishment of a republican government and the adoption of a permanent constitution? Until that should really come to pass, recognition would be meaningless. For the sake of caution the Wilson administration had to wait until the Assembly could be so organized as to be able to discuss and solve its basic problems. In that sense the unfavorable response of the powers had not affected Wilson's program, which was essentially one of independent action.

On the day of the opening of the Chinese National Assembly the Brazilian government promptly accorded recognition.[58] The next day the government of Peru formally followed suit.[59] The action of Brazil and Peru was probably attributed to a misunderstanding of the situation in Peking, because neither of them had a representative there. Having previously assented to act in concert with the American government and having also learned of the punctual opening of the Assembly, they had quite credibly concluded that the American recognition had already taken place and that they were bound to follow the lead in due time.[60] At any rate, either by misjudgment or on purpose, they had anticipated the United States in accomplishing an act of historical significance for the nascent Republic of China.

Wilson continued to give attention to the developments in China. He told his cabinet that April fifteenth would be the appropriate occasion for recognition if the Assembly were completely organized by that time. But the Assembly failed to meet this expectation. At the cabinet meeting of April eighteenth, the Chinese problem was brought up again. As the organization of the Assembly was yet to be accomplished, it was decided that recognition should be temporarily postponed.[61] From then on Wilson seemed to leave it to the judgment of the American chargé d'affaires at Peking to choose the proper moment for recognizing China in accordance with the conditions previously laid down.

It was not long before the Chinese Senate and Lower House were both satisfactorily organized for business.[62] Considering that all conditions had been fulfilled, E. T. Williams immediately informed the Chinese foreign office that he had been instructed to deliver to President Yüan a message of recognition from the President of the United States.[63] Foreign Minister Lou Tseng-tsiang at once replied that Yüan had designated the second of May as the day for Williams' reception.[64] For this special occasion the Chinese government had prepared an unusually elaborate program. When the appointed time arrived, the American chargé d'affaires, accompanied by the staff of his legation, drove to the President's Palace in a state carriage escorted by a Chinese guard of honor. His route was lined with uniformed police and soldiers, and the houses on both sides were bedecked with fluttering flags. As he entered the palace, he was greeted with military salutes and welcoming anthems. Many if not all high Chinese officials were present at the ceremony, and everything was marked with signal honors.[65]

After being formally received by the Chinese President, Williams presented the following message from Woodrow Wilson:

President of China: The Government of people of the United States of America, having abundantly testified their sympathy with the people of China upon their assumption of the attributes and powers of self-government, deem it opportune at this time, when the representative National Assembly has met to discharge the high duty of setting the seal of full accomplishment upon the aspirations of the Chinese people, that I extend, in the name of my Government and of my countrymen, a greeting of welcome to the new China thus entering into the family of nations. In taking this step I entertain the confident hope and expectation that in perfecting a republican form of government the Chinese nation will attain to the highest degree of development and well being, and that under the new rule all the obligations of China which passed to the Provisional Government will in turn pass to and be observed by the Government established by the Assembly.[66]

Then Williams made a brief address giving assurances of sympathy for the new Republic. In reply Yüan Shih-k'ai most heartily expressed his gratification and stressed the common faith of the Chinese and American peoples in the soundness of democratic government.[67] After a lunch given in their honor the chargé d'affaires and his staff took leave and were escorted back to the American legation. Thus ended this historically important ceremony of recognition, marked by pomp and display.

Although at the ceremony Yüan said nothing about the observance of China's obligations, he did make this point plain in his formal reply to the message of Wilson. After a reiteration of his thanks for the American act of friendliness and goodwill he pledged to preserve the newly established republican form of government and to perfect its operation to the end that the Chinese people "may enjoy its unalloyed blessings, prosperity, and happiness within, through union of law and liberty

and peace and friendship without, through the faithful execution of all established obligations." [68]

American recognition was a great boon to Yüan, who was
then confronted by the bitterly hostile Kuomintang leaders.
They had done everything in their power to oppose the centralization of power in the hands of the President. This ceaseless
enmity had especially manifested itself in the Assembly where
followers of both sides were represented. It explains the delay
in organizing the Assembly for effective work. On April twenty-
sixth, Yüan signed the reorganization loan with the quintuple
group. The signature of this loan without the previous consent
of the constituent body instantly called forth indignant protests
from the opposition party. It was reported that Sun Yat-sen
and other leaders, aside from making open denouncements,
were even plotting a revolution to overthrow Yüan's government. [69] Under such conditions the President was particularly
anxious to have his regime strengthened through recognition
by the great powers. The American act of recognition therefore
came just at the psychological moment. With his financial situation greatly improved through the conclusion of the loan and
with his political status formally recognized by one of the big
powers, the United States, Yüan was enabled to battle through
the opposition in the National Assembly and the provinces and
finally to establish at least the semblance of constitutional government with himself as its Chief Executive.

Practically all China greeted American recognition with
gratitude and delight. First of all, the Chinese Senate and
Lower House respectively adopted a vote of thanks to the
American government for its friendly act. [70] The provincial
legislative bodies were equally gratified and some of them took
identical action. Many local administrative authorities like the
governors of Shansi, Chihli, Chekiang and Kansu sent telegrams to Wilson, offering their heartfelt thanks. [71] Even the
Kuomintang governor of Kiangsi, General Li Lieh-chün, who

was bitterly opposed to the personal rule of Yüan Shih-k'ai, also formally acknowledged his gratitude in a message addressed to the American consul-general at Hankow.[72]

Numerous public meetings were held in various cities in celebration of this memorable event. In Peking, for instance, on May 8, 1913, three or four thousand delegates from the principal local schools and commercial and industrial guilds paraded with flags and banners through the streets to the music of several bands, and requested E. T. Williams to convey their appreciation to the American government.[73] The same kind of joy and enthusiasm was demonstrated in Hankow and Wuchang, the cradles of the Chinese Revolution. People ran about the streets with gongs, announcing American recognition.[74] In Shanghai, the greatest port on the Chinese coast, people put up flags and other decorations. The various commercial houses held a special celebration under the auspices of the Chinese-Anglo-American Friendship Association.[75] In Nanking, the former capital, the Kuomintang local branch called a special meeting and sent several representatives to the American consulate to express its cordial thanks.[76] The voluntary participation of so many classes of people in a nation-wide celebration was ample evidence of the growing popularity of republicanism and of a general attitude of appreciation and friendliness toward the United States.

Despite public rejoicing, recognition was really not so acceptable to the political enemies of Yüan Shih-k'ai. Some Kuomintang leaders including Sun Yat-sen feared that it could serve merely to strengthen the hands of Yüan. They had accused Yüan of perpetrating the murder of Sung Chiao-jen, of concluding the unconstitutional reorganization loan, and of intriguing to plunge China into another civil war. Now they could not help thinking that recognition, though granted by the United States, was actually detrimental to China because it might encourage the old sinister forces which, symbolized by the President, were still working devastation in the new Republic.[77]

As was to be expected, the other powers, particularly Japan, were displeased that the United States had once more broken the principle of international concert. The Japanese press acrimoniously called Wilson's independent action arbitrary and arrogant.[78] With a view to gaining time both to confirm Chinese internal strife and to secure satisfactory terms from China, the Japanese government attempted to continue the policy of concerted delay. Great Britain, France, and Russia were all ready to cooperate with Japan. But Germany, in spite of her stand for the general principle of cooperation, was disinclined to make any definite commitment. Impatient of the undue delay on the part of other powers, she chose to recognize China as soon as the election of Yüan Shih-k'ai as President was approved by the Chinese Assembly.[79]

Wilson's action, in contrast to its unfavorable reception in Europe and Japan, elicited great applause in the United States. Thousands of business men, manufacturers, bankers, and others offered congratulations to Wilson on what he had done for China.[80] A great number of Chinese students, residents, and organizations in America also heartily expressed their thanks. Numerous newspapers and magazines gave favorable comments. The New York *Times* remarked that the act of the President could hardly be regarded as precipitate and that through recognition the United States had given China the highest assurance of a friendly feeling.[81] The *Nation* considered the American recognition of the Chinese Republic another manifestation of "democratic diplomacy" as opposed to dollar diplomacy.[82] The *Independent* thought it to be a sign of the universal victory of American republicanism in the world.[83]

When the American chargé d'affaires delivered the message of recognition at Peking, Bryan was on an official mission in the West, negotiating with the California legislature for a satisfactory solution to the problem of alien land ownership. He immediately expressed his satisfaction upon learning of the news. He called the American action epoch-making.[84] Wilson was even more satisfied. In a letter to Julean Arnold, the American consul at Chefoo, he remarked that his thoughts constantly turned to the great Chinese nation "now struggling to its feet as a conscious self-governing people," and he felt proud that the Chinese people "should look to the United States as to their friend and exemplar in the great tasks which lie ahead of them." Furthermore he earnestly expressed the hope that "not once in the recognition and first greeting of the Republic, but many times in the years to come, this country may have the opportunity to show its cordial friendship for China and all those who work for her lasting benefit.[85]

As we have seen, Wilson's policy of recognition for China was basically one of independent action. Within about seven weeks after his withdrawal from the consortium, he had boldly dealt another hammer-like blow to the principle of international concert as set forth by the Taft administration. But it is to be noted that although he did not conform to Taft's formula of the constitutional test Wilson's recognition of the Chinese Republic was by no means unconditional. He had made it perfectly plain that he would grant recognition only after the National Assembly should have convened with a quorum and become organized for business. He had in fact waited for the satisfactory fulfillment of that condition.

Then the question arises: Why did Wilson not act in accordance with Taft's formula? Why did he not wait until a permanent constitution had been adopted and a permanent form of government established? What was his real motive of recognizing China as soon as the National Assembly had completed its organization?

The answer can be found in the actual situation then existing in China. Before the American recognition took place,

Yüan Shih-k'ai had been confronted with almost insuperable
difficulties. The designs of the powers upon Tibet, Mongolia,
Sinkiang, and Manchuria had threatened to dismember China.
The long bargaining by the consortium countries for economic
and political advantages had kept the Chinese government in
painful straits. Most serious of all had been the ever-present
danger of another revolution, aiming at the overthrow of Yüan's
government. E. T. Williams had realized the seriousness of the
situation and had thus repeatedly reported it to Wilson. As
Williams saw it, the continuance of Yüan in power was the only
hope for the preservation of peace and order in the whole
country, and having opposition leader, Sun Yat-sen, as an alternative was not advisable. For the sake of strengthening Yüan
in the eyes of the Chinese people and helping to prevent foreign
intervention and to quiet the prevailing unrest, he recommended
the immediate recognition of the Peking government.

Williams' representations must have greatly influenced Wilson, whose basic desire was also to see the establishment in
China of a stable government, a government strong enough to
resist aggression or intervention from without and to maintain
peace and order at home. Although Wilson did not accept the
suggestion as to immediate recognition, he did come to realize
the necessity of taking action as early as conditions would
permit. Chiefly for this reason he worked out his new formula
providing for prompt but still conditional recognition.

So far as the stabilization of Yüan's power was concerned,
Wilson's recognition policy seems to have been temporarily
justified. With moral support from the United States and
financial aid from the quintuple consortium, Yüan soon succeeded in consolidating his position. In the summer of 1913
he suppressed a Kuomintang uprising in the Yangtze Valley
with remarkable ease. Then the National Assembly elected him
President of the Republic of China, and all the other powers
formally granted him recognition.[86] But Yüan still retained

his imperialistic leanings. As time went on, he began to take more and more despotic measures against his political enemies. Repeatedly he resorted to indiscriminate arrest and summary execution. As a result he aroused so great a hatred in the country that a few years later his authority almost totally collapsed. In the long run, therefore, Wilson's support of Yüan in an effort to establish a stable government proved to be a failure.

Our account of Wilson's efforts to bring the United States into *de jure* and normal relations with Yüan's government would be incomplete without mention of his final selection of an American minister to China. To take up the tale begun in the first chapter, we should recall the fact that Wilson was very much disappointed after John R. Mott had declined his offer. He felt that it was a great blow,[87] but his eagerness to solve the problem was not diminished. The real difficulty was to find a nominee with both personal abilities and a religious background. Before accepting the ambassadorship to Turkey, Henry Morgenthau, a capable man of Jewish descent, had shown a preference for the Chinese post. Wilson had to refuse the offer, because the applicant was not an evangelical Christian.[88] Colonel House had also suggested Norman Hapgood, a noted author and editor, but nothing came out of the suggestion for the same religious reason.[89] Charles R. Crane, a well-known industrialist and Wilson's supporter, highly recommended Edward A. Ross, a celebrated sociologist and the author of *The Changing Chinese*.[90] The recommendation interested Wilson very much but does not seem to have convinced him.[91]

After China was recognized, the need for the appointment of a formal representative to Peking became more pressing. In June the name of William T. Ellis was mentioned. Although Ellis had been active in church affairs and of good moral character, he was said to be "an undiplomatic man." [92] Probably for this reason Wilson did not appoint him.[93] Finally Professor

83

Paul S. Reinsch of the University of Wisconsin was taken into consideration.

Reinsch had achieved a national reputation as a proficient and productive scholar of political science and had gained a profound understanding of the international politics in the Orient. His father was a Lutheran clergyman, and his religious background was naturally acceptable to the American Protestant missionaries in China. Most noticeable was the fact that like Wilson he had professed himself to be an opponent of imperialism and a champion of the under-developed countries. He was certainly an ideal choice for the Peking post. At the end of June, Wilson requested him to come to Washington for a conversation on "a matter of important public business." [94] It was not long before Wilson broached the matter and, with his consent, formally appointed him minister to China.

With the recognition of the Chinese Republic and the appointment of Reinsch as minister to Peking, the United States had resumed regular diplomatic relations. But many new difficulties still lay ahead. Most spectacular of these was the Japanese effort to seize control of China during the First World War.

NOTES:

1 Wu T'ing-fang to William R. Hearst, November 15, 1911, SD, 893.00/634.

2 Roger S. Greene to W. J. Calhoun, November 22, 1911, *ibid.*, 893.00/894.

3 Foster Rhea Dulles, *China and America: the Story of Their Relations since 1784* (Princeton, 1946), pp. 138-139. Hereafter cited as F. R. Dulles, *China and America.*

4 "Recognition of the Chinese Republic," *Independent*, vol. 72 (1912), pp. 209-211.

5 W. J. Calhoun to the secretary of state, December 28, 1911, SD, 893.00/832.

6 In response to a request from the Japanese government for an expression of views as to the situation in China, the American government replied that it shared apprehension regarding the seriousness of the Chinese situation, but that it still stuck to "the attitude of strict neutrality thus far adopted by the common consent of the powers." See the secretary of state to the American embassy at Tokyo, December 21, 1911, *ibid.,* 893.00/785.

7 For the text of the note, see *For. Rels., 1912,* p. 62.

8 "The Chinese Revolution," *Independent,* vol. 72 (1912), p. 71.

9 For the text of the resolution, see SD, 893.00/1146a. The resolution was actually drafted by Huntington Wilson, acting secretary of state, who had sought to remove from it the objectionable features of the earlier Sulzer resolution. See Huntington Wilson to President Taft, February 26, 1912, SD, 893.00/1105.

10 Wen Hwan Ma (Ma Wen-huan), *American Policy toward China* (Shanghai, 1934), p. 239. Hereafter cited as W. H. Ma, *American Policy.*

11 See SD, 893.00/634.

12 See W. J. Calhoun to the secretary of state, February 13, 1912, *ibid.,* 893.00/1468; and the Chinese minister at Washington to the secretary of state, February 14, *For. Rels.,* 1912, p. 66.

13 Huntington Wilson to Charles D. Hilles, February 25, 1913, Taft Papers, presidential series no. 2, box 33.

14 Huntington Wilson to President Taft, February 26, 1912, SD, 893.00/1105.

15 *For. Rels., 1912,* pp. 69-70.

16 *Ibid.,* pp. 68-70, 74, and 79.

17 *Ibid.,* pp. 78-79.

18 Lou Tseng-tsiang (Lu Cheng-hsiang) to the secretary of state, July 7, 1912 (date of receipt), SD, 893.00/1364.

19 The secretary of state to the American ambassadors to France, Germany, Great Britain, Italy, Japan, Russia and Austria, July 20, 1912, *For. Rels., 1912,* p. 81.

20 *Ibid.,* pp. 82-86. For a brief summary of the correspondence between the powers and the United States relating to the Knox proposal, see Knox Correspondence, vol. 19.

21 *For. Rels., 1912,* p. 84.

22 See the memorandum enclosed in a letter from Knox to Senator Shelby Moore Cullom, February 4, 1913, SD, 893.00/1529a.

23 According to Huntington Wilson, it would be in accordance with established precedents to delay recognition until China should have adopted a permanent constitution, have duly elected a president, and have established a permanent government with constitutional authority. However, he further remarked: "Whether formal action in the matter of recognition shall be deferred until the above programme is carried out,—a course which it is understood is favored by the other powers having important interests in China,—or whether the Executive shall, owing to certain exigencies of the situation both here and abroad and for reasons deemed sufficient by him, take individual action, remains to be decided." See Huntington Wilson to Louis Livingston Seaman, August 16, 1912, *ibid.,* 893.00/634. He repeated the same statements in his instructions to the American minister at Peking. See Huntington Wilson to W. J. Calhoun, September 20, 1912, *ibid.,* 893.00/1447. Later in answer to letters inquiring about or appealing for recognition of China the American government made it unequivocally clear that the policy of concert would never involve any commitment to the prejudice of such freedom of action as might at any time be necessary for individual recognition. See, for example, Alvey A. Adee to E. F. Baldwin (editor of the *Outlook*), February 26, 1913, *ibid.,* 893.00/1534.

24 *For. Rels., 1913,* p. 91. For the American recognition of the Portuguese Republic, see *For. Rels., 1911,* pp. 689-694.

25 *For. Rels., 1912,* the annual message of the President, XXI-XXII.

26 *For. Rels., 1913,* p. 92.

27 See *Congressional Record,* January 2, 1913, p. 914.

28 *For. Rels., 1913,* pp. 88-91.

29 J. W. Bashford to Huntington Wilson, January 20, 1913, SD, 893.00/634. For Bashford's stand for the immediate recognition of China, also see J. W. Bashford to Secretary of State Knox, August 17, 1912, *ibid.,* 893.00/634; the same to President Taft, September 16, 1912, *ibid.,* 893.00/1464; and the same to President Taft, November 11, 1912, *ibid.,* 893.00/634.

30 See a clipping from Burlington *Free Press,* January 27, 1913, and a typewritten copy of an article from Worcester *Telegram,* January 12, 1913, SD, 893.00/634.

31 New York *Times,* January 1, 1913.

32   Louis Livingston Seaman, "A Plea for Fair Play and the Recognition of the Chinese Republic," in George H. Blakeslee, ed., *Recent Developments in China* (New York, 1913), p. 64.

33   Austin P. Brown to Woodrow Wilson, March 4, 1913, SD, 893.00/634.

34   J. N. Butler to William Jennings Bryan, March 6, 1913, *ibid.*, 893.00/634.

35   Chicago *Tribune*, March 10, 1913.

36   Austin P. Brown to Bryan, March 12, 1913, SD, 893.00/634.

37   The petition is dated March 14, 1913. See *ibid.*, 893.00/634.

38   William Sulzer to Wilson, March 20, 1913, *ibid.*, 893.00/634.

39   The Chamber of Commerce of the United States to Bryan, March 24, 1913, *ibid.*, 893.00/634.

40   For all these letters and telegrams, see *ibid.*, 893.00/634.

41   E. T. Williams to Bryan, March 18, 1913, *For. Rels., 1913*, pp. 96-98.

42   Lou Tseng-tsiang to Bryan, March 25, 1913, *ibid.*, pp. 98-99.

43   E. T. Williams to Bryan, March 28, 1913, *ibid.*, p. 100; and the same to the same, April 1, 1913, *ibid.*, pp. 106-108.

44   Bryan to E. T. Williams, March 28, 1913, *ibid.*, p. 100.

45   Alvey A. Adee to Bryan, March 28, 1913, *ibid.*, pp. 100-103.

46   D. F. Houston, *Wilson's Cabinet*, I, 49.

47   Bryan to the representatives in Washington of countries having relations with China, April 2, 1913, Wilson Papers, II, 34. Also see *For. Rels., 1913*, p. 108.

48   E. T. Williams to Bryan, April 3, 1913, SD, 893.00/1591.

49   E. T. Williams to Bryan, April 1, 1913, *For. Rels., 1913*, pp. 106-108.

50   D. F. Houston, *Wilson's Cabinet*, I, 49.

51   Bryan to E. T. Williams, April 6, 1913, *For. Rels., 1913*, pp. 109-110.

52   See *ibid.*, pp. 109-111; and *Die grosse Politik*, XXXII, 270-273.

53   The Japanese embassy to the state department, April 4, 1913, *For. Rels., 1913*, p. 109.

54   The Austro-Hungarian embassy to the state department, undated, *ibid.*, pp. 114-115.

55   *Ibid.*, p. 110.

56   *Ibid.*, p. 109.

57   E. T. Williams to Bryan, April 11, 1913, *ibid.*, p. 112.

58   Brazil effected her recognition of China through a formal note communicated on April 8, by the Brazilian chargé d'affaires in Japan to the Chinese diplomatic representative there. See Lou Tseng-tsiang to E. T. Williams, April 10, 1913, SD, 893.00/1645.

59   Lou Tseng-tsiang to E. T. Williams, April 11, 1913, *ibid.*, 893.00/1656.

60   E. T. Williams to Bryan, April 11, 1913, *For. Rels., 1913,* pp. 113-114.

61   D. F. Houston, *Wilson's Cabinet,* I, 59-60.

62   The Senate completed its organization on April 25, and the Lower House elected its speaker on April 30, and its vice-speaker on May 1, thus also completing its organizational work. See E. T. Williams to Bryan, May 6, 1913, *For. Rels., 1913,* pp. 116-117.

63   E. T. Williams to Lou Tseng-tsiang, May 1, 1913, SD, 893.00/1681.

64   Lou Tseng-tsiang to E. T. Williams, May 1, 1913, *ibid.*, 893.00/1681.

65   See a clipping from Shanghai *North China Daily News,* May 3, 1913, SD, 893.00/1726; and E. T. Williams to Bryan, May 6, 1913, *For. Rels., 1913,* p. 117.

66   *Ibid.,* p. 110.

67   For Williams' remarks and Yüan's response, see *ibid.,* pp. 118-119.

68   Yüan Shih-k'ai to Wilson, May 2, 1913, *ibid.,* p. 116.

69   E. T. Williams to Bryan, *ibid.,* p. 118.

70   *Ibid.,* pp. 120-121.

71   See Yen Hsi-shan (governor of Shansi) to Wilson, May 7, 1913, SD, 893.00/1654; Feng Kuo-chang (governor of Chihli) to Wilson, May 9, 1913, *ibid.,* 893.00/1662; Chu Jui (governor of Chekiang) to Wilson, May 6, 1913, *ibid.,* 893.00/1660; and Chao Wei-hsi (governor of Kansu) to Wilson, May 10, 1913, *ibid,* 893.00/1661.

72   Li Lieh-chün to the American consul general at Hankow, May 4, 1913, *ibid.,* 893.00/1704.

73   E. T. Williams to Bryan, May 22, 1913, *ibid.,* 893.00/1722.

74   E. T. Williams to Bryan, May 6, 1913, *For. Rels., 1913,* p. 118.

75   E. T. Williams to Bryan, May 19, 1913, SD, 893.00/1719.

76   A. Gilbert (American vice-consul at Nanking) to Bryan, May 19, 1913, *ibid.,* 893.00/1753.

77   Austin P. Brown to Bryan, June 12, 1913, *ibid.*, 893.00/ 1714.

78   A. Rex (German ambassador to Japan) to Bethmann-Hollweg, May 9, 1913, *Die grosse Politik*, XXXII, 277.

79   John G. A. Leishman (American ambassador to Germany) to Bryan, May 5, 1913, SD, 893.00/1650. It was reported from St. Petersburg on May 21, 1913 that while Great Britain, France, Japan, and Russia were acting together with regard to the recognition of China, Germany did not seem to be associated with them in the matter. See London *Times,* May 22, 1913. For more information about the attitude of Germany, see *Die grosse Politik,* XXXII, 274-289.

80   John B. Jeffery to Wilson, May 21, 1913, SD, 893.00/1679.

81   New York *Times,* May 3, 1913.

82   *Nation,* vol. 96 (1913), p. 457.

83   "Recognition at Last," *Independent,* vol. 74 (1913), pp. 1009-1010.

84   Bryan to John B. Moore, May 2, 1913, SD, 893.00/1644.

85   Wilson to Julean Arnold, May 23, 1913, Wilson Papers, VI, 227.

86   *For. Rels.,* 1913, pp. 131-132.

87   R. S. Baker, *Wilson,* IV, 31.

88   J. Kerney, *Political Education,* p. 313.

89   Entry of April 3, 1913 and entry of April 4, 1913, House Diary.

90   See a brief summary of a letter from Charles R. Crane to Wilson, April 3, 1913, Wilson Papers, VI, 252. Also see Charles R. Crane to Wilson, April 8, 1913, *ibid.,* VI, 252. Charles R. Crane was the president of the Crane Company in 1913. In 1920 he succeeded Reinsch as American minister to China.

91   Wilson to Charles R. Crane, April 3, 1913, *ibid.,* VI, 252. Also see Wilson to Charles R. Crane, April 10, 1913, *ibid.,* VI, 252.

92   Winthrop M. Daniels to Wilson, June 15, 1913, Wilson Papers, II, 36. Attached to Daniels' letter is a summary of a letter (missing from the file) from W. C. Robinson, which says that Ellis "is known as an undiplomatic man."

93   Wilson to Winthrop M. Daniels, June 18, 1913, *ibid.,* II, 36. In this letter Wilson remarked that he agreed with Robinson's judgment about the appointment to China.

94   Wilson to Paul S. Reinsch, June 30, 1913, *ibid.,* VII, 3.

CHAPTER FOUR

The Threatened Japanese Protectorate

1.

With Europe aflame in war in August, 1914, China became daily apprehensive of being engulfed in the fast spreading conflagration. She was especially aware of the fact that Japan, long inclined toward territorial expansion on the Asiatic continent, had a defensive and offensive alliance with Great Britain. Should Japan enter the war under the pretext of fulfilling the obligations of the alliance, the immediate object of her attack would most probably be the German foothold in Chinese territory. In such an eventuality China, too weak to keep an inviolate neutrality, would be placed in the same extremely unenviable position she was in during the Russo-Japanese War, which had been fought chiefly in Manchuria. This soon turned out to be the case.

In the event of war among the powers which possessed leaseholds in China, the best way for China to avoid involvement in trouble would be to persuade the belligerents to pledge themselves not to undertake hostilities in Chinese territory. As the friendship of the United States had always been counted upon, the Chinese foreign minister approached the American chargé d'affaires at Peking, John V. A. MacMurray, with the request that the American government "endeavor to obtain the consent of the belligerent European nations to an undertaking not to engage in hostilities either in Chinese territory and marginal waters or in adjacent leased territories." [1] At the same time the

Chinese minister at Washington left a memorandum with the state department to the same effect.[2]

A few days later, on August sixth, China formally declared her neutrality by a presidential mandate.[3] Anxious to preserve her neutrality, she repeated the above-mentioned request to the American government, and also simultaneously asked for the good offices of Japan.[4] She specifically asserted to the Japanese government that if possible China, Japan, and the United States should jointly dissuade the belligerents from extending the war to the Far East.[5]

From the outset the idea of restricting the area of hostilities seemed to be acceptable to the United States. When MacMurray asked for authorization to participate in the arrangements which were being made by the diplomatic body at Peking for the neutralization of all foreign settlement concessions excluding leased areas, Bryan readily granted the request.[6] At the same time he gave careful consideration to the broader aspect of the proposal which the Chinese government had made twice.[7] He decided to sound all interested powers on the possibility of preserving the *status quo* in China and even in the entire Far East.[8] As no general agreement could be reached, his overture came to nothing.[9]

To Japan the Chinese proposal was absolutely unacceptable; she was determined on war without hindrance. In an interview with the Chinese minister at Tokyo on August eighth, the Japanese premier, Count Okuma, plainly stated that the German fleet at Tsingtao would inevitably fight against England and France, and that Japan, bound by the Anglo-Japanese alliance, could not maintain neutrality.[10] The day Okuma was making this statement, the Japanese fleet appeared in waters near Tsingtao.[11] Obviously Japan was prepared to attack the German stronghold in Shantung.

The United States was then the only neutral power which could effectively help to insure Chinese neutrality against violation. On this account Japan was unusually sensitive to every move that the American government might make in China. When the rumor spread that Chinese ports were going to be guarded with the assistance of American troops, Okuma seriously put a question to the Chinese minister at Tokyo concerning the matter.[12] Again when it was known that China, before making a simultaneous overture to both the Japanese and the American governments with respect to the delimiting of the area of hostilities, had sought American good offices in the first instance, the Japanese government reprimanded China for having disregarded Japan in "such a matter of great concern to the Far East." [13] To her satisfaction Japan soon found out that the American government really had no intention of maintaining the *status quo* in China by force and that all peaceful Chinese and American efforts to keep the Far East out of the area of war were doomed to failure.[14] Even more gratifying was the fact that the Chinese government, confronted with the fruitless American peace efforts and the insurmountable Japanese opposition, finally withdrew its proposal for a joint appeal to the belligerent nations for the exclusion of the Far East from the war zone.[15]

Another initial concern of the Japanese government was England's lack of enthusiasm for invoking the Anglo-Japanese Alliance of 1911. Sir Edward Grey had informed the Japanese ambassador to London on August first that if England should intervene on the side of France and Russia it would not be likely for her to apply to Japan for assistance under the alliance.[16] This was merely a general statement; apparently Grey had not yet given thought to the specific condition under which Japanese assistance could be applied for. Presently he sought counsel from William Tyrrell of the British foreign office, and in accordance with the latter's advice made it specifically known to the Japanese government that England would rely upon the support of Japan if an enemy attack on Hongkong or Weihaiwei should take place in the Far East.[17] Here he obviously meant that Japanese assistance would be needed only to protect those two territorial possessions from enemy attack. The Japanese government promptly agreed to this, adding that Japan would also readily support England in case of "a similar concrete act of aggression." [18] They thus resourcefully enlarged the scope of assistance or increased the chance to enter the war. On August fourth, Grey, while thanking Japan for her "generous offer of assistance," formally expressed his intention to avoid "drawing Japan into any trouble." [19] It became evident that Grey had decided, although temporarily, not to invoke the alliance.

But Grey changed his mind a few days later. He told the Japanese government on August seventh: "As some time will be needed in order that our ships of war may find and destroy German ships in Chinese waters, it is most important that the Japanese fleet should hunt out and destroy the armed German merchant cruisers who are now attacking our commerce. . . . This, of course, means an act of war against Germany but this is, in our opinion, unavoidable." [20] Japan agreed to enter the war on the side of England, but opposed the limitation of her belligerent actions to the destruction of the German cruisers. She wanted to extend the war to the Chinese mainland by eliminating the German base of Kiaochow. In spite of Grey's opposition she insisted that her wish be respected. After a futile attempt to convince Japan to limit her activities only to the protection of commerce on the high seas, Grey was finally forced to agree on an attack on the German leasehold in the Province of Shantung.[21]

Germany too, of course, tried to keep Japan out of the war and thus avoid a Japanese attack on Kiaochow. In answer to the American inquiry as to the possibility of circumscribing the area of hostilities in the Far East, the German government indicated to the United States that it did not seek war with

Japan, and that Japan, England, and Germany should agree "that none of these three shall attack warships, colonies, territory, or commerce of any of the others in the East." By the East she meant "all lands and seas between parallels London 90 east and all Pacific to Cape Horn." [22] When the United States received this reply, Japan had already decided to join the war and to remove the Germans from Kiaochow. On August fifteenth the Japanese government delivered an ultimatum to Germany, requiring the latter to give a reply to the following two demands by noon of August twenty-third:

(1) To withdraw immediately from the Japanese and Chinese waters German men-of-war and armed vessels of all kinds and to disarm at once those which cannot be so withdrawn.

(2) To deliver on a date not later than September 15, 1914, to the Imperial Japanese authorities without condition or compensation the entire leased territory of Kiaochow, with a view to eventual restoration of the same to China. [23]

Aside from the above-mentioned suggestion made by the German government to the United States, the German chargé d'affaires at Peking had also worked out a formula for preventing Kiaochow from falling into the enemy hands. On his own authority he had approached the Chinese government with the proposition that Kiaochow should be immediately and directly retroceded to China. He had done this in the hope that at the conclusion of the war Germany could either recover that leasehold or claim an equivalent leased territory as a compensation. [24] The Japanese government, which was always on the alert, soon got wind of this matter. It immediately instructed its representative at Peking to warn the Chinese foreign office against the acceptance of any such proposition. [25] The British minister at Peking also indicated that his government could not recognize the direct transfer of Kiaochow from Germany to China. [26] In view of Japan's threatening attitude and England's opposition the Chinese government refrained from entering into further negotiations with the German chargé d'affaires, thus allowing the latter's plan for direct transfer finally to come to nothing.

The Chinese government was certainly anxious to have Kiaochow retroceded to her one way or another. As direct transfer proved impossible, it at once thought of recovering the leasehold through the medium of the United States. Thereupon Liang Tun-yen, the Chinese minister of communications, requested the American government to approach England and Germany "with a proposal that, in order to avert hostilities, the German rights in Kiaochow might be ceded to the United States for immediate transfer to China." [27] But the state department rejected Liang's request, because, as Bryan put it, "such a course would do more to provoke than to avert war." [28] Thus the Chinese attempt at an immediate but indirect transfer of the German leasehold through the good offices of the United States came to naught.

So hostilities came to the Far East. As the German government failed to comply with the Japanese demands within the time limit assigned for it, Japan formally declared war on August twenty-third. Only a few days later the Japanese fleet, aided by British vessels, began actions against the German base of Tsingtao. In the meantime the Japanese government was planning an attack on that port from the land side. Under the pretext of facilitating military operations on land it attempted to impose upon China the creation of a special war zone south of the Yellow River in Shantung Province. If created, this zone would include the larger part of Shantung. To this excessive demand China certainly would not agree. China, however, did consent to delimit a small war zone along the coast for the landing and passage of the British and Japanese troops.[29] Therefore on September third, the next day after Japan landed troops at Lungkow, the Chinese government declared that "at such points within Lungkow, Laichow, and the neighborhood of Kiaochow Bay adjoining thereto as are absolutely necessary for the passage and use of belligerent troops it cannot hold itself responsible for the obligations of strict neutrality." [30] It took such a step in the hope that the Japanese actions in Shantung would be restricted to a specially designated area. But before long this hope was completely shattered. As the Japanese troops also aimed at the seizure of the German railway possessions, they soon carried their warlike activities beyond the delimited war zone by first occupying the railway station at Weihsien and then extending their control over the whole line as far west as Tsinan. With the capitulation of the German troops at Tsingtao on November seventh, they then came into possession of not only the German leasehold but also the entire Tsingtao-Tsinan Railway.[31]

While the above events took place, the United States was watching all developments in the Far East with great care. It was particularly aware of the possibility that Japan might take advantage of the situation to intervene in Chinese affairs in case internal disorders should occur in China. As it always felt concern for China's internal stability, it would like to be first consulted by Japan before the latter took any such action of intervention. This line of thought had been expressed explicitly by Bryan even before the Japanese declaration of war against Germany. In a statement with regard to the Japanese ultimatum to the German government Bryan had said on August nineteenth:

Should disturbances in the interior of China seem to the Japanese Government to require measures to be taken by Japan or other powers to restore order, the Imperial Japanese Government will no doubt desire to consult with the American Government before deciding upon a course of action. This would be in accordance with the agreement made in the exchange of notes on the 30th of November, 1908 by His Excellency, Baron Kogoro Takahira, then

Japanese Ambassador to the United States, and Hon. Elihu Root, then American Secretary of State.[32]

The suggestion of consultation between the United States and Japan in accordance with the Root-Takahira Agreement seems to have been regarded among some Chinese circles as indicating a determination on the part of the American government to insist upon a previous approval of any Japanese action in Chinese territory. For this reason V. K. Wellington Koo (Ku Wei-chün) of the Chinese foreign office, in an interview with MacMurray on August twenty-seventh, "specified the possible landing of an expeditionary force in Shantung (beyond the limits of the zone of condominium established by the treaty of lease of the Kiaochow territory) as constituting a question in regard to which the Japanese Government would thereby be required to seek the approval of the United States." [33] At that time Japan was pressing for the creation of a large war zone for her military operations which were expected to take place in the Shantung area at any moment. Koo was apparently requesting the United States to intervene on China's behalf.

The broad interpretation that some Chinese including Koo gave to the American suggestion of consultation with Japan was in fact merely wishful thinking. In answer to Koo's request MacMurray said that the suggested consultation applied only to "the case of internal disorders in China," and that the exchange of notes between Root and Takahira was only "a joint declaration of policy rather than a convention establishing a legal status which either party might invoke against the other." [34] To this statement the state department later gave its full endorsement. In his instructions to Paul S. Reinsch the acting secretary of state, Robert Lansing, further expounded the American policy in China:

The United States desires China to feel that American friendship is sincere and to be assured that this Government will be glad to exert any influence, which it possesses, to further, by peaceful methods, the welfare of the Chinese people, but the Department realizes that it would be quixotic in the extreme to allow the question of China's territorial integrity to entangle the United States in international difficulties.[35]

It became quite clear that the American government, in pursuance of a policy of strict neutrality, was definitely reluctant to run into any great trouble with Japan by interfering with the latter's belligerent actions against the Germans in Shantung. Its main concern now seemed to be China's internal stability rather than China's territorial integrity. Unless the occurrence of disorders in the Chinese interior gave rise to intervention on the part of Japan, it preferred not to take any action to irritate Japanese feelings. With its hands full with many other problems it could not resort to anything but peaceful means in dealing with Japan. The extravagant hope entertained by the Chinese at the beginning of the war to the effect that the United States would use force to guard China against territorial infringements, therefore, had little chance of realization.

Militarily weak, China did not dare to put up an armed resistance to the Japanese troops for their violation of her neutrality. All she could do in the midst of helplessness was to register protests to which the Japanese government seldom paid any serious attention. Her anxiety increased daily with the extension of the Japanese military actions in Shantung. The surrender of the Germans at Kiaochow, however, gave her a temporary relief because she thought that the original status of the war zone could be restored as a result of the cessation of hostilities. With this view in mind she addressed a note to the British and Japanese ministers at Peking on January 7, 1915, cancelling the war zone which she had previously delimitated.[36] In answer to this note the Japanese government flatly refused to recognize such an act of cancellation which it denounced as "improper, arbitrary, betraying, in fact, want of confidence in international good faith and regardless of friendly relations." [37] Before any settlement of this question could be brought about, it presented to China the Twenty-One Demands—a *démarche* much more daring and alarming than its seizure of Kiaochow.

The United States had refused to entangle itself in "international" difficulties in China occasioned by the First World War. It would not come to the defense of Chinese neutrality or Chinese territory. It had never espoused other than "peaceful means" to support the integrity of China. It had rationalized the Root-Takahira Agreement into a mere understanding of policy between the United States and Japan to consult each other in case of "internal disorder" in China. Now, in the name of law and order in the Far East, Japan threatened to impose a protectorate over all of China. At one stroke she would have torn down the new edifice of Chinese nationality so painfully propped up by Yüan Shih-k'ai following his victory over the Kuomintang Revolt of 1913. In one dramatic coup the Japanese, taking advantage of Europe's distresses and America's pacifism, would have wiped away the whole China policy of the United States from John Hay to Elihu Root, the only obstacle left standing in their way of conquest over that vast country, the dream-domain of the Japanese empire. The Twenty-One Demands were a challenge to the United States as a world power as well as to China as the intended victim of Japanese aggression and expansion.

2.

The presentation of the Twenty-One Demands took place at a psychological moment when China, without the previous consent of the Japanese government, had just cancelled the Shantung war zone. But the cancellation of the war zone was by no means the real cause of Japan's new diplomatic *démarche,* which reflected a basic desire to secure a recognition of her alleged paramount interests in Chinese territory as well as her controlling voice in Chinese affairs. The demands as presented were a clear and comprehensive expression of the so-called policy of continental expansion which Japan had energetically pursued but had not fully realized owing to the existence of an international balance of power in China. Now that the balance was upset as a result of the war in Europe, a fortunate opportunity had come for Japan to carry out her traditional policy.

Of all Japanese governmental authorities the foreign minister, Baron Kato, was mainly responsible for the decision to present the Twenty-One Demands. As early as January, 1913, he, before leaving his post as ambassador at London in order to become foreign minister at home, had disclosed to Edward Grey the necessity under which Japan was to retain the Kwantung leased territory permanently and to extend the agreements for the South Manchuria and Antung-Mukden railways. Grey, although reticent on the problem of the extension of the railway agreements, was warmly sympathetic with the proposal for a permanent retention of the said leased area.[38] Upon his return to Japan, Kato repeated Grey's words to Premier Katsura, who felt so pleased as to decide to solve the Manchurian problem along the proposed lines. But the Katsura ministry fell before any direct negotiations could be opened with China. Kato did not have the chance to proceed with his plan until he became foreign minister under the leadership of Count Okuma in 1914.[39] Under the favorable circumstances resulting from the outbreak of the war in Europe, his plan for the control of Manchuria was soon broadened into a scheme for the hegemony of the whole of China.

After the fall of Tsingtao in November, 1914, the Japanese minister at Peking, Eki Hioki, was recalled to Tokyo for consultation. On December third, Kato handed him the Twenty-One Demands to be presented to the Peking government.[40] The written instructions which the Japanese foreign minister gave

101

him at the same time did not specify when the demands should be presented. It was presumably up to Hioki to decide upon the opportune time for their presentation.

The manner in which Hioki presented the demands after his return to Peking was unusual. Bypassing the Chinese foreign office he handed the text of the demands directly to President Yüan Shih-k'ai on January 18, 1915. In the course of his interview with the latter, he made several significant remarks. In the first place, he enjoined strict secrecy on pain of grave consequences to China. In the second place, he stated that the majority of the Japanese people were hostile to Yüan because the latter had adopted a policy of antagonizing Japan and befriending European countries and America. He hinted that a speedy acceptance of the demands would remove the hostile feelings of the Japanese people toward Yüan. Furthermore he remarked that the Chinese revolutionists had kept close and intimate relations with some influential Japanese advocating the adoption of strong measures with regard to China, and that if China failed to give a prompt and satisfactory answer the Japanese government would find it impossible to restrain those Japanese from instigating the Chinese revolutionists to cause trouble in China. Obviously he was capitalizing on the Chinese internal dispute as a leverage to attain Japan's goals.[41]

The demands as presented to Yüan Shih-k'ai were divided into five groups. Group I had to do with the settlement of the Shantung question. It required China's assent in advance to any agreement that Japan might make with Germany for the disposition of all German rights, interests, and concessions in the Province of Shantung; to agree not to cede or lease to any other power any territory or island within Shantung or along its coast; to permit Japan to construct a railway from Chefoo or Lungkow to meet the Tsingtao-Tsinan Railway; and to open certain cities and towns in that province as commercial ports.

Group II aimed at defining Japan's special position in South

Manchuria and Eastern Inner Mongolia and required China's recognition thereof. It stipulated that China should agree to extend for a period of ninety-nine years the term of the lease of Port Arthur and Dairen and the term relating to the South Manchuria and Antung-Mukden railways. Further, the control and management of the Kirin-Changchun Railway should be delivered over to Japan also for a period of ninety-nine years. Japanese subjects should be permitted in South Manchuria and Eastern Inner Mongolia to lease or own land "required either for erecting buildings for various commercial and industrial uses or for farming"; to reside and travel, and to engage in various kinds of business; and to open mines. The Chinese government should obtain the previous consent of Japan if it intended (1) to grant permission to other nationals to build a railroad or to obtain from other nationals a loan for constructing a railroad in South Manchuria and Eastern Inner Mongolia, and (2) to pledge to a third power the local taxes of these two areas as security. Whenever the Chinese government employed political, financial, or military advisers or instructors in the said territories, it should first consult Japan.

Group III was concerned with the Han-Yeh-Ping Company. Under the provisions of this section the said company should be made a joint concern of the two countries, and without the consent of Japan the Chinese government should not dispose of any right or property of the company. Besides, all the mines in the neighborhood of those owned by the company should not be worked by other persons without the consent of the company, which should retain a monopoly in the area around its own mines.

According to the single article of Group IV the Japanese and Chinese governments, "with the object of effectively preserving the territorial integrity of China," were to agree that China should engage "not to cede or lease to a third Power any harbour or bay or island along the coast of China."

The Japanese intention of establishing a protectorate over China was far better revealed in Group V than in the first four groups. In this group of articles the Chinese government was required to employ influential Japanese as political, financial, and military advisers; to grant the right of owing land to Japanese hospitals, temples, and schools in the interior of China; to place the police in important places in China under joint Japanese and Chinese administration or to employ numerous Japanese in police offices in such places; and to purchase from Japan a fixed quantity of arms and to establish in China a jointly worked Sino-Japanese arsenal in which Japanese technical experts were to be engaged and Japanese materials to be used. Furthermore China should agree to give Japan "the right of constructing a railway connecting Wuchang and Kiukiang and Nanchang, another line between Nanchang and Hangchow, and another between Nanchang and Chaochou." Finally China was asked to grant Japanese subjects the right to preach throughout Chinese territory.[42]

In accordance with the written instructions given by Kato to Hioki, the latter should negotiate treaties and agreements with China mainly along the lines set forth in the first four groups. With regard to the proposals included in the fifth group, they were to be presented as the "wishes" of the Japanese government. The problems treated under this class were "entirely different in character" from the problems contained in the other groups.[43] It is to be noted, however, that upon presenting the Twenty-One Demands to Yüan Shih-k'ai, Hioki did not make any such distinction. Throughout his discussions with the Chinese government he pressed for the acceptance of all the demands that he had presented. Only when an ultimatum was delivered to China on May seventh did the Japanese government formally withdraw the whole fifth group (except the article relating to Fukien) from negotiations and reserve it for future consideration.[44]

Although the Chinese government was enjoined not to give out any information about the Japanese demands until Japan and China had settle the questions between themselves, the news of the Japanese diplomatic *démarche* came out through secret channels. It was one of the Chinese ministers who first divulged the "astonishing nature" of the Japanese demands to the American diplomatic representative at Peking, Paul S. Reinsch. He confidentially told the latter that Japan had presented "categorical demands" which, if accepted, would reduce China to a state of vassalage. He further remarked that the demands meant to control Chinese natural resources, finances, and army.[45] It was most likely that the Chinese government intentionally let information leak out so as to avoid the disadvantage of negotiating with Japan in secrecy. From the Chinese point of view, publicity was the most effective means to counter Japanese secret diplomacy.

Reinsch, who was highly sympathetic to the Chinese people and greatly suspicious of Japanese designs upon China, immediately realized the seriousness of the situation. On January twenty-third, soon after he learned of the general character of the Japanese proposals, he made a report to the state department to the effect that China's open door and independence were threatened as a result of the new Japanese move. He expressed the fear that in case China should fail to comply Japan would instigate revolutionary uprisings which, in turn, "would offer pretext for military occupation." [46]

At the same time Reinsch tried to keep in close touch with the Chinese government, which was anxious to seek his help. From January twenty-fifth on, the question of the Japanese demands began to be discussed by the Peking press, and it was no more possible to keep the matter locally secret. Therefore high Chinese officials began to consult with him "almost daily" about their difficulties.[47] Although they could not obtain as much official support as they desired, they did gain much invaluable private advice as to the technique of dealing with the individual demands. Without instructions from Washington, Reinsch could not offer the full support of his government to China. All he could do under the circumstances was to give a sympathetic hearing to whatever they wished to discuss, and to give them his carefully weighed opinion.[48] Throughout the Sino-Japanese discussions of the Twenty-One Demands he played the part of a diplomat who gave counsel more in his individual capacity than as the official representative of his own government. In this way he rendered an effective advisory service to the government to which he was accredited.

In pursuance of its secret diplomacy the Japanese government at first did everything in its power to hide the truth about the demands. While prohibiting comment in the Japanese press, it denounced outside reports concerning the basis of the proposed negotiations with China as absolutely unfounded. The Japanese minister at Peking even protested against "inaccuracies" in the dispatch sent by the acting correspondent of the American Associated Press, but did not point out what they were.[49] The Japanese foreign office, on February second, authorized newspapers to state that the demands neither contemplated infringement upon Chinese territory nor impaired foreign rights in China.[50] For a short period of time both British and American newspapers were so convinced by the repeated Japanese denials that they withheld publication of the reports received from their correspondents at Peking. Only gradually did the truth become known to the British and American press.

3.

From the beginning the American government viewed Japan's new move with great concern. Soon after Reinsch's first report reached the state department, E. T. Williams, chief of the division of Far Eastern affairs, wrote a memorandum to Bryan on January twenty-fifth, discussing the critical situation as newly created by Japan in China. He pointed out that the Japanese action violated both the open door policy and the Root-Takahira Notes and that the United States should not let this violation pass without protest. In his opinion, consultation with Great Britain whose interests were likewise affected might be necessary, but this might not be all that the United States should do.[51] In another memorandum which he wrote to Bryan two days later, he further expounded his views about the Chinese situation and urged firm action toward Japan:

Japan's present action not only violates the pledge as to the preservation of "the common interests of all powers," but practically repudiates the pledge to consult the United States and is the more regrettable since the United States in August last intimated an expectation that it would be consulted in case further action in China should be found by Japan to be desirable.

In our own interest and in that of the powers who have at our request entered into the "Open Door" agreements, it seems to be our duty to ask explanation from Japan and insist firmly upon our rights.

I believe that any lack of firmness will but encourage further disregard of our rights.

Our present commercial interests in Japan are greater than those in China, but the look ahead shows our interest to be a strong and independent China rather than one held in subjection by Japan.

China has certain claims upon our sympathy. If we do not recognize them, as we refused to recognize Korea's claim, we are in danger of losing our influence in the Far East and of adding to the dangers of the situation.[52]

By that time the Chinese situation had aroused the attention of Woodrow Wilson. He remarked to Bryan on January 27, 1915, that among the many things which the United States should consider with regard to Japan were "her present attitude and intentions in China and her willingness or unwillingness to live up to the open door in the East." [53] Both Wilson and Bryan seem to have been cautious. They would not make any definite decision before more information was available. Bryan telegraphed Reinsch that the Chinese matter was receiving "careful and prompt attention" and the latter should have the state department "fully informed." [54]

Unlike Wilson and Bryan, Reinsch was anxious to take action. He thought that as Japan was expected to urge quick submission upon China it was essential for the United States to make an early decision as to its policy.[55] He made two concrete suggestions to Bryan. In the first place, China should be asked to ignore the Japanese injunction of secrecy to make the United States officially cognizant of the demands. He believed that China would readily grant such a request "if assured that the Government of the United States would assume moral and consequent political responsibility for insistence upon the disclosure of matters affecting its rights." In the second place, the United States should reach an understanding with Great Britain in order to moderate the Japanese course of action. He thought that the British government held the key to the critical situation. In its own interest it would be willing to support the United States in opposing Japanese supremacy in China. In consideration of the position of the United States both as a friendly neutral power and as an approachable base of supplies it would not be inclined to disregard an intimation from the American government "that it could not regard with indifference the usurpation of political, military and economic domination of China by Japan nor dissociate Great Britain from responsibility for such a situation created by its ally under circumstances incidental to purposes professedly dictated by the Anglo-Japanese Alliance." If the British government should take the suggested position, it would most probably help to put a quietus upon the Japanese schemes.[56]

The next day E. T. Williams, in spite of illness, wrote a letter to Bryan, making more comments on the Japanese demands. On the basis of the information obtained and sent back by Reinsch he pointed out the dangers which the demands held for American interests. In agreement with Reinsch he suggested that China should publish all the demands so that the whole world might pronounce judgment on them and no violation of American rights might occur. As to the attitude of Great Britain he remarked that she "probably has her blind eye on the telescope and does not desire to see the danger signal." But she would certainly be happy to assist in modifying the Japanese proposals if the United States could have them officially published by China. In conclusion Williams said: "If we can succeed in reducing the demands, it seems to me that we ought to insist upon China's putting her house in order and making herself able to defend herself. We can and ought to assist her in this, and in so doing we shall be building up a strong defense for ourselves." [57]

The suggestions of both Reinsch and Williams were referred to Wilson. Although anxious to aid China and to protect American interests, the President and his secretary of state did not seem to think it advisable to assume the responsibility of insisting upon an official disclosure by China of the demands. Therefore they did not make any official request to the Chinese government as it was suggested. With regard to the problem of consultation with Great Britain, a prompt action was taken. Bryan telegraphed to Ambassador Page at London, instructing the latter to find out if the British government had been informed about the nature and extent of the reported Japanese demands and to report what he could learn from the British foreign office.[58] Page received a reply from Edward Grey on February twelfth to the effect that the British government had inquired of Japan but so far had received no comment.[59] E. T. Williams, in a note to Bryan, described the British answer as "very curious and unsatisfactory." [60] The American attempt to exchange views with Great Britain was fruitless.

As time went on, more information about the demands leaked out chiefly through Chinese channels.[61] The press reports, which had been sent out from Peking but temporarily withheld from publication, soon appeared in both British and American newspapers. Japanese designs upon China quickly became a topic of discussion all over the world. This situation compelled the Japanese government to admit part of the whole truth. A memorandum handed to Bryan by the Japanese ambassador at Washington on February eighth revealed an expurgated list of its demands, incompletely covering the first four groups and entirely omitting the fifth one.[62] The next day, February 9, 1915, Baron Kato handed to Ambassador Guthrie a slightly different text of the same list of demands, which he said had been handed in the same manner to the British, French, and Russian ambassadors in Tokyo.[63] The Chinese government at once perceived the moral advantage which it gained as a result of the garbled version given by Japan to her allies and the United States; and it therefore decided to communicate to these same nations a translation of the original document presented to Yüan Shih-k'ai by the Japanese minister on January eighteenth.[64] Through "one of the staff of the Foreign Office" it handed such a translation to Reinsch on February twentieth.[65]

Before Reinsch obtained the above-mentioned translation, Bryan had already received from the Chinese minister at Washington a complete statement of the Twenty-One Demands.[66] The secretary of state was quick to see that the fifth group of proposals, if made as demands, would have threatened China's administrative integrity and independence as well as the principle of equal treatment for other nations. He thought, however, that owing to strong opposition from China the Japanese government, before its ambassador at Washington handed out a shorter statement of the demands, might have withdrawn the fifth group from the negotiations which had commenced on February second. To give emphasis to this suggestion he instructed Reinsch to cable at once whether or not the Japanese were still pressing the proposals of Group Five.[67] At the same time he instructed Guthrie to thank the Japanese government for its memorandum of the demands, which he interpreted as "a complete denial" of press reports about the existence of five objectionable demands of the fifth group.[68] Thus under the cover of expressing thanks, he intended to effect a virtual official inquiry about the fifth group at Tokyo.

Reinsch, who had watched the Sino-Japanese negotiations with special care and had secured much inside information through his intimate contact with the Chinese foreign office,[69] replied on February twentieth that all the demands were being urged not excepting "the more obnoxious ones" classified under Group Five.[70] His report was accurate, because in fact the Japanese had been repeatedly insisting upon discussions of the fifth group of proposals.[71] Now he had clearly seen how the Japanese, by insistence upon the most unacceptable demands, were actually threatening Chinese integrity and American interests. In the hope that his Chief Executive would understand and give direct attention to this critical situation in China, he sent the following telegram to President Wilson:

In consideration of the momentousness of the present crisis in Chinese affairs, of the consequent danger to the hard-earned position, rights and legitimate prospects of Americans here and of the hope entertained by the President and his advisors that in maintaining the independence and free government of this country they may count on your active sympathy, I venture to invite your personal attention to the present difficulties and have requested the Secretary of State to communicate to you my telegram of today and previous reports relating to the Japanese demands.[72]

The personal views of Wilson in regard to the Chinese-Japanese negotiations had already been expressed to Reinsch in a letter of February second, which of course had not reached Peking by the time the above telegram was sent.

I have had the feeling that any direct advice to China, or direct intervention on her behalf in the present negotiations, would really do her more harm than good, inasmuch as it would very likely provoke the jealousy and excite the hostility of Japan, which would first be manifested against China herself. . . . For the present I am watching the situation very carefully indeed, ready to step in at any point where it is wise to do so.[73]

The cautious tone expressed therein was apparently not in accord with Reinsch's desire for prompt action. Nevertheless, as he later pointed out in a reply, he felt encouraged to learn that the President's hand was actually "at the helm" in dealing with the difficult situation out in China.[74]

As to Bryan's skillfully worded telegram to Tokyo inquiring about the fifth group, it promptly produced the desired effect. Guthrie reported on February twenty-first that the Japanese foreign minister admitted the presentation of some "requests" or "wishes" together with the "demands." [75] The next day the Japanese ambassador at Washington handed to Bryan a memorandum listing in brief terms the seven "requests" of the fifth group which, he explained, were considerably different from the demands of the other groups.[76]

4.

Now that the existence of the fifth group had been officially verified, Bryan immediately reported the matter to the President. He did not consider the section regarding the Japanese propagation of religious teachings and the section concerning the right of the Japanese hospitals, churches, and schools to own lands, because he thought they were not objectionable. He was opposed to all the remaining "requests," particularly the one concerned with the employment of Japanese police officers. For his opposition to them, he found two main reasons: one was that they threatened China's political integrity, and the other was that they violated the principle of the equal treatment of all nations. In conclusion he suggested to Wilson: "If you think it wise to bring this matter to the attention of Japan we can follow the plan adopted in the last telegram and express gratification that these are not made as demands but merely presented as requests, and thus, our discussion of them upon their merits will not be objectionable." [77]

Although Bryan did not discuss the Japanese proposals of the first four groups in his letter to the President, the state department was giving them careful consideration. Williams suggested to Bryan that before deciding definitely not to oppose the demands as distinguished from the requests it was proper to obtain a *quid pro quo*. While disapproving the demands about Manchuria, Williams considered it necessary to recognize the Japanese "special interests" in that region. He did not think it advisable for the United States to protest against the Japanese action in Manchuria as well as in Shantung. Curiously enough, this tone of compromise was in clear contrast to that of firmness shown in his previous memoranda to the secretary of state. He pointed out that Japan needed a place for her surplus population and that a diversion of the flux of the Japanese immigrants into Manchuria would relieve the California land question then harassing the American government. Furthermore the South Manchuria Railway was discriminating in freight rates against other nations, and the removal of such a discrimination was especially desirable. Finally he made his objection to the proposal requiring Japan's consent to the working of other mines in the neighborhood of the Han-Yeh-Ping properties, because the granting of such a proposal might exclude American citizens from opening and operating the mineral deposits of the provinces of Hupeh, Kiangsi, and Hunan. He implied that the American government, prior to an expression of its acquiescence in the "demands," should reach an understanding with Japan about all these problems.[78]

Robert Lansing, counsellor of the state department, approved of the idea of securing a *quid pro quo* from Japan. Following Williams' thoughts, the legal-minded counsellor made three concrete suggestions to the secretary of state. According to him American acquiescence in the demands relative to South Manchuria and Shantung should be reciprocated by a declaration on the part of the Japanese government to the effect that the latter:

(1) Will make no further complaint in regard to legislation affecting land tenures in the United States unless such legislation is confiscatory in character, or materially affects vested rights;

(2) Will reaffirm explicitly the principle of the "Open Door," making it particularly applicable to the territories affected by the demands;

(3) And will prevent any monopolization by Japanese subjects of particular trades in these territories, and any preferential rates of treatment by Japanese railways or other transportation concerns for the benefit of Japanese subjects or merchandise.[79]

He further states: "If a bargain along these lines could be struck it would relieve us of the vexatious California land controversy, and prevent in large measure future disputes which seem almost inevitable if the 'demands' of Japan are permitted at the present time to pass unchallenged." [80]

Presumably Wilson and Bryan did not find it advisable to link up the California problem with the Japanese demands upon China and to strike a bargain with Japan at this juncture. So they did not adopt the plan for securing an official declaration from the Japanese government along the suggested lines. But they did think it necessary to present a full statement of the American views on all the proposals, particularly those of the fifth group. As a result Bryan sent the Japanese ambassador at Washington a lengthy note on March thirteenth, embodying, among other things, most of his ideas as already expressed to the President in the letter of February twenty-second.[81]

The above-mentioned note was intended to be a reply to the two memoranda which the Japanese ambassador had left with Bryan on February eighth and February twenty-second. First of all it stressed the difference between the "demands" and the "requests." From this distinction it drew the inference that the Japanese government would not press the "requests" should China refuse to discuss them. Then after a detailed review of all the statements, agreements, and treaties upon which the United States had based its policy in China, it stated:

While on principle and under the treaties of 1844, 1858, 1868 and 1903 with China the United States has ground upon which to base objections to the Japanese "demands" relative to Shantung, South Manchuria, and East Mongolia, nevertheless the United States frankly recognizes that territorial contiguity creates special relations between Japan and these districts. This Government, therefore, is disposed to raise no question, at this time, as to Articles I and II of the Japanese proposals.[82]

Without a *quid pro quo* in California, Bryan acquiesced in the demands relating to Shantung, South Manchuria, and Eastern Inner Mongolia. His recognition of the special relations between Japan and these regions constituted a distinct diplomatic concession inconsistent with the American stand against the creation of new spheres of influence in China. Ambiguous as it was, later the term "special relations" was made use of by both Japan and the United States, and was formally written into the Lansing-Ishii Notes of November 2, 1917, after the United States had entered the European war.

Bryan did not object to the provision of Group III requiring a joint Sino-Japanese control of the Han-Yeh-Ping Company. Nor did he question the second, fifth, and seventh articles of Group V, namely, the right of the Japanese hospitals, churches, and schools to own lands in the Chinese interior; the specified railway concessions south of the Yangtze River; and the Japanese right to propagate religious teachings in China.[83] His tacit consent to all these proposals again sounded like a diplomatic concession.

Bryan also raised objections, but only with regard to Group V. With great severity he dwelt upon the four remaining "requests" of Group V: the employment of Japanese advisers, the joint policing of China, the purchase of Japanese arms and ammunition, and the Japanese monopoly of the development of Fukien. To Group IV requiring China not to alienate or lease any port, bay, or island on her coast,[84] he also insinuated his opposition. He cleverly quoted Baron Kato as saying that Japan desired no naval station along the Chinese coast but would stand against any other nation possessing such a station. He strongly argued that all these proposals, if acceded to, would be derogatory to American interests and Chinese independence.[85]

As it was expected, Bryan's note aroused the Japanese government. At first the Japanese foreign minister, Baron Kato, suspected that the document might have been sent at the request or suggestion of China or some other power.[86] But this suspicion was promptly dispelled by Guthrie's explanation and Bryan's denial.[87] On March twentieth, Kato had a "full and frank" talk with Guthrie, during which the former, aside from reemphasizing the distinction between the "demands" and the "requests," especially brought up the Fukien question.

It is to be remembered here that ever since 1900 the Japanese government had been haunted by Secretary Hay's suggestion as to the procurement by the United States of a coaling station in Samsah Bay. Recently it had felt very uneasy about the rumor that the Bethlehem Steel Company had made a contract with China for the improvement of a harbor along the coast of Fukien. Evidently it had begun to fear the possibility of a revival of the American plan to obtain a foothold in that province. From this fear had resulted the stringent Fukien demand upon China. Now that this demand had been officially discussed in the American note, the Japanese foreign minister found it opportune to clear away all difficulties with the American government. For this reason he proposed that "the United States and Japan should agree upon a frank and friendly statement concerning this province by which all possibility of future uneasiness might be eliminated." [88] Through the ambassador in Washington, the Japanese government indicated its willingness to reconsider the Fukien proposal if the United States agreed not to participate in any development on the Fukien coast which would threaten Japan.[89]

Bryan viewed the Japanese sensitiveness about Fukien with a good deal of sympathy. The present American government really desired no coaling station in that province. So he believed that much difficulty with Japan could be smoothed out through an exchange of notes which would relieve the Japanese people of their anxiety about any revival of the Hay suggestion. But such an exchange of notes, in his opinion, should be so worded as merely to approve a direct agreement between China and Japan, under which "all investment of foreign capital in harbor improvement, or the establishment of coaling stations or naval bases, should be prevented." [90] In other words an agreement designed to prevent all powers, not the United States alone, from securing concessions on the coast of Fukien should be first reached between China and Japan and then approved by America. In this way the American government could avoid the disadvantage of making a direct arrangement with Japan simply at its own expense.

Wilson readily consented to Bryan's suggestion and added: "I am happy to think that we can easily come to an understanding on this point, and remove an impression which ought not to have been so long to exist; I mean the impression created by Mr. Hay's suggestion as to a coaling station in Fukien." [91] Then Bryan put his proposition into a concrete form and also wrote out an addition concerning railway concessions in the interior of Fukien.[92] When the whole was approved by the President,[93] he telegraphed Guthrie as follows:

... It is evident that the Japanese Government has regarded the suggestion made by Mr. Hay in regard to a naval coaling station as evidence of a continuing desire upon the part of the United States to secure a concession on the coast of Fukien, whereas this Government has no such purpose or desire. . . .

You are, therefore, authorized to inform the Government that this Government will view without the slightest objection any arrangement which Japan may make with China looking toward the withholding of any concession to any foreign Power which contemplates the improvement of any harbor on the cost of Fukien or the establishment of a coaling station or naval base along said coast by any foreign Power. Such an agreement entered into between Japan and China, and approved by the United States in an exchange of notes, would put an end to any speculation that may have been indulged, or fears that may have been entertained in regard to this nation's desires or intentions. As Japan's desire to be consulted in regard to concessions granted to Fukien was based upon her wish to prevent the development of any foreign influence on the coast of Fukien we may assume that this fear being removed she will not feel it necessary to insist upon any special advantage in regard to the development of the interior of Fukien. In fact, this is intimated in both your despatch and the communication made by Ambassador Chinda.

If the Japanese Government has any uneasiness as to the development of the interior of Fukien you might inquire whether it would not be advisable to propose that no railroad concession be granted to any foreign Power, with the understanding that the Chinese Government shall, itself, build, own and operate any railroads that may be deemed necessary for the development of Fukien, such railroads, if built with borrowed money, not to be mortgaged or in any way pledged to the creditors.[94]

In giving the above instruction Bryan did not in any way recognize Fukien as a Japanese sphere of influence. The gist of his proposition lay in the withholding by China of concessions to all foreign powers including Japan. To his satisfaction the Japanese government finally did modify its request for a preferred position in Fukien.[95] Apparently it did so in accordance with the American wishes. But it must also have felt satisfied, because all its professed apprehensions originating from the Hay suggestion had been removed in consequence of Bryan's statement and Japan's final arrangement with China. Thus the United States succeeded in helping to check a threatened Japanese monopoly of Fukien, whereas Japan was able to nullify the supposed American designs upon that province. In that sense both countries must have felt content.

Now let us return to the other Japanese "requests" which the United States opposed. In the previously-mentioned oral statement made to Bryan by Chinda on March twenty-second, the problems of advisers, arms, and police supervision came up. Wilson did not find Chinda's explanations convincing, and construed the Japanese propositions as constituting "a serious limitation upon China's independence of action, and a very definite preference of Japan before other nations."[96] Bryan was equally dissatisfied with the Japanese views; nevertheless he would like Japan and China to make a mutual compromise in respect to those problems. Thus he remarked to Wilson: "As Japan and China must remain neighbors it is of vital importance that they should be neighborly, and neighborly spirit cannot be expected if Japan demands too much, or if China concedes too little."[97]

In line with his principle of mutual compromise Bryan made three concrete suggestions for the consideration of the Japanese government. First, Japan and China should come to an agreement whereby the latter, in employing foreign advisers, should make no discrimination against the former as compared with other powers. Second, in the matter of arms the two countries should reach a similar agreement by which China would promise not to discriminate against Japan in the amount and kind of arms purchased. Third, police supervision, if China was inclined to concede it, should be applied only to those places in Manchuria and Eastern Mongolia that had a considerable percentage of Japanese subjects. It might be specifically stipulated that when Japanese people constituted a certain percentage of the population in any place in those two regions the provision for joint supervision would automatically go into effect.[98]

Here we can see that according to Bryan, Japan might gain an equal treatment in the matter of advisers and arms. With regard to police supervision, Japan, he hinted, might seek such concessions as affected only Manchuria and Eastern Mongolia. He first submitted those suggestions to the President for approval.[99] Then he telegraphed them to Guthrie to the effect that they should be used as the basis for discussion in case of Japanese inquiry.[100] Soon in a conference between the Japanese foreign minister and Guthrie the matters were formally discussed. Following this, an outline of these suggestions was officially communicated to the Japanese ambassador at Washington.[101] As we know, Japan finally reserved for future negotiation all the demands about arms, advisers, and police supervision.

While giving attention to the above problems of Group V, the United States was also concerned about the future development of the mines near the properties of the Han-Yeh-Ping Company. At this time it was reported that the Japanese had demanded the right of veto over competing mining enterprises in the Yangtze region. With the approval of the President,[102] Bryan immediately instructed Guthrie to make inquiry as to the matter.[103] In the final settlement of the demands of Group III, Japan dropped this objectionable veto feature.[104] As Bryan saw it, she did so out of consideration for the American suggestion.[105]

5.

From all the representations that Bryan had made to Japan as to the demands, the Japanese government seemed to gain the impression that the United States meant to be conciliatory and certainly would not resist the first four groups of the demands. As to the fifth group which constituted a Japanese protectorate over China and negated the China policy of the United States, there was still some doubt. Japan now proceeded to take advantage of known situations to bring more pressure to bear upon Peking to accept at least Groups I, II, III, and IV. During recent conferences the Japanese negotiators time and again indicated that the American government had given consent to Japanese policy in China.[106] Their intention was to bring the Peking authorities to a quicker submission by impressing upon them the futility of dependence on American support. When the Fukien question was discussed, Hioki specifically made reference to the "complaisance" of the United States.[107] Back in Japan even Count Okuma was reported to have mentioned American acquiescence in the Japanese demands.[108]

Reinsch had detected the Japanese attempt to alienate the Chinese confidence in the United States. For the purpose of offsetting the Japanese propaganda he requested "authorization to give informally, impersonally and unofficially, publicity to the view that the American Government had not abandoned either its material interests or its moral obligations in respect to China." [109]

Wilson had now come to view the Chinese situation with the greatest solicitude. He felt particularly worried about the report that Japan had been repeatedly insisting upon China's acceptance of the "requests." In a letter he frankly told Bryan:

I am very uneasy about what is going on, as reported by Mr. Reinsch, and must frankly admit that I do not credit the assurances the Japanese have sought to give us. I wish that you might find an opportunity to express to the Japanese ambassador the grave concern we feel at hearing that his government is insisting upon the acquiescence of the Chinese government in the "requests," because they are so clearly incompatible with the administrative independence and autonomy of the Chinese Empire and with the maintenance of the policy of an open door to the world.

In short, I feel that we should be as active as the circumstances permit in showing ourselves to be champions of the sovereign rights of China, now as always, though with no thought of seeking any special advantage or privilege for ourselves. . . . [110]

At the end of the letter Wilson asked if Reinsch had been told that the American government had not acquiesced in the Japanese demands.[111] Thereupon Bryan, on April fifteenth, authorized Reinsch to give out something informally and unofficially in this sense: "The American Government has not surrendered any of its treaty rights in China or abated one iota of its friendly interest in all that concerns the industrial and political welfare of China. It is awaiting the results of the present negotiations in the confident expectation that the rights, and obligations of the United States will not be affected or its interests impaired." [112]

As time went on, Wilson more and more realized the importance of giving publicity to American views about the Japanese demands. The privacy of the American representations to Japan, he thought, accounted for the real weakness of the American influence. Besides, he also realized the necessity of cooperation with other powers in dealing with Japan. So he told Bryan on April twenty-seventh that it was needful to make American views public "perhaps in conjunction with other nations whose interests and sympathies are equally involved." [113] Following the same line of thought, he mentioned the next day that the American government might make its position clear by means of a circular note to the leading European powers.[114]

While Wilson considered the question of making American views known to other powers equally interested in and friendly to China, the Sino-Japanese negotiations were nearing a climax. On April twenty-sixth, the Japanese minister at Peking presented to the Chinese government a list of revised demands requiring full and prompt acceptance.[115] After careful consideration China gave a detailed reply on May first.[116] Failing a full acceptance of the revised demands, the Chinese reply at once proved unsatisfactory to the Japanese government. Impatient of further delay the foreign office at Tokyo began to draft the text of an ultimatum and to make preparations for war.

With a view to preventing an open armed conflict between Japan and China, Bryan, after consulting the President,[117] took three steps on May sixth, the day before the Japanese ultimatum was presented to the Chinese government. In the first place he sent a personal message to Count Okuma, urging that the Sino-Japanese negotiations should be continued in a spirit of patience until a peaceful settlement could be reached. He also made it clear that it would be most unfortunate should Japan and China come into an armed conflict at a time when a large part of the world was already at war.[118] In the second place he, in the name of the President, instructed Reinsch to appeal to the Chinese foreign office to the same effect.[119] Lastly he requested Great Britain, France, and Russia to join the United States in making "a friendly but earnest appeal to Japan and China to continue their negotiations in the spirit of patience and friendship until a satisfactory conclusion is reached." [120]

Bryan's personal appeal to Okuma did not reach Tokyo until the morning of May seventh, the day on which the British passenger liner *Lusitania* with American citizens on board was sunk by a German submarine in the North Atlantic. The Japanese government had already made the final decision as to the issuance of an ultimatum, requiring China's unconditional acceptance of all but Group V of the demands, and threatening "necessary" measures against China if she failed to give a satisfactory reply by six o'clock in the afternoon on the ninth day of May.[121] When Chargé d'Affaires Wheeler presented Bryan's appeal to Okuma at noon on May seventh, the latter simply expressed his courteous thanks for the American advice and furthermore indicated the hope that China would yield to the Japanese ultimatum as already sent out to Peking.[122] Needless to say, Bryan's message had failed to produce its desired result. The *Lusitania* affair could not but strengthen the hand of Japan in the Far East, particularly *vis-a-vis* the United States.

Bryan's appeal to the Chinese government was delayed in transmission; therefore Reinsch did not act on it.[123] Even if he had been able to act in time, he would not have done much help to the critical situation. After all, it was not China but Japan who decided to discontinue the negotiations. As a matter of fact the Chinese government, before receiving the ultimatum, had tried to make further concessions in order to avert the imminent danger.[124] Bryan's invitation to Great Britain, France, and Russia for a joint representation to Tokyo also came too late. It likewise became an abortive attempt, because none of these powers accepted it.[125] On May seventh, Lansing expressed the fear that these three European powers would refuse to unite in the proposed joint action.[126] Unfortunately enough, his fear proved well founded.

Among the Entente Powers, Great Britain, despite her disinclination for a joint admonition to her ally, was the only one that had independently offered appreciable opposition to the Japanese course of action in China. She had already taken steps to urge moderation upon the Japanese government. Toward the end of April and at the beginning of May she had several times warned Japan against an open break with China.[127] Sir Edward Grey had personally told the Japanese ambassador at London that the British government would view with concern any rupture between Japan and China.[128] In his memorandum handed to the Japanese ambassador on May sixth, he had pointed out that the Japanese government should consult Great Britain first before it finally closed the door upon a peaceful settlement with China.[129] Grey's action, independent as it was, pleased the American government just as well. Wilson thought that Grey had acted very wisely.[130] Bryan believed that Grey's memorandum had helped to reduce the severity of the Japanese demands.[131]

On the whole, Great Britain disapproved Group V, and her repeated strong warnings had played a part in securing its withdrawal.[132] But the modified demands, excluding this group, it seemed to her, would be acceptable to China. Grey expressed the hope to the Chinese minister at London on May seventh that the Chinese government would be able to accept them.[133] This was part of the reason why Great Britain, after Japan's presentation of the ultimatum which left the fifth group for future consideration, did not take any action, either independent or joint, to show further opposition to the Japanese demands. On the contrary she tried her best to persuade China to yield. The British minister at Peking insistently and convincingly urged China to accept the Japanese ultimatum. His advice had a significant influence upon the final Chinese decision to give in.[134]

The Chinese government, finding itself militarily weak and helpless, reluctantly decided to back down as a result of a meeting held on May eighth by its high officials under the chairmanship of Yüan Shih-k'ai.[135] The next day it officially informed the Japanese minister at Peking of its unconditional acceptance of the ultimatum as presented on May seventh at three o'clock in the afternoon, thus bringing to a close more than three months of strenuous negotiations with Japan.[136]

The United States did not view with indifference what had just happened in China. Only two days after China acceded

to the Japanese demands unconditionally, Bryan sent the following identic note to Tokyo and Peking:

> In view of the circumstances of the negotiations which have
> taken place and which are now pending between the Government
> of Japan and the Government of China, and of the agreements
> which have been reached as a result thereof, the Government of
> the United States has the honor to notify the Imperial Japanese
> Government that it cannot recognize any agreement or undertak-
> ing which has been entered into or which may be entered into
> between the Governments of Japan and China, impairing the treaty
> rights of the United States and its citizens in China, the political or
> territorial integrity of the Republic of China, or the international
> policy relative to China commonly known as the open door policy.[137]

This note was originally drafted by Lansing. He suggested
to Bryan on May seventh that in case Great Britain, France,
and Russia refused to unite in a joint warning to Japan the
United States should independently address to Tokyo and Peking
a caveat in the sense of his draft. Lansing said of his proposed
document: "While it might not prevent Japan from carrying
out her purpose of coercing China to submit to her demands,
it would constitute a complete reservation of all possible rights
affecting American interests and Chinese interests as well, so
that any agreement forced upon China at the present time
could properly become the subject of discussion in the future
when the conditions are more propitious." [138]

Bryan submitted the proposal to the President who, in view
of the world's political situation as a whole, thought it wise to
lodge such a caveat, if not to take any further action at the time.
It was also Wilson's view that the United States should not leave
any of the American rights indefinite or seem to concur in any
portion of the Japanese program which violated international
understandings about China. Besides, he thought that the suggested notification might "favourably affect the Japanese official

mind with regard to the wisdom of postponing the discussion of Group V for a very long time indeed." [139]

In fact the American note of May eleventh, after its text had leaked out from Peking, did not gain a favorable response in Japan. ,By this time the German torpedoing of the *Lusitania* had startled the world and produced a first-class German-American war crisis. Japanese newspaper editorials were generally resentful in tone and denounced the American note as unnecessary.[140] Even Baron Kato referred to it as "impudent." [141] In China its general effect was reassuring, although it did not cause much public comment. The Chinese government felt relieved to see that the basic principles of American Far Eastern policy had been partly reasserted.[142] In the final analysis, this note was tactically advantageous to the United States which, through filing such a caveat, placed itself in a position from which it did not have to recognize any results of the Sino-Japanese negotiations which might impair its rights and policies in China. Indirectly it threw doubt upon Bryan's previous recognition of the Japanese "special interests" in China. After the *Lusitania* affair, which obviously strengthened Japan's position, to lodge such a caveat with the Japanese government was the best the United States could do in the midst of the imbroglio with Germany.

Reinsch fully grasped the importance of the American caveat and furthermore wanted to carry its spirit into the final treaty to be concluded between China and Japan. When he presented the document to China on May thirteenth, he suggested to the Chinese foreign minister that in the definitive Sino-Japanese agreement there should be an article explicitly binding both contracting parties not to construe any provision in such a way as to impair China's integrity and the principle of equality of commercial opportunity.[143] Bryan did not think such an article necessary, because the United States had officially made its position known to both parties.[144]

In his conversation with the Chinese foreign minister, Reinsch also mentioned that under the most-favored-nation principle any rights of residence granted to Japanese subjects in Manchuria would accrue in similar terms to the United States. He thought that the Chinese government should inform the United States of any Sino-Japanese arrangement which would change the status and rights of foreign residents in China.[145] Bryan promptly confirmed this view.[146] Thereupon Reinsch communicated it to the Chinese government by a formal letter.[147]

On May twenty-fifth, China and Japan signed two treaties and exchanged a number of notes.[148] As a result the Chinese government granted far-reaching concessions respecting Shantung, South Manchuria, Eastern Inner Mongolia, and the matter of Han-Yeh-Ping. The fifth group, with the exception of the Fukien article, was left for subsequent consideration. From beginning to end the policy of Yüan Shih-k'ai had been to refuse to discuss this group.[149] Through patience, insistence, delay, public opinion, and tactful diplomacy he finally secured the suspension of those "requests" the acceptance of which would mean placing China under Japanese sovereignty. In this respect China salvaged something in her negotiations with Japan. Besides, the Japanese resort to the measure of delivering an ultimatum constituted the grounds of *force majeure* upon which the Chinese government, later at the Paris Peace Conference, demanded the abolition of the 1915 agreements. What was more noticeable, those agreements were never ratified by the Chinese Parliament and were therefore considered invalid by the Chinese people themselves.

6.

No other Chinese questions had thus far drawn so much of the attention of the Wilson administration. In the beginning its attitude toward the Japanese *démarche* in China was cautious and conciliatory. Its opposition to the Twenty-One Demands was restricted largely to a few of the "requests." Even its objection to these few "requests" was quite flexible. It rendered little help in solving the actual points at issue except the Fukien question. Later when news came that Japan had been pressing the entire group, it began to realize the importance of taking a stronger stand. Nothing short of armed intervention would have much restraining influence upon Japan who soon decided to resort to extreme measures. President Wilson, like any American President before him, would not resort to other than "peaceful means" for the preservation of Chinese territorial, administrative, or political integrity. His only peaceful recourse, aside from direct appeals to Japan and China, was to request the cooperation of the warring Entente powers of Europe, enemies of·Germany, nominally bound to Japan by the Anglo-Japanese Alliance. Failing in such an attempt, he objected to Group V, was indeed complaisant about Groups I, II, III, and IV, and fell back on the general caveat of May eleventh. With his mind more and more preoccupied by the European situation and the German submarine warfare against Great Britain, he had at least attempted to save China from complete Japanese mastery, no matter how little his diplomacy actually achieved.

After all, it was mainly China's internal weakness which invited foreign aggression. In the mind of Wilson, China should first have to set her own house in order before she could effectively have her sovereign rights respected. In the following chapter we shall see how Wilson, in consideration of China's internal unity, supported the Peking government under the leadership of Yüan Shih-k'ai against the ideals of republican government.

NOTES:

1   John V. A. MacMurray to Bryan, August 3, 1914, *For. Rels., 1914, Supplement,* p. 162.

2   Bryan to MacMurray, August 7, 1914, *ibid.*, p. 163.

3   For the text of the mandate, see Wang Yün-sheng, *Liu-shih-nien-lai Chung-kuo yü Jih-pen, China and Japan during the Last Sixty Years* (7 vols., in Chinese, Tientsin, 1932-1934), VI, 40-41. Hereafter cited as Wang Yün-sheng, *China and Japan.*

4   MacMurray to Bryan, August 6, 1914, *For. Rels., 1914, Supplement,* p. 162.

5   The Chinese foreign office to Lu Tsung-yü (the Chinese minister to Japan), August 6, 1914, Wang Yün-sheng, *China and Japan,* VI, 46.

6   MacMurray to Bryan, August 3, 1914, *For. Rels., 1914, Supplement,* p. 162; and Bryan to MacMurray, August 7, 1914, *ibid.*, p. 163.

7   Bryan to MacMurray, August 7, 1914, *ibid.*, p. 163.

8   See *ibid.*, pp. 165-167.

9   A. Whitney Griswold, *The Far Eastern Policy of the United States* (New York, 1938), p. 179. Hereafter cited as A. W. Griswold, *Far Eastern Policy.*

10   Lu Tsung-yü to the Chinese foreign office, August 8, 1914, Wang Yün-sheng, *China and Japan,* VI, 46-47.

11   *Ibid.*, VI, 48.

12   Lu Tsung-yü to the Chinese foreign office, August 8, 1914, *ibid.*, VI, 47.

13   The Chinese foreign office to Lu Tsung-yü, August 10, 1914, *ibid.*, VI, 47.

14   On August 12 Bryan instructed MacMurray to deny the rumor that the United States was considerably reënforcing its Asiatic fleet to aid China in case of need. See *For. Rels., 1914, Supplement,* p. 168.

15   The Chinese foreign office to the Chinese legation at Tokyo, August 12, 1914, Wang Yün-sheng, *China and Japan,* VI, 48.

16   Edward Grey to Conyngham Greene, August 1, 1914, G. P. Gooch and Harold Temperley, eds., *British Documents on the Origins of the War, 1898-1914* (11 vols., London, 1926-1936), XI, 256. Hereafter cited as G. P. Gooch and H. Temperley, *British Documents.*

17   Edward Grey to Conyngham Greene, August 3, 1914, *ibid.*, XI, 298. Also see Thomas Edward LaFargue, *China and the World War* (Stanford and London, 1937), p. 9. Hereafter cited as T. E. LaFargue, *China and World War.*

18 Conyngham Greene to Edward Grey, August 4, 1914, G. P. Gooch and H. Temperley, *British Documents*, XI, 327.

19 Edward Grey to Conyngham Greene, August 4, 1914, *ibid.*, XI, 329.

20 Ito Masanori, *Kato Takaaki* (2 vols., in Japanese, Tokyo, 1929), II, 78. Also see T. E. LaFargue, *China and World War*, pp. 11-12; and Charles Nelson Spinks, "Japan's Entrance into the World War," *Pacific Historical Review*, V (1936), p. 303, hereafter cited as C. N. Spinks, "Japan's Entrance into War."

21 T. E. LaFargue, *China and World War*, pp. 12-14. Also see C. N. Spinks, "Japan's Entrance into War," pp. 304-308.

22 James Watson Gerard (American ambassador to Germany) to Bryan, August 13, 1914, *For. Rels., 1914, Supplement*, pp. 169-170.

23 George Wilkins Guthrie (American ambassador to Japan) to Bryan, August 15, 1914, *ibid.*, p. 170.

24 T. E. LaFargue, *China and World War*, p. 16.

25 Wang Yün-sheng, *China and Japan*, VI, 49.

26 MacMurray to Bryan, August 20, 1914, *For. Rels., 1914, Supplement*, p. 173.

27 MacMurray to Bryan, August 20, 1914, *ibid.*, pp. 173-174.

28 Bryan to MacMurray, August 20, 1914, *ibid.*, p. 174.

29 For the Sino-Japanese negotiations about the creation of a special war zone, see Wang Yün-sheng, *China and Japan*, VI, 53-57; and Chang Chung-fu, *Chung-hua Min-kuo Wai-chiao Shih, A Diplomatic History of the Chinese Republic* (only the first volume in print, in Chinese, Chungking, 1933), I, 126-127. Hereafter cited as Chang Chung-fu, *Diplomatic History*.

30 *For. Rels., 1914, Supplement*, pp. 188-189.

31 Wang Yün-sheng, *China and Japan*, VI, 60-74.

32 Bryan to George Wilkins Guthrie, August 19, 1914, *For. Rels., 1914, Supplement*, p. 172.

33 MacMurray to Bryan, September 10, 1914, *ibid.*, p. 187.

34 MacMurray to Bryan, September 10, 1914, *ibid.*, p. 187.

35 Lansing to Reinsch, November 4, 1914, *ibid.*, p. 190.

36 J. V. A. MacMurray, *Treaties and Agreements*, II, 1157.

37 *Ibid*, II, 1158.

38 For the conversations between Grey and Kato, see Ito Masanori, *Kato Takaaki*, II, 132-140; Wang Yün-sheng, *China and*

Japan, VI, 83-84; and T. E. LaFargue, *China and World War,* 49-50.

39   Wang Yün-sheng, *China and Japan,* VI, 84-85.

40   *Ibid.,* VI, 85. Also see Ito Masanori, *Kato Takaaki,* II, 154; and T. E. LaFargue, *China and World War,* p. 50.

41   For the interview between Yüan and Hioki, see Paul S. Reinsch, *An American Diplomat In China* (Garden City, N. Y. and Toronto, 1922), pp. 129-130. Hereafter cited as P. S. Reinsch, *An American Diplomat.* Also see *For. Rels., 1915,* p. 132; Wang Yün-sheng, *China and Japan,* VI, 87; and Thomas F. Millard, *Our Eastern Question* (New York, 1916), pp. 130-131.

42   For the complete text of the Twenty-One Demands, see Carnegie Endowment for International Peace, Division of International Law, *The Sino-Japanese Negotiations of 1915: Japanese and Chinese Documents and Chinese Official Statement* (Washington, 1921), pp. 2-8. Hereafter cited as *Sino-Japanese Negotiations of 1915.* Also see Wang Yün-sheng, *China and Japan,* VI, 87-90.

43   *Sino-Japanese Negotiations of 1915,* pp. 1-2.

44   Wang Yün-sheng, *China and Japan,* VI, 86.

45   P. S. Reinsch, *An American Diplomat,* p. 131. Also see P. S. Reinsch, "Secret Diplomacy and the Twenty-One Demands," *Asia,* XXI (1921), p. 939.

46   Reinsch to Bryan, January 23, 1915, *For. Rels., 1915,* p. 79.

47   P. S. Reinsch, *An American Diplomat,* p. 132.

48   *Ibid.,* p. 144.

49   Reinsch to Bryan, February 1, 1915, *For. Rels., 1915,* pp. 81-82.

50   Guthrie to Bryan, February 3, 1915, *ibid.,* p. 82.

51   E. T. Williams to Bryan, January 25, 1915, SD, 793.94/498.

52   E. T. Williams to Bryan, January 27, 1915, SD, 793.94/211.

53   Wilson to Bryan, January 27, 1915, Bryan Papers, letter book for December 1, 1914 to June 27, 1915.

54   Bryan to Reinsch, January 28, 1915, *For. Rels., 1915,* p. 80.

55   Reinsch to Bryan, January 29, 1915, *ibid.,* p. 81.

56   Reinsch to Bryan, February 1, 1915, Wilson Papers, II, 75.

57   Williams to Bryan, February 2, 1915, Wilson Papers, II, 75.

58   Bryan to Page, February 2, 1915, *For. Rels., 1915,* p. 82.

59   Page to Bryan, February 13, 1915, *ibid.,* p. 88.

60   Williams to Bryan, February 15, 1915, SD, 793.94/225.

61   The Chinese vice-minister of foreign affairs, Ts'ao Ju-lin, admitted on March 5, 1915, that the Chinese government had clandestinely given out information to the powers about the whole set of Japanese demands. He also mentioned that Wellington Koo had contacted foreign correspondents and had been active in the matter of publicity. See Ts'ao Ju-lin to Lu Tsung-yü, March 5, 1915, Wang Yün-sheng, *China and Japan*, VI, 216.

62   For the text of the Japanese memorandum, see *For. Rels., 1915*, pp. 83-84.

63   Guthrie to Bryan, February 9, 1915, *ibid.*, pp. 84-85.

64   John V. A. MacMurray to Wilson, April 5, 1915, Wilson Papers, II, 78.

65   Reinsch to Bryan, March 6, 1915, *For. Rels., 1915*, p. 99. Reinsch transmitted this translation to Bryan on March 6, 1915. For this document, see *ibid.*, pp. 99-103.

66   For the Chinese statement, see *ibid.*, pp. 93-95.

67   Bryan to Reinsch, February 19, 1915, *ibid.*, p. 95.

68   Bryan to Guthrie, February 19, 1915, *ibid.*, p. 93. The five objectionable demands of the fifth group listed in Bryan's instructions to Guthrie were worded in the same manner as in the statement handed by the Chinese minister at Washington. See *ibid.*, pp. 94-95.

69   Reinsch said of his contact with the Chinese foreign office throughout the Sino-Japanese negotiations: "Dr. Wellington Koo all through this time acted as liaison officer between the Minister for Foreign Affairs and myself, although I also saw many other members of the Ministry. In discussing the consecutive phases of the negotiations, as they developed, Doctor Koo and I had many interesting hours over diplomatic tactics and analysis, in which I admired his keenness of perception. Some objection was hinted by the Japanese Legation to Doctor Koo's frequent visits to my office and house, but his coming and going continued, as was proper." See P. S. Reinsch, *An American Diplomat*, p. 144.

70   Reinsch to Bryan, February 20, 1915, *For. Rels., 1915*, pp. 95-96.

71   See Wang Yün-sheng, *China and Japan*, VI, 140-143.

72   This telegram was to be communicated to Wilson by the secretary of state. See Reinsch to Bryan, February 20, 1915, SD, 793.94/510.

73   P. S. Reinsch, *An American Diplomat*, p. 137.

74 Reinsch to Wilson, March 22, 1915, Wilson Papers, II, 78.

75 Guthrie to Bryan, February 21, 1915, *For. Rels., 1915,* p. 96.

76 Bryan to Wilson, February 22, 1915, Bryan Papers, letter book for December 1, 1914 to June 27, 1915. For the Japanese memorandum, see *For. Rels., 1915,* p. 97.

77 Bryan to Wilson, February 22, 1915, Bryan Papers, letter book for December 1, 1914 to June 27, 1915.

78 Williams to Bryan, February 26, 1915, *ibid.,* letter book for December 1, 1914 to June 27, 1915.

79 Lansing to Bryan, March 1, 1915, *ibid.,* letter book for December 1, 1914 to June 27, 1915.

80 Lansing to Bryan, March 1, 1915, *ibid.,* letter book for December 1, 1914 to June 27, 1915.

81 For the complete text of the note from Bryan to the Japanese ambassador, see *For. Rels., 1915,* pp. 105-111.

82 Bryan to the Japanese ambassador, March 13, 1915, *ibid.,* p. 108. By "Articles I and II" Bryan meant Groups I and II.

83 In the note Bryan stated: "Further, as to Article IV, and Article V, paragraphs 2, 5 and 7, this Government perceives no special menace to the existing rights and interests of the United States or of its citizens in China." See *ibid.,* p. 108. What he called "Article IV" is simply Group III. In the Japanese memorandum handed on February 8, 1915, this group is arranged as the fourth part of the demands; hence he called it "Article IV." For the said memorandum, see *ibid.,* pp. 83-84. By "Article V" he meant Group V. The Japanese memorandum handed on February 22, 1915 includes seven "paragraphs," that is, seven "requests." See *ibid.,* p. 97.

84 Group IV is what Bryan called "Article III." See *ibid.,* p. 110. This group is arranged as the third part of the demands in the Japanese memorandum handed on February 8, 1915. See *ibid.,* pp. 83-84.

85 For Bryan's objection to these proposals, see Bryan to the Japanese ambassador, March 13, 1915, *ibid.,* pp. 108-111.

86 Guthrie to Bryan, March 17, 1915, *ibid.,* p. 112.

87 Bryan to Guthrie, March 17, 1915, *ibid.,* p. 113.

88 Guthrie to Bryan, March 21, 1915, *ibid.,* pp. 113-115.

89 Bryan to Wilson, March 22, 1915, Bryan Papers, letter book for December 1, 1914 to June 27, 1915.

90   Bryan to Wilson, March 22, 1915, Bryan Papers, letter book for December 1, 1914 to June 27, 1915.

91   Wilson to Bryan, March 24, 1915, *ibid.,* letter book for December 1, 1914 to June 27, 1915.

92   Bryan to Wilson, March 25, 1915, SD, 793.94/283½.

93   Wilson to Bryan, March 25, 1915, *ibid.,* 793.94/283½.

94   Bryan to Guthrie, March 26, 1915, *For. Rels., 1915,* p. 117.

95   The final settlement of the Fukien problem took the form of an exchange of notes in which the Chinese government declared "that it has given no permission to foreign nations to construct, on the coast of Fukien Province, dock-yards, coaling stations for military use, naval bases, or to set up other military establishments; nor does it entertain an intention of borrowing foreign capital for the purpose of setting up the above-mentioned establishments." See *Sino-Japanese Negotiations of 1915,* pp. 61-62. It is also noticeable that in modifying her Fukien request Japan made no reference to the development of the interior of Fukien. This was also in line with American suggestions. See Bryan to Wilson, May 3, 1915, Bryan Papers, letter book for December 1, 1914 to June 27, 1915,

96   Wilson to Bryan, March 24, 1915, *ibid.,* letter book for December 1, 1914 to June 27, 1915.

97   Bryan to Wilson, March 25, 1915, *ibid.,* letter book for December 1, 1914 to June 27, 1915.

98   Bryan to the American embassy at Tokyo, March 26, 1915, SD, 793.94/294a.

99   Bryan to Wilson, March 25, 1915, Bryan Papers, letter book for December 1, 1914 to June 27, 1915.

100   Bryan to the American embassy at Tokyo, March 26, SD, 793.94/294a.

101   Bryan to Sutemi Chinda, March 30, 1915, Bryan Papers, letter book for December 1, 1914 to June 27, 1915.

102   See Bryan to Wilson, April 2, 1915; and Wilson to Bryan, April 3, 1915, *ibid.,* letter book for December 1, 1914 to June 27, 1915.

103   Bryan to Guthrie, April 2, 1915, *For. Rels., 1915,* p. 119.

104   See the Sino-Japanese "Exchange of Notes Respecting the Matter of Hanyehping," May 25, 1915, *Sino-Japanese Negotiations of 1915,* pp. 58-60.

105   Bryan to Wilson, May 3, 1915, Bryan Papers, letter book for December 1, 1914 to June 27, 1915.

106 Reinsch to Bryan, April 12, 1915, SD, 793.94/293.

107 Reinsch to Bryan, April 14, 1915, *ibid.*, 793.94/294.

108 See Wilson to Bryan, April 14, 1915, Bryan Papers, letter book for December 1, 1914 to June 27, 1915.

109 Reinsch to Bryan, April 14, 1915, SD, 793.94/294.

110 Wilson to Bryan, April 14, 1915, Bryan Papers, letter book for December 1, 1914 to June 27, 1915.

111 Wilson to Bryan, April 14, 1915, *ibid.*, letter book for December 1, 1914 to June 27, 1915.

112 Bryan to Reinsch, April 15, 1915, SD, 793.94/294.

113 Wilson to Bryan, April 27, 1915, Bryan Papers, letter book for December 1, 1914 to June 27, 1915.

114 Wilson to Bryan, April 28, 1915, *ibid.*, letter book for December 1, 1914 to June 27, 1915. In this letter Wilson suggested that Bryan should inform the Japanese ambassador of the American intention of sending a circular note to the chief European powers.

115 For the Japanese revised demands, see *Sino-Japanese Negotiations of 1915,* pp. 10-19.

116 For the Chinese reply to the Japanese revised demands, see *ibid.,* pp. 23-31.

117 Bryan to Wilson, May 6, 1915, Bryan Papers, letter book for December 1, 1914 to June 27, 1915.

118 Bryan to the American embassy at Tokyo, May 6, 1915, SD, 793.94/405a.

119 Bryan to the American legation at Peking, May 6, 1915, *ibid.*, 793.94/400a.

120 Bryan to the American embassies at London, Paris and Petrograd, May 6, 1915, *ibid.*, 793.94/393a.

121 The delay in the transmission of Bryan's message to Okuma was caused by the break of cable. See Chargé d'Affaires Wheeler to Bryan, May 8, 1915, *ibid.*, 793.94/392½. The Japanese final decision as to the issuance of the ultimatum was made on May 6, 1915. See Wang Yün-sheng, *China and Japan,* VI, 301. For the text of the Japanese ultimatum, see *ibid.*, VI, 305-307; and *For. Rels., 1915,* pp. 194-195.

122 Chargé d'Affaires Wheeler to Bryan, May 8, 1915, SD, 793.94/392½.

123   Reinsch to Bryan, May 9, 1915, *For. Rels., 1915,* p. 145. Also see Wang Yün-sheng, *China and Japan,* VI, 330; and P. S. Reinsch, *An American Diplomat,* p. 148.

124   For the Chinese efforts to avert the danger by making further concessions, see Wang Yün-sheng, *China and Japan,* VI, 301-303.

125   See A. W. Griswold, *Far Eastern Policy,* p. 194; Ito Masanori, *Kato Takaaki,* II, 196; and T. E. LaFargue, *China and World War,* p. 74.

126   Lansing to Bryan, May 7, 1915, SD, 793.94/339½.

127   See Wang Yün-sheng, *China and Japan,* VI, 293-296; A. W. Griswold, *Far Eastern Policy,* pp. 195-196; Ito Masanori, *Kato Takaaki,* pp. 190-191; and T. E. LaFargue, *China and World War,* p. 74.

128   See Edward M. House to Wilson, May 7, 1915, Wilson Papers, II, 80.

129   See Ambassador Page to Bryan, May 7, 1915, *For. Rels., 1915,* p. 144.

130   Wilson to Bryan, May 10, 1915, SD, 793.94/392½.

131   Bryan to Wilson, May 8, 1915, *ibid.,* 793.94/392½.

132   See Wang Yün-sheng, *China and Japan,* VI, 296; and A. W. Griswold, *Far Eastern Policy,* p. 196.

133   Ambassador Page to Bryan, May 7, 1915, *For. Rels., 1915,* p. 145.

134   On May eighth, the British minister had an interview with Lu Tseng-tsiang, the Chinese foreign minister, just before the Chinese government held a conference to make the final decision as to the Japanese ultimatum. The British minister did not take leave until Lu Tseng-tsiang definitely promised to do everything in his power to have the ultimatum accepted. The latter reported the interview at the conference held a little later on the same day. See Ts'ao Ju-lin to Lu Tsung-yü, May 10, 1915, Wang Yün-sheng, *China and Japan,* VI, 310-311.

135   For an account of the meeting, see Ts'ao Ju-lin to Lu Tsung-yü, May 10, 1915, *ibid.,* VI, 310-312.

136   The Chinese government gave to Hioki its official reply to the ultimatum on May ninth at eleven o'clock in the evening, five hours later than the Japanese time limit. See Ts'ao Ju-lin to Lu Tsung-yü, May 10, 1915, *ibid.,* VI, 313. According to Reinsch's report, the Chinese reply was delivered at midnight of May eighth.

See Reinsch to Bryan, May 17, 1915, *For. Rels., 1915,* p. 148. For the Japanese ultimatum, see *Sino-Japanese Negotiations of 1915,* pp. 31-36.

137   Bryan to Guthrie (and to Reinsch), May 11, 1915, *For. Rels., 1915,* p. 146.

138   Lansing to Bryan, May 7, 1915, SD, 793.94/339½. The original draft, which is a little different in wording from the note quoted above, is annexed to this letter. For information, also see Robert Lansing, *War Memoirs of Robert Lansing* (Indianapolis and New York, 1935), p. 284. Hereafter cited as R. Lansing, *War Memoirs.*

139   Wilson to Bryan, May 10, 1915, Bryan Papers, letter book for December 1, 1914 to June 27, 1915.

140   Chargé d'Affaires Wheeler to Bryan, May 24, 1915, *For. Rels., 1915,* p. 156. Also see the same to the same, May 26, 1915, *ibid.,* p. 158.

141   A. W. Griswold, *Far Eastern Policy,* p. 196.

142   Reinsch to Bryan, May 31, 1915, SD, 793.94/420.

143   Reinsch to Bryan, May 14, 1915, *For. Rels., 1915,* p. 147.

144   Bryan to Reinsch, May 15, 1915, *ibid.,* p. 147.

145   Reinsch to Bryan, May 14, 1915, *ibid.,* p. 147.

146   Bryan to Reinsch, May 15, 1915, *ibid.,* p. 147.

147   For the text of Reinsch's letter to the Chinese government, see Reinsch to Bryan, May 25, 1915, *ibid.,* pp. 157-158.

148   For those treaties and notes, see *Sino-Japanese Negotiations of 1915,* pp. 39-63.

149   Wang Yün-sheng, *China and Japan,* VI, 398. Yüan's policy could be better seen from his personal comments on the original Twenty-One Demands of January 18 and on the Japanese revised demands of April 26. *See ibid.,* VI, 91-95 and 283-286.

CHAPTER FIVE

Wilson's Support of Yüan Shih-k'ai

The Chinese Republic, founded upon the extensively decentralized Manchu Empire, simply could not be consolidated into a cohesive whole at one stroke. Intermittently it suffered from internal disunity which accounted mainly for its administrative inefficiency, military weakness, financial straits, and, above all, inferior position in the family of nations. Unless effectively united, it would be in no position to become a strong modern state and to free itself from the yoke of foreign invasion and oppression. Yüan Shih-k'ai who was then at the helm of government realized this and, in spite of his personal weakness, strove hard to bring about the unification of his country. For a time he seemed successful in stabilizing his regime. But that stability did not last very long and was finally destroyed by his own selfish ambitions. After his death the whole country fell into a state of confusion which was bound to continue for some time to come and which made real internal solidarity even harder of realization.

Woodrow Wilson favored any sincere efforts by the Chinese government to entrench its position, because he considered national unity the outstanding problem for that country. He was always willing to give direct or indirect moral support to the central governmental authorities, stopping short of intervention in Chinese domestic affairs. He never assisted the Kuomintang leaders like Sun Yat-sen and others in their insurgent plottings, although he was sympathetic with their democratic principles.

He realized that only a really unified and stabilized China could effectively withstand Japanese aggressive designs and safeguard American interest in the integrity of Chinese territory and sovereignty. For the sake of both China and the United States he found it wise to encourage the Chinese government to promote internal peace and stability. He maintained this stand persistently throughout the eight years of his regime, particularly in those years when Yüan Shih-k'ai was the Chief Executive of the Peking government. This policy found its full expression in his attitude toward Yüan's monarchical movement.

The Wilson administration at Washington seemed to have much confidence in Yüan's ability and power as the leader of a new and united China. As we have previously mentioned, American recognition of the Chinese Republic in 1913 was in fact an act of support for Yüan who as the head of the newly established government promised to unify and regenerate his country. Wilson viewed with favor whatever measures Yüan took to consolidate his rule and thus strengthen his nation against foreign pressure.

During the summer of 1913 the Kuomintang started a rebellion in the South and threatened to overthrow Yüan. But American faith in Yüan did not weaken. In spite of strict neutrality in the ensuing brief Chinese civil war, the United States showed much sympathy for and gave moral support to the cause of the Peking government. E. T. Williams, American chargé d'affaires at Peking, described Yüan as the real founder of the Chinese Republic. As he saw it, Sun Yat-sen's statement that the Kuomintang uprising was merely a protest against Yüan's dispatch of troops into the South was "ridiculous." He also refuted the idea that the insurrection resulted from any desire on the part of the Kuomintang to avenge the murder of Sung Chiao-jen. The revolutionary leaders including Sun Yat-sen were reported either to be "impracticable" men or to be of "disreputable" character.[1] On the whole Williams regarded Yüan as the only man strong enough to guarantee the unity that China needed; and the chargé's views must have impressed his government favorably. As a matter of fact all Americans and Europeans in China generally pinned their faith on Yüan and distrusted the inexperienced young men in the Chinese Parliament, most of whom were Kuomintang members.[2]

At the beginning of the revolt the insurrectionists used the foreign settlements of Shanghai as a base of sedition. Williams took the position that no belligerents of either side should use the foreign settlements for the purpose of planning warlike actions.[3] The Consular Body of Shanghai made a proclamation to that effect.[4] Such an attitude of neutrality was of great help to Yüan; it prevented the revolutionaries from hiding themselves safely in the settlements from which to plan military operations against the government.

With the defeat of the Kuomintang revolt of 1913 the power of Yüan Shih-k'ai was greatly strengthened. The National Assembly formally elected him President of the Chinese Republic on October sixth.[5] The next day the ministers for Russia, Great Britain, Germany, Japan, Italy, Austria-Hungary, and several other countries informed the Chinese minister of foreign affairs that they had been instructed to accord recognition to the Chinese Republic.[6]

Upon hearing of the election of Yüan Shih-k'ai as China's constitutional President, Secretary of State Bryan expressed gratification that things had come out so well. He suggested that President Wilson should send congratulations on the day of Yüan's inauguration, October tenth.[7] Wilson thereupon sent Yüan a message in which he expressed his "pleasure to cooperate with you in preserving and still more firmly cementing the friendly and cordial relations between the two countries." [8] In reply the newly inaugurated Chinese President indicated his whole-hearted willingness to cooperate in tightening "the bonds of friendship and good understanding that unite the two sister republics." [9]

After Paul S. Reinsch reached Peking and assumed the post of American minister, he had an interview with Yüan Shih-k'ai, during which the latter was pleased to learn of Wilson's personally sympathetic attitude toward China. A few days later Yüan, through the kindness of Williams who was to return to the United States to become the chief of the division of Far Eastern affairs of the state department, sent Wilson his renewed thanks and best regards together with a copy of his autographed photograph.[10] Wilson soon presented Yüan with a copy of his own photograph and took occasion to point out that the American-Chinese friendship should be solidified by China's adoption of representative government and that the peoples of the United States and China would "find their growing intercourse of increasing mutual benefit." [11]

An autocrat at heart, Yüan Shih-k'ai never really cared much about the development of republicanism in China. By first expelling the Kuomintang members of the National Assembly and then dissolving the Assembly itself and promulgating a revised Provisional Constitution, he succeeded in centralizing great powers in his own hands. Dictatorial as he seemed, his government gained thereby efficiency and strength. Reinsch interpreted Yüan's centralization of power not as a reaction against democracy but rather as a necessary step to bring about national unity and internal peace under which constitutional government could be safely developed.[12] Even Bryan, who had been startled at the dissolution of the Kuomintang and had spoken of Yüan as adopting "something of Huerta's methods," [13] later toned down his criticism when social and financial conditions in China improved. According to the state department, China's "substantial people" were all supporting their President. The secretary of state therefore asserted that although Yüan's methods might smack of dictatorship one could

142

hardly pass judgment upon the matter without knowing all the circumstances.[14]

Wilson, the champion of democratic self-government in the Western world, the sworn opponent of the Mexican dictator Huerta, never openly criticized Yüan's undemocratic methods. Like Reinsch he thought it justifiable for the Chinese President to assume such great powers as were necessary to strengthen the government and to bring about internal peace. As far as circumstances permitted, he afforded Yüan his support for constructive work in China. He had told Reinsch before the latter left for the Peking post that the United States should extend to China both moral and financial aid.[15] He was willing to approve military assistance in the person of American officers for training the Chinese army. It was Lindley M. Garrison, the secretary of war, who first suggested that the United States could lend accomplished officers for this purpose.[16] Wilson completely approved of the idea.[17] Thereupon Bryan instructed the American legation at Peking to take up this matter unofficially with the Chinese government.[18] As China then did not intend to employ foreign training officers but meant to reduce her troops and expenses,[19] the American offer, although greatly appreciated, was not accepted.

Aside from the above-mentioned manifestations of friendliness on the part of the United States, what gratified Yüan Shih-k'ai most was the American attitude of non-assistance to his political opponents. Increasingly consolidated as his government was, he was now and then beset with the thought that the Kuomintang revolutionaries might come back to power with the help of some foreign power. After the defeat of the uprising of 1913 some Kuomintang members took refuge in the United States. It was repeatedly reported that they, together with American-born Chinese, had been plotting against the Peking government by using the United States both as a base and as an asylum. For this reason Yüan felt ill at ease and was anxious

143

to make sure that the American government would not give any encouragement or aid to such plotters.

To the satisfaction of Yüan Shih-k'ai the American government was not in any way disposed to encourage or assist the Kuomintang agitators in the United States. One or two cases may be cited by way of illustration. On June 4, 1914, the Chinese minister at Washington sent to the state department a translation of a telegram from the Chinese foreign office complaining that certain members of the Kuomintang had bought two airplanes in America and were sending them to China for the use of the revolutionaries.[20] On June thirtieth, he called the attention of the state department to the report that Chinese "rebels" had also contracted for twelve more airplanes to be shipped to China.[21] Although the American government under its laws at that time could do nothing to prevent the sale and shipment of arms and munitions of war, it did assist in detecting such illegal exportations and informing the Chinese government about them.[22]

In the same year of 1914 the famous revolutionist, Huang Hsing, and some of his associates set forth for the United States to begin agitation against the Peking government. The Chinese minister, on October first, informed Bryan of the impending visit of Huang Hsing to Washington and expressed the hope that American officials at the capital would give no encouragement to the Chinese revolutionists.[23] The secretary of state assured him that there would be no encouragement to persons intriguing against a friendly government and that President Wilson would not receive Huang Hsing in any audience.[24] The American government consistently viewed with disfavor Sun Yat-sen's Kuomintang opposition. Once Bryan remarked that if Sun's plans for revolution were carried out, the Chinese situation would be so much worsened that foreign intervention would almost inevitably follow.[25] Such an eventuality would be most undesirable in the eyes of Wilson, who had always wished for internal peace and stability in China.

No further Kuomintang revolution took place in the year 1914, and the Peking government became stronger despite the extension of the First World War into Chinese territory. The increasing stabilization of the Chinese government pleased China's well-wishers, especially President Wilson. For the third anniversary of the Republic he sent Yüan Shih-k'ai "cordial felicitations and fervent wishes for the continued prosperity of your great friendly republic and for your Excellency's personal welfare and happiness." [26] Yüan reciprocated with most heart-felt greetings. [27] Although such an exchange of messages was largely a matter of protocol, it undoubtedly testified to the friendly ties between China and the United States, which both Wilson and Yüan had tried hard to tighten.

During the Sino-Japanese discussions of the Twenty-One Demands, relations between China and the United States remained as cordial as ever, although the American government, owing to its preoccupation with European affairs, could not lend Yüan Shih-k'ai as much diplomatic support as was expected. The Japanese *démarche* threatened but did not destroy China's internal stability and peace. The prestige of Yüan Shih-k'ai was not much weakened in the eyes of the Chinese people, because, as a result of the Japanese ultimatum, he had escaped full responsibility for the acceptance of the demands and the Kuomintang charge that he had intentionally intrigued with Japan at the expense of China's birthrights did not seem to be justified. Elated with tiding over the great national crisis, Yüan soon embarked upon a monarchical movement which shook the very foundation of his government and at last cost him his life.

Feeling already had it in Peking during the years 1913 and 1914 that republicanism was not suited to the conditions in China. In January of 1915 one of Yüan's trusted followers,

Yang Tu, and Yüan's eldest son, Yüan K'o-ting, secretly initiated a movement for the reinstitution of the monarchical form
of government.[28] But the movement did not spread widely during the national crisis caused by the Japanese presentation of
the Twenty-One Demands. After the conclusion of the Sino-
Japanese negotiations it was revived with renewed vigor and
gained momentum rapidly. It was first supported by some leaders of the so-called Anhui party, a political clique consisting
mainly of men with great military influence. It aimed at making Yüan Shih-k'ai the emperor of China with all power concentrated in his hands. No provision was then made for representative institutions; the militarists thought they would thrive
more under a regime patterned after the Manchu Dynasty.
President Yüan, despite his repeated disclaimers of imperial
aspirations, looked upon the movement with tolerance and
complacency. His eldest son, from a desire to be the future
heir apparent, was particularly enthusiastic in bringing the
monarchical scheme to a head.

The ascendancy of the Anhui party meant loss of power
for the rival clique, the Cantonese party, composed chiefly of
comparatively progressive civilian leaders. Despite an immediate threat to their own interests, the leaders of the latter party
stole the thunder of their rivals and came to the full support of
the monarchical movement. They seemed to have convinced
Yüan Shih-k'ai that they could help to realize his personal
ambitions. To gain popular support they tried to give the
movement a constitutional appearance; that is to say, they
promised to establish a monarchy based on representative institutions. Their assumption of leadership angered the Anhui
faction, some leaders of which either resigned or kept aloof
from the political plots which had once had their support.[29]

The development of the monarchical agitation was also
associated with a memorandum prepared by the famous American educator and constitutional advisor, Frank J. Goodnow,

shortly after his return to Peking in the middle of July, 1915, for a brief stay. Goodnow was concurrently the president of Johns Hopkins University and was highly respected in official circles at Peking. The memorandum was written at the request of Yüan Shih-k'ai for his own information. It was on the comparative merits of the republican and monarchical forms of government with special reference to Chinese conditions.[30] According to Goodnow, a monarchical form of government was, without doubt, better suited to a China for centuries habituated to autocratic rule. The American adviser, however, refrained from expressing opinions on the expediency of an actual change of the form of government under the circumstances then existing in China. As he pointed out, any reversion to the monarchy could be successfully carried out only if it met with no opposition from the Chinese people and foreign powers; if the law of succession was satisfactorily fixed; and if the development of constitutional institutions under the monarchy was provided for: it was for those responsible for the destinies of the Chinese nation to decide whether those conditions were present in China.[31]

The fact that an eminent scholar and citizen of the senior republic of the world favored a monarchy for China seemed to be of great significance. The Peace Planning Society, newly organized by Yang Tu and others for the purpose of promoting the monarchical movement, immediately made use of the memorandum as the basis of its propaganda. It quoted or misquoted Goodnow's views to give an impartial appearance to its own agitation for the re-establishment of a monarchical form of government.[32]

As the tide of monarchism rose, Goodnow's opinions were more and more widely quoted, exaggerated, and perverted. By giving the movement an objective and constitutional form, the promoters of the monarchical plan daily won new adherents. Most provincial governors as well as many commercial and educational organizations throughout China telegraphed their support of the movement.[33] Apparently the upper classes of the Chinese people for the most part approved of a constitutional monarchy.

John V. A. MacMurray, then in charge of the American legation at Peking during the absence of Minister Reinsch, had watched all the above developments with great care. For the purpose of ascertaining the nature and effects of the monarchical agitation in the provinces, he had instructed the consuls to make reports on the subject.[34] He hoped to gather all available information so as to adopt a proper attitude toward the impending change of the form of government in China. At the same time he suggested to the state department that American policy should be determined by such factors as the acceptability of the projected new regime to the Chinese people, and its ability to keep order and protect foreign rights.[35] This suggestion had the entire approval of the state department.[36]

The reports of the American consuls showed that the monarchist movement in the provinces had been inspired by the highest governmental authorities at Peking. The official classes either actively supported it or at least paid lip-service to it. The merchants and the majority of the gentry did not sympathize with, but did acquiesce in, the proposed change of the form of government. The Chinese masses were indifferent. Hostile as the student classes and the professed revolutionists were, they could not easily offer any organized opposition.[37] These reports seemed to indicate that the planned new government, once established, would deserve recognition on the part of the United States.

It is to be recalled that Yüan Shih-k'ai, upon inauguration as President, had solemnly sworn to support the Republic. To find a way to revoke his oath required careful consideration and planning. The best solution would be to have the imperial throne imposed upon him through a popular vote. In his message to the Council of State he adroitly insinuated the advisability of consulting the people about a change in the form of government.[38] Upon his promptings the said council decided to institute a national referendum on this momentous issue.[39]

While Yüan Shih-k'ai, for the time being, had the internal situation well in hand, the Japanese government was contemplating measures of intervention which finally doomed his movement to failure. It was to the advantage of Japan to keep the different political factions or parties at loggerheads and thus reduce their will to resist foreign invasion. As long as China was divided and decentralized, Japan could have her own way in that country. The development of a strong central Chinese national authority in monarchical form would be, therefore, most troublesome to Japan's aggressive policy toward China.

In the main, Yüan Shih-k'ai miscalculated the attitude of Japan, which soon took the lead in opposing his restoration of the monarchy. After the conclusion of the Sino-Japanese negotiations of the Twenty-One Demands, Yüan held the erroneous belief that Japan was well contended with what she had exacted from him and would not be hostile to his personal ambitions.[40] But when the monarchist movement came to the open, the Japanese government unexpectedly looked upon it with great disfavor. In a conversation with the Chinese minister at Tokyo on September 6, 1915, Count Okuma had warned against the proposed change of form of the government lest it should give rise to internal disturbances in China and affect detrimentally Japanese trade there.[41] This warning, in all fairness, was well-intentioned, and at that time the Japanese government had not yet seriously thought of intervention. Later when Yüan Shih-k'ai decided to proceed with his plan without any regard for foreign opposition, some Japanese extremists, especially the militarists who had detected in the Chinese situation a good excuse for armed intervention on the part of Japan, began to attack their government upon its impotent China policy. Under such circumstances the Japanese government was compelled to change its moderate course of action.[42] The assumption by Kikujiro Ishii of the post of foreign minister marked the beginning of such a change.[43]

It was not long before the Japanese government formally decided upon a course of intervention in China. It first tried to strengthen its stand by securing the cooperation of the other powers. The Japanese foreign minister informed Guthrie on October twenty-sixth that the Japanese government, in view of the danger which appeared to threaten foreign interests and commerce in China, had requested Great Britain, Russia, and France to join with Japan in a caveat to Yüan Shih-k'ai against continuance of the monarchical plan.[44] A similar communication had been despatched to Washington to the effect that the United States would tender Yüan the same advice.[45] Great Britain readily accepted the Japanese suggestion and furthermore advised the United States to cooperate without delay.[46]

Before a definite reply was received from Washington, Japan, in cooperation with Great Britain and Russia, had already presented a warning to Peking. On October twenty-eighth, the Japanese chargé d'affaires, accompanied by his British and Russian colleagues, called upon the Chinese foreign minister and emphatically drew the attention of the latter to the signs of disquietude in the Yangtze region and other southern provinces. With a view to preserving "the perpetual peace of the Orient" he counseled delay in the change of policy.[47] The Chinese government did not formally reply to the joint caveat until November second when it denied the reported undercurrent of opposition and unrest in South China and reiterated its ability to maintain internal peace and order. It implied its determination to carry through the projected referendum according to the wishes of the people.[48] The Tokyo government considered this answer unsatisfactory and continued to bring diplomatic pressure to bear upon Peking.[49] France and Italy also added some weight to the Japanese argument by participating in the joint action of admonition to China.[50] But the Chinese government had not yet fully realized the strength of Japanese opposition.

The United States was the only power that decided to abstain from the *démarche* initiated by Japan. This decision was made only after prudent consideration on the part of President Wilson and his new secretary of state, Robert Lansing. When the Japanese and British ambassadors requested American cooperation in the matter of what amounted to a virtual protest to China, Lansing was very cautious and did not make any commitment. Later he confessed to Wilson that he was puzzled about the real purpose of the Japanese action. Personally he thought that if the Japanese protest to China accomplished its avowed aims, it would produce good effects. With a keen eye he saw that Yüan's movement was due merely to "ambition for the continuance of his family in power for the assumption of the title." However, he did not find it advisable for the United States to intervene in the matter.[51] Thus he telegraphed Guthrie on October twenty-eighth that according to information in the possession of the state department the monarchical restoration in China would not bring on serious uprisings or jeopardize foreign life or property. In his opinion, interference in the internal affairs of other countries ran counter to American policy.[52] Obviously he would not fall in with the Japanese scheme for intervention, although he was unsympathetic with Yüan's personal aspirations to the throne.

In answer to Lansing's request for instructions Wilson suggested the following course of action which represented the gist of the American policy toward the Chinese monarchical movement:

Could we not give a very plain intimation to the Japanese government and the governments which seem to be acting with it in this matter that we agree with the Chinese in their position that a change in their form of government, however radical, is wholly a domestic question and that it would in our opinion be a serious breach of China's sovereignty to undertake any form of interference or even protest without such evidences as are now wholly lacking that foreign interests would be imperiled which it is our privilege to safeguard; and at the same time intimate to the Chinese government in the most friendly manner, our feeling that this is a most critical time in the affairs of the whole world and that her own international and national interests are in danger of being seriously compromised unless the present changes there can be guided with a very firm and prudent hand.[53]

As we can see, Wilson strongly disapproved of taking any action toward intervention or in protest jointly with Japan and other powers. He would have liked to leave China free to manage her own domestic affairs. It was his hope that China, for the sake of her own interests, would be able to handle the impending drastic change with great caution.

Consonant with the above instructions of Wilson, Secretary Lansing officially replied to Japan and Great Britain on November fourth, courteously declining their invitation to join in the tender of a warning to China.[54] American abstention from invasion of China's sovereignty impressed all classes of the Chinese people favorably. To quote the words of Reinsch: "The attitude of our Government is highly appreciated, and it is currently stated in the public press that at no time has America enjoyed greater popularity among the Chinese than at present." [55]

The Japanese government was not in any way discouraged by the American attitude of non-cooperation. It kept on exerting weighty diplomatic pressure upon Peking. This made Wilson very suspicious of Japanese motives. On December fifth, he suggested that Lansing should have "a very serious conversation with the Japanese ambassador about the Chinese situation." He thought Japan should be frankly told how the United States would view the Japanese efforts to place China under further control.[56]

In defiance of the Japanese and Entente opposition the Chinese monarchists carried through the referendum. Thanks to their skilful manipulation they won a superficially universal approval of the proposed restoration of the monarchy. Thereupon the Council of State, on December 11, 1915, asked Yüan Shih-k'ai to ascend the throne in response to the demand of the popular vote. After the customary polite refusal he acceded to the offer the next day. It was now simply a matter of days before the Empire would be formally promulgated. At this juncture Reinsch found it necessary to ask for instructions with regard to recognition and took occasion to suggest that, in view of the satisfactory conditions existing in China, the new regime, once officially established, should be recognized as a matter of course.[57] Secretary Lansing telegraphed Reinsch on December twenty-first as follows:

When Empire is proclaimed, if no serious organized opposition exists and you see no other reason to doubt permanence of new order, you are instructed to recognize new Government of China and say that, while the Government of the United States may feel a natural sympathy for republican forms of government which fulfill the hopes of the people of other countries, we recognize right of every nation to determine form of its government and that the people of China have our good wishes for undisturbed peace and prosperity.[58]

These instructions were in keeping with the thinking of Wilson and must have had his approval.

The much vaunted unanimous support for the monarchy was only temporary and ostensible. A well-planned revolt in Yunnan Province soon invalidated it. During the latter part of December when Yüan Shih-k'ai was preoccupied with preparations for the coronation, the governmental and military authorities of that province suddenly demanded the cancellation of the monarchy and, upon being rejected, declared their independence of the central government. Toward the end of January, 1916, the Province of Kweichow also announced its independence. Without question the tide of opposition was speedily moving throughout China.

But before the armed forces of revolt marched invincibly beyond the mountain fastnesses of Yunnan, there was still great hope of the success of the monarchical regime. People of moderate views, though having no special affection for Yüan Shih-k'ai, preferred the peaceful establishment of a monarchy to internal uprisings and disturbances. The prevailing fear of Japanese intervention on behalf of the secessionists made many staunch advocates of republicanism hesitate to oppose the coming change in government. Besides, the attitude of the powers, with the exception of Japan, was favorable to Yüan Shih-k'ai at this time. Their diplomatic representatives at Peking were all in favor of recognizing the new government at an early date and felt that any delay would serve merely to encourage "irresponsible elements" to make further troubles.[59] The American minister, Reinsch, was ever-ready to accord recognition upon the proclamation of the Empire, if no material change should take place in the Chinese situation and no further instructions should be received from his home government.[60]

At the same time the secessionists were gaining in strength. At a surprisingly quick speed the expeditionary forces of Yunnan marched into the southern part of Szechwan Province. Troops of the central government hastened to meet the attack but did not make any headway. Sporadic uprisings broke out in several other provinces in China.

Yüan Shih-k'ai had failed to announce a definite constitutional program to be carried out under the new regime. Many people who had suppressed their doubts were now encouraged by the prospect of the victory of the revolters and began to cry out against despotism. Yüan's authority weakened daily as the popular ill-will increased. Even under such circumstances it might not have been too late to save the critical situation, if he could have given concrete constitutional guaranties promptly and promulgated the Empire on them as a foundation.[61] But he held back in indecision and the chance slipped by. On February twenty-third, he issued a mandate postponing the date of accession.[62] About one month later, on March twenty-second, he ordered the total cancellation of the change of policy, thus putting an end to the monarchical movement altogether.[63]

Aside from the Chinese internal situation, outside opposition from Japan likewise contributed a great deal to the failure of the monarchical movement. The seriousness of Japanese hostility dawned upon the mind of Yüan only after the Japanese government several times warned him against the change in government. With a view to winning the Japanese favor he proposed to despatch a special envoy to present the Japanese Emperor with a decoration, only to meet with refusal from Tokyo.[64]

Report had it that Japan would intervene by arms in case of Yüan's failure to drop the monarchical plan.[65] Foreign Minister Ishii frankly blamed the Chinese government for failing to listen to the Japanese warning and furthermore expressed the Japanese determination not to recognize the new regime.[66] At the same time the Tokyo government energetically assisted the revolters in the South by supplying them with both funds and arms. It also connived at the use of Tsingtao by the Chinese revolutionists as a base for rebellious action.[67] The Japanese Yokohama Specie Bank even refused to pay over the surplus from current income from the salt revenue, thus adding difficulties to the already strained financial condition of the Chinese government.[68] Japan's hostility to a powerful Chinese monarchy doomed Yüan's political ambitions to failure.

The Japanese attitude caused the United States grave concern. The European powers were no less worried, because the upset of the Far Eastern *status quo* in favor of Japan was equally injurious to their interests in China. With this general picture in mind Reinsch proposed to the state department on April 1, 1916, that the powers should each send China an identical note "which while impressing on the Chinese Government the necessity of protecting foreign life and property during this crisis would give assurance that the *status quo* as guaranteed by international engagements would not be changed during the present war." [69] Two days later he suggested two alternatives to be considered. First, America, as it had done to China and Japan in May of 1915, should file a caveat to the effect that "the American Government reserves specific objection to any infringement of treaty rights and might, therefore, bring up, at the end of the war, the question of the status of the rights as affected by new agreements." Second, there should be a joint international control of Chinese finance. Even the Chinese government had for some time regarded international control as a last resort to cope with internal disorganization and the Japanese menace. Under any form of government whatsoever inefficiency and corruption would probably last in China until honest and expert administration was imposed upon her either by Japan alone or by the powers in concert. [70] All these proposals were designed primarily to balance the Japanese predominance in Chinese affairs.

Presumably after consultation with Wilson, Lansing accepted Reinsch's suggestion of April first, and immediately took steps to sound out London and Paris on the advisability of cooperation among interested powers through identical notes to China. [71] Since Great Britain and France were too busy with the war to join in any effort to resist the Japanese in China, the American proposal was ignored by them. Playing a lone hand, the United States could not at that time by peaceful means effectively oppose the threatened Japanese hegemony in the Far East. For this reason Reinsch's first alternative suggestion was put aside. As to the problem of an international control of Chinese finance the American government, though taking no prompt action, did give it serious consideration. Its approval of this idea later led to the American participation in the new international banking group in complete repudiation of Woodrow Wilson's earlier opposition.

In China, Yüan Shih-k'ai position was becoming more and more precarious. His abandonment of the monarchy did not fully satisfy his enemies. They demanded his utter elimination. Nor did it please his followers. They regretted to see him make a unilateral concession without a guaranteed *quid pro quo* on the part of the revolutionists.[72] His prestige thus fell immeasurably. To appease growing disfavor he yielded his administrative and military power to a responsible cabinet and retained himself merely as the nominal head of the government.[73] This failed to placate his opponents. They urgently required his immediate removal. For a time he did contemplate tendering his resignation and visiting the United States.[74] According to Reinsch, the American legation at Peking, when appealed to, should give him the required protection and hospitality, if circumstances permitted.[75] Japan had offered him asylum, but he had not accepted it, obviously because of his lack of confidence in that country.[76]

In the midst of internal strife and confusion Yüan Shih-k'ai died of illness and despair on June 6, 1916. His death settled once for all the problem of his ejection. According to the provision of the Chinese Constitution, the Presidency devolved upon Vice-President Li Yüan-hung. As Li was acceptable to both Yüan's adherents and the revolutionists, the North and the South were again united.

When the news of the death of Yüan reached Washington, Wilson expressed both his own sympathy and that of the American government and people.[77] He personally attended and offered a wreath at the memorial services held on June twenty-sixth, by the Chinese legation in memory of the late

President. For his friendly and sympathetic action the Chinese government declared itself most grateful.[78]

With the succession of Li Yüan-hung to the Presidency the rump parliament dissolved by Yüan Shih-k'ai was revived and the Nanking Constitution was restored to force. Despite the fact that factional conflicts were still going on, the authority of Peking did not collapse. Wilson continued to support the Chinese central government, and the cordial relations between the United States and China remained unchanged. Toward the close of Wilson's first administration, Li Yüan-hung, to quote Reinsch, "expressed his highest appreciation of the personal attention which President Wilson has given to Chinese affairs during the last four years, and especially the fact that whenever agreements concerning China had been made, the American Government had taken steps to safeguard the rights of China and the principle of equal opportunity." [79] Li's words must have represented the true sentiments of the Chinese government. Wilson had now won China's gratitude for his moral encouragement.

As we have seen above, Wilson never flinched from his moral support of the Peking government under the guidance of Yüan Shih-k'ai. He did so not because he favored the latter's dictatorial inclinations and monarchical ambitions, but because the Peking government was the only actual authority in sight which promised peace and order in China, and the consequent bolstering of that country against Japanese aggression. In formulating his policy concerning the Chinese political situation he always stressed China's internal stability rather than her form of government. For this reason the proposed restoration of the monarchy was unobjectionable to Wilson. Unlike Japan, the United States never encouraged any secessionists hostile to Yüan's government. It was an interesting episode in history when the monarchical schemes of Yüan Shih-k'ai were opposed by one of the world's most conservative monarchies and supported by one of the world's most progessive republics.

So far we have not dwelt upon American financial and industrial activities in China during the period of Wilson's independent diplomacy. This does not mean that the economic aspect of the American policy toward China was then unimportant. There were quite a few independent loans and engineering enterprises that are worthy of review in a separate chapter.

NOTES:

1 Williams to Bryan, August 22, 1913, *For. Rels., 1913,* pp. 128-129.

2 See James Bryce to Wilson, June 12, 1913, Wilson Papers, II, 36.

3 Williams to Bryan, July 26, 1913, SD, 893.00/1790.

4 The proclamation is dated July 26, 1913. See Shanghai *Gazette,* July 31, 1913.

5 The Chinese chargé d'affaires to Bryan, October 6, 1913, *For. Rels., 1913,* p. 131.

6 Williams to Bryan, October 8, 1913, *ibid.,* p. 132.

7 Bryan to Wilson, October 6, 1913, Wilson Papers, VI, 226.

8 Wilson to Yüan Shih-k'ai, October 9, 1913, *For. Rels., 1913,* pp. 132-133.

9 Yüan Shih-k'ai to Wilson, October 13, 1913, *ibid.,* p. 135.

10 Yüan Shih-k'ai to Wilson, December 2, 1913, Wilson Papers, VI, 226.

11 Wilson to Yüan Shih-k'ai, February 11, 1914, *ibid.,* VI, 226.

12 Reinsch to Bryan, May 5, 1914, *For. Rels., 1914,* pp. 51-52.

13 Bryan to Wilson, November 5, 1913, Wilson Papers, II, 41.

14 Bryan to Joseph P. Tumulty, December 2, 1914, *ibid.,* II, 68.

15 P. S. Reinsch, *An American Diplomat,* p. 63.

16 Lindley M. Garrison to Wilson, October 11, 1913, Wilson Papers, VI, 227. It was then rumored that the Peking government was calling upon Germany to assist it in instructing its army. Garrison thought that American participation in the work of in-

struction would help to strengthen the friendly ties between China and the United States.

17 Wilson to Bryan, October 14, 1913, *ibid.,* VI, 227.

18 Bryan to Williams, October 14, 1913, SD, 893.20/24.

19 Williams to Bryan, October 20, 1913, *ibid.,* 893.20/25. On the same day Bryan reported the matter to Wilson by a letter enclosing Williams's cable. See Bryan to Wilson, October 20, 1913, Wilson Papers, VI, 227.

20 The Chinese minister to E. T. Williams, June 4, 1914, SD, 893.00/2132.

21 William Phillips (third assistant secretary of state) to the secretary of the treasury, July 3, 1914, *ibid.,* 893.00/2141.

22 W. P. Malburn (assistant secretary of the treasury) to Bryan, July 9, 1914, *ibid.,* 893.00/2142. Also see Bryan to the Chinese minister, July 15, 1914, *ibid.,* 893.00/2141.

23 The Chinese minister to Bryan, October 1, 1914, *ibid.,* 893.00/2188.

24 Bryan to the Chinese minister, October 6, 1914, *ibid.,* 893.00/2188.

25 Bryan to Joseph P. Tumulty, December 2, 1914, Wilson Papers, II, 68.

26 Wilson to Yüan Shih-k'ai, October 9, 1914, *ibid.,* VI, 226.

27 Yüan Shih-k'ai to Wilson, October 12, 1914, *ibid.,* VI, 226.

28 Chang Chung-fu, *Diplomatic History,* I, 175.

29 For a brief description of the rivalry between the Anhui and Cantonese parties in connection with the monarchical movement, see John V. A. MacMurray to Lansing, September 24, 1915, *For. Rels., 1915,* p. 63; P. S. Reinsch, *An American Diplomat,* pp. 172-174; and T. E. LaFargue, *China and World War,* pp. 79-80.

30 John V. A. MacMurray to Lansing, September 7, 1915, *For. Rels., 1915,* pp. 48-49.

31 For Frank J. Goodnow's memorandum, see *ibid.,* pp. 53-58.

32 In a manifesto which appeared in the Peking press on August 16, 1915, the Peace Planning Society indicated its preference for the monarchical form of government and based its argument on views attributed to Goodnow. For the manifesto, see *ibid.,* pp. 58-59.

33 MacMurray to Lansing, September 2, 1915, *ibid.,* p. 47.

34 MacMurray to Lansing, September 7, 1915, *ibid.,* p. 53.

35 MacMurray to Lansing, September 4, 1915, *ibid.,* p. 47.

36   Lansing to MacMurray, September 7, 1915, *ibid.*, p. 60.
37   MacMurray to Lansing, September 24, 1915, *ibid.*, pp. 62-63.
38   The message was conveyed to the Council of State on September 6, 1915. For its English text, see *ibid.*, p. 61.
39   Reinsch to Lansing, October 11, 1915, *ibid.*, pp. 65-66. Also see P. S. Reinsch, *An American Diplomat*, p. 176.
40   Wang Yün-sheng, *China and Japan*, VII, 3.
41   Lu Tsung-yü to the Chinese foreign office, September 6, 1915, *ibid.*, VII, 4-5.
42   *Ibid.*, VII, 3, 6.
43   *Ibid.*, VII, 6.
44   Guthrie to Lansing, October 26, 1915, SD, 893.01/38.
45   The Japanese embassy to the state department, October 27, 1915, *For. Rels., 1915*, pp. 69-70.
46   The British embassy to the state department, October 27, 1915, *ibid.*, p. 70.
47   For the text of the advice verbally communicated by the Japanese chargé d'affaires to the Chinese foreign minister, see *ibid.*, p. 73.
48   For the Chinese reply to the chargé d'affaires of Japan and the ministers of Great Britain and Russia, see *ibid.*, pp. 74-76.
49   See Wang Yün-sheng, *China and Japan*, VII, 14-19.
50   *Ibid.*, VII, 14.
51   Lansing to Wilson, October 27, 1915, SD, 893.01/73.
52   Lansing to Guthrie, October 28, 1915, *ibid.*, 893.01/38.
53   Wilson to Lansing, October 31, 1915, *ibid.*, 893.01/78½.
54   See the memoranda from the state department to the Japanese and British embassies, dated November 4, 1915, *For. Rels., 1915*, pp. 76-77.
55   Reinsch to Lansing, November 19, 1915, *ibid.*, p. 78.
56   Wilson to Lansing, December 5, 1915, SD, 793.94/488½.
57   Reinsch to Lansing, December 18, 1915, *For. Rels., 1915*, pp. 78-79.
58   Lansing to Reinsch, December 21, 1915, *ibid.*, p. 79.
59   Reinsch to Lansing, January 15, 1916, *For. Rels., 1916*, pp. 53-55. Also see Reinsch to Lansing, February 24, 1916, *ibid.*, p. 63.
60   Reinsch to Lansing, January 19, 1916, *ibid.*, p. 55.
61   Reinsch to Lansing, February 23, 1916, *ibid.*, pp. 59-60.

62   For the mandate, see *ibid.,* p. 61.

63   Reinsch to Lansing, April 4, 1916, *ibid.,* p. 67. For the mandate cancelling the monarchy, see *ibid.,* pp. 69-71.

64   See Wang Yün-sheng, *China and Japan,* VII, 29-35.

65   Lu Tsung-yü to the Chinese foreign office, January 21, 1916, *ibid.,* VII, 36-37.

66   Lu Tsung-yü to the Chinese foreign office, January 21, 1916, *ibid.,* VII, 37.

67   Willys R. Peck (American consul at Tsingtao) to Lansing, April 11, 1916, *For. Rel., 1916,* pp. 71-73.

68   Reinsch to Lansing, April 18, 1916, *ibid.,* p. 76.

69   Reinsch to Lansing, April 1, 1916, Wilson Papers, II, 96.

70   Reinsch to Lansing, April 3, 1916, *ibid.,* II, 96.

71   Lansing to Reinsch, April 4, 1916, *ibid.,* II, 96. Also see Lansing to the American embassy at London, April 4, 1916, *ibid.,* II, 96.

72   Reinsch to Lansing, April 4, 1916, *For. Rels., 1916,* pp. 67-68.

73   Reinsch to Lansing, April 24, 1916, *ibid.,* p. 77. Also see Reinsch to Lansing, April 27, 1916, *ibid.,* p. 79.

74   P. S. Reinsch, *An American Diplomat,* p. 192.

75   Reinsch to Lansing, May 24, 1916, *For. Rels., 1916,* p. 82. Also see Reinsch to Lansing, May 25, 1916, *ibid.,* p. 82.

76   Reinsch to Lansing, May 6, 1916, *ibid.,* p. 79.

77   See Lansing to the Chinese minister at Washington, June 8, 1916, *ibid.,* pp. 98-99.

78   Wellington Koo to Lansing, June 26, 1916, *Wilson Papers,* VI, 226. Also see Reinsch to Lansing, July 3, 1916, *ibid.,* VI, 226.

79   Reinsch to Lansing, December 8, 1916, *For. Rels., 1916,* p. 102.

CHAPTER SIX

American Economic Activities
in China during the First
Wilson Administration

1.

Wilson's first term of office as President corresponded roughly to the period between the American abandonment of the six-power loan and the American revival of the consortium. It marked an interregnum during which American commercial, financial, and industrial interests in China followed a course of independent action, and, in the absence of international cooperation, more than once met with strong opposition or obstruction from other powers and to a large extent failed to offset their imperialistic designs.

Wilson's withdrawal of government support for the American banking group from the consortium did not in the least imply his lack of interest in the development of American economic enterprises in China. On the contrary, he would by all means encourage American entrepreneurs in the opening of China's untouched and unrivaled resources.[1] It was his idea that the United States, independently of other powers, should render China both moral and financial assistance. Personally he assured his diplomatic representative in Peking, Reinsch, of his active support for constructive work in China.[2] But he also made it clear that in promoting the legitimate enterprises of American citizens and developing the trade relationship between the United States and China his administration would do nothing to interfere in Chinese internal affairs. He had no preference for any particular group of merchants or bankers, but would encourage all interested American individuals to compete on an equal footing for contractual favors. As he saw it, the United States government was not the endorser of any particular group of competing American capitalists, and for that reason was not a responsible party to the enterprises in which they were engaged. They should depend principally upon their own efforts and seek from their government only such aid and protection as were customarily given to legitimate business enterprises abroad. In other words, Wilson, in advancing his economic policy, always bore in mind the independence and sovereignty of China. He was reluctant to give American citizens any improper assistance which might impair China as a nation. Throughout this period he stuck closely to this benevolent policy of hands-off.

It was Minister Reinsch who actively executed Wilson's economic policy in China. Although realizing the importance of moral encouragement and political example as suggested by Wilson, Reinsch concentrated most of his energy upon American participation in Chinese industrial and economic development. He thought that an American diplomat in China should be occupied not only with political affairs but also with commerce, finance, and industry.[3] He agreed with many Chinese high authorities that only through modernization and industrialization could China substantially and effectively maintain her independence and sovereignty which it was incumbent upon the powers to respect in accordance with international agreements, but which most powers surreptitiously attempted to undermine for their own selfish ends. The fact that the United States had had no political designs upon China would help China to stand on her own feet, especially in the economic field. It would be disappointing to the Chinese, if America should refuse to extend a helping hand here. Besides, an extension of American enterprises throughout all the important parts of China would essentially undermine the old spheres of influence, secure American opportunities of commerce, and counterbalance the sinister forces of the aggressive powers, particularly Japan. Thus, both for the benefit of the United States and for the welfare of the Chinese nation, American economic opportunities in China should be greatly advanced. With this view in mind, Reinsch staunchly asserted American interests throughout China in the face of both the covert and open antagonism of the other powers. Out of a desire to carry out the economic policy of his country, he oftentimes moved ahead of his home government and the American investors.

2.

American economic assistance to China from 1913 to 1917 took the form chiefly of private loans. Generally speaking these loans fell into three categories: (1) educational loans, (2) administrative loans, and (3) industrial loans. Of the first kind only one small loan was made during this period. Administrative loans were allowed but not specially encouraged, because the American government was not enthusiastic in supporting loan contracts tied up with political matters as in the case of the reorganization loan. It was the last group of loans that the Wilson administration whole-heartedly favored. Most loans contemplated or actually negotiated during these years were industrial in nature.

Before the Wilson administration began, two educational loans had been made to China by the American banking group. One had been signed on November 26, 1912, for the sum of $200,000, and the other on January 14, 1913, for the sum of $185,000. Both loans were to be used for the maintenance of Chinese students in the United States and to be paid from the remitted portion of the Boxer Indemnity.[4] A few months after the withdrawal of the American group from the consortium the Chinese government paid off both loans together with accrued interest.[5] In the summer of 1913 Andrew Carnegie loaned to China the sum of $200,000 for the same purpose of maintaining the Chinese indemnity students in the United States. This loan was to be reimbursed also from the portion of the Boxer Indemnity to be remitted by the American government.[6] But unlike the above two loans it did not bear interest.[7] It was the only educational loan made to China during Wilson's first term of office as President.

3.

From the point of view of the new administration in Washington, American citizens should be encouraged to make investments in China only to such an extent as not to imply forcible interference in Chinese political and financial affairs. Loan contracts with objectionable conditions similar to those of the reorganization loan were to be discouraged. For this reason the American government, after its severance of connections with the international banking group, was very cautious in dealing with Chinese loans of an administrative nature. American bankers clearly understood this new policy of their government and became equally prudent in making decisions in answer to Chinese requests for such loans.

The Chinese government was on the brink of bankruptcy in the first half of the year 1913. The five-power loan signed in April, 1913, relieved only in part its fiscal distress. Should it turn again to the quintuple group for another loan, it would most probably have to accept even more stringent and disastrous terms. Under such circumstances it naturally looked for help to the United States which had just proclaimed its benevolent economic policy toward China. Even if large loans were not forthcoming from banking groups in the United States, the existence of competition between American financiers and those of the quintuple group might induce the latter to moderate their demands.

Before Minister Reinsch took up his post at Peking, requests for administrative loans had been made not only by the Chinese central government but also by some Chinese provincial authorities. In the first place the Province of Chekiang had approached the International Banking Corporation with a request for a loan to be secured upon its silk tax. The corporation declined, because the loan was to be used for political purposes and the security offered was insufficient. In the second place the military governor of Mukden had sought a loan also for political purposes.[8] He did not gain a favorable response, because the very nature of the requested loan did not meet with the approval of the American investors.

The administrative loan that the Chinese central government had solicited was intended for the improvement of the Chinese currency. Several times the Chinese premier, Hsiung Hsi-ling, had broached the subject to the American chargé d'affaires, E. T. Williams. At that time there was in circulation a vast amount of depreciated paper money issued by the provinces, and the central government desired to replace this currency with notes of the Bank of China secured by a foreign loan. If such a loan could be contracted for with American financiers, China would be able to avoid the undesirable course of negotiating another loan from the consortium. In order to arouse American interest the Chinese premier even described this contemplated loan as being industrial not political in nature, on the ground that it would give impetus to commerce and industry by reforming and stabilizing the national currency. E. T. Williams realized the possibility that China's financial straits might lead to foreign interference. He suggested that due weight must be given to that possibility when the advisability of an American loan was considered.[9]

It is to be recalled that as early as April 15, 1911, a currency reform loan agreement had been entered into between the Manchu government and the American, British, French, and German banking groups.[10] Owing to the outbreak of the Chinese Revolution the loan was not issued. After its withdrawal from the negotiations for the reorganization loan in 1913 the American group, while retaining its interest in an advance already made, abandoned its option on the currency reform loan altogether.[11] Thus all its obligations and rights were assumed by the British, French, and German groups who still held the option on the currency reform loan. Later these three groups decided to have Russian and Japanese bankers participate in any currency loan that might be financed for China.[12] It was now the Five-Power Consortium which was to handle the currency loan problem.

In fact the Five-Power Consortium did contemplate the inclusion of a sum for currency reform in a supplementary reorganization loan which China had solicited for the purpose of defraying short-term obligations. But the Peking government was unwilling to grant the consortium the option for a currency loan. It preferred to resume negotiations with American bankers in the hope that the latter, either independently or jointly with the British, French, and German groups, would undertake the loan for currency reform.[13] But at this time the American group was disinclined to re-enter into transactions from which it had withdrawn following President Wilson's disapproval of the consortium.

The Chinese government had also approached American investors outside the American group. It had asked the Standard Oil Company to arrange for a loan of G$15,000,000 to strengthen the capital of the Bank of China. It hoped that by improving the credit of this bank it would be able to start the reorganization of the national currency. The Standard Oil Company, primarily interested in oil concessions, did not want to make this loan a part of its contemplated arrangements with China. However, the company promised to give tacit support to a loan of this nature.[14]

At this juncture a New York contractor, G. M. Gest, became interested during his short stay at Peking in the problem of Chinese domestic financing. Before his departure from China he had secured an option for the Bank of China loan contract.[15] Upon his return to the United States he attempted to enlist the support of both the state department and the American group with a view to realizing the loan. The state department, seeing that no interference in Chinese internal affairs was involved, fully endorsed the proposed loan and promised to give it "all proper diplomatic support." [16] But the American group refused to underwrite this transaction on the ground that it was still bound by the provisions of the agreement signed by the Six-Power Consortium on June 20, 1912, and consequently was not supposed to compete with the other groups of the consortium for loan contracts of an administrative nature.[17] Later Gest appealed to President Wilson for help in finding a solution to the difficulty.[18] In spite of this the American group remained adamant in its decision not to take up the loan.

Soon the European War broke out, and, as a result, the world financial situation made it more difficult for China to place a loan even in the neutral United States. In a letter to the American chargé d'affaires at Peking, J. V. A. MacMurray, Counselor Robert Lansing remarked: "It is regretted that recent efforts to secure a loan in the United States in aid of the Bank of China appear to have been unsuccessful. The present war in Europe seems about to disturb the financial equilibrium of the world and it seems unlikely that China will be able to negotiate in the near future a loan for any considerable amount of money." [19]

Months passed before the Chinese government ventured on another move toward administrative loans in the United States.

First, it authorized G. M. Gest to negotiate a short-term loan of G$15,000,000 to be secured upon the unpledged portion of the likin tax of the provinces of Kiangsu and Chekiang.[20] Secondly, it inquired through W. W. Willoughby about the possibility of placing a loan of from one hundred to two hundred millions of dollars in the United States. The purpose of the large loan was to reform the Chinese banking and currency system.[21] Neither of its attempts met with any final success.

But the Chinese government did not give up the hope of securing American financial assistance. Through G. M. Gest it appointed Messrs. Lee, Higginson and Company as its fiscal agents for the purpose of placing bond issues and maintaining the price of the Chinese bonds on the American market and performing other financial services at China's instance.[22] In making this appointment, however, it by no means delegated that banking firm to negotiate all loans for it in the United States. It meant to float general loans for administrative purposes through this agency and still reserved the right to place special industrial loans with other banking houses.[23]

Negotiations for a loan were undertaken shortly between the Peking government and its new fiscal agency, Messrs. Lee, Higginson and Company. At this time open opposition to Yüan Shih-k'ai's monarchical movement was spreading rapidly in China, and the revolutionists stood strongly against any general loans to the Peking government whose authority they repudiated. Under such circumstances Reinsch found it inexpedient for American bankers to give financial support to the Peking authorities as against the opposition leaders. He advised that loan negotiations should be delayed until the China's internal strife was settled.[24] He insisted that no new loans should be made to China unless the proceeds were assigned to industrial purposes.[25]

The loan that the Chinese government was negotiating with Messrs. Lee, Higginson and Company was a short-term loan of $5,000,000 bearing interest at six per cent and payable in three years. In an official letter to Reinsch, Liang Shih-yi, president of the Chinese loan bureau, stated that the loan was to be devoted to "advances to the Provinces for industrial developments, municipal improvements, and education." [26] As a matter of fact its purpose was to meet the deficit in the expenditures of the central government, and the contemplated advances were already in the budget for the year 1916. Later it was even intended to satisfy the most urgent necessities of bank and military payments.[27] It was really an administrative loan. The Chinese statement of the industrial nature of the loan was intended chiefly to invalidate Reinsch's opposition and thus to get the money. In accordance with the wishes of the Chinese government, Messrs. Lee, Higginson and Company made an advance of $1,000,000 on April 3, 1916, and four days later formally signed the loan contract.[28] Owing to Reinsch's repeated warnings, however, further advances were delayed.[29]

Soon the Chinese political situation became somewhat clarified. Yüan Shih-k'ai, against whom the southern provinces had raised the banner of revolt, abandoned his monarchical scheme and transferred his administrative powers to a newly organized cabinet under the premiership of Tuan Ch'i-jui. The new premier and several other influential men like Hsü Shih-ch'ang and Li Yüan-hung were trying to re-unite the country and win over dissident elements by peaceful means. Seeing that this new program adopted by the Peking government constituted "the most practical solution in view," Reinsch reversed his previous stand and advocated immediate financial aid. By that time he thought that the completion of the Lee-Higginson loan would be desirable and in the interest of China.[30] But in order to relieve the grave consequences of disorganization resulting from the Chinese civil war, larger loans would be more effective than small advances. As the United States was the only chief neutral power interested in China's independence and internal unity, it should lose no time in putting China on her own feet through sufficient financial assistance. First of all, the Chinese national banks were to be rehabilitated, and a banking loan of $15,000,000 of American capital was necessary for that purpose. In the second place, Chinese financial adequacy was to be restored, and a large American reorganization loan of $30,000,000 would serve that purpose. These loans should be so adequately secured as to attract and satisfy American bankers.[31]

In expounding the urgency of relieving Chinese internal disruption, Reinsch had in mind the international significance of his proposal. The fact that Japan had been attempting exclusive control of Chinese financial affairs and had been furnishing assistance to the Chinese revolutionists presented such a threat to Chinese independence and American interests as to require immediate counter-action on the part of the United States. He remarked:

> Though American activity in China is not welcomed by Japan a last opportunity is afforded. A just, straightforward policy of the United States, strongly supported, would compel respect and prevent developments extraterritorially perilous to our future. Menacing ambitions of Japan though given much scope by the complications in Europe still rest on slender basis and could be held in check by display of active interest in China. Once realized, however, they could not be controlled except by great force. . . .
>
> In its results the moderate investment suggested would equal military expenditure of hundred millions because it would prevent realization of exclusive control in the Far East inevitably hostile to America. The issues involved exceed those in Europe in ultimate importance.[32]

Soon came the sudden death of Yüan Shih-k'ai which further aggravated the financial distress of the Chinese government. Japan took advantage of this situation to offer a large loan on injurious conditions, including the demand to serve as the exclusive fiscal agent of China throughout the world. With a view to holding in check the imminent Japanese domination of Chinese finance and to maintaining American interests in China, Reinsch again urged that American financiers take prompt and favorable action. By telegraph he told Lansing that unless a favorable decision was made now American opportunity would be "irrevocably lost." [33]

The state department fully realized the seriousness of the Chinese financial situation as well as the Japanese menace to American rights. But financial assistance to China could not be immediately effected in the United States. It would take time to interest enough bankers in that matter and more time for them to work out a principle of cooperation among themselves. At that time there was a great danger of conflict between the bankers represented by Messrs. Lee, Higginson and Company and those connected with the old American group. Messrs. Lee, Higginson and Company as China's fiscal agents claimed a right to place all Chinese government loans on the American market, whereas the American group as a party to the six-power loan agreement claimed an option on any new reorganization loan although it had withdrawn from the consortium.[34] The state department thought that if the two groups of American bankers actually struggled with each other the Japanese might "secure the prize." It seemed reasonable that both groups should be combined in a joint effort to render financial aid to China.[35] Apparently this idea had the approval of Wilson.

Reinsch continued to send back telegrams pressing for immediate advances on the proposed reorganization loan of $30,000,000. He also urged Messrs. Lee, Higginson and Company to make further advances on the loan contract already concluded with China. The banking firm hesitated to comply, because it said that it could not place the loan without the cooperation of other banking houses in New York, especially the American group.[36] Thus the state department now found it opportune to bring about cooperation between the two rival groups of bankers.

Prompted by the state department, J. P. Morgan, on June 27, 1916, summoned a meeting of the old American group, the Guaranty Trust Company, and Messrs. Lee, Higginson and Company, at which Third Assistant Secretary of State William Phillips, on behalf of Secretary Lansing, reiterated the Chinese need for a reorganization loan and also expressed the hope for a mutual understanding and cooperation among the various interested bankers.

During the discussions, Lee, Higginson and Company and the Guaranty Trust Company made it clear that they were willing to make the advance of one or two millions of dollars as urged by Reinsch on June 26, 1916,[37] if the cooperation of the members of the American group could be obtained. The latter declined on the ground that they were under obligation to consult the other groups of the consortium in connection with administrative loans to China.[38] They stated that they could make an advance on a reorganization loan only in conjunction with or on behalf of the other members of the six-power international banking group. As a matter of fact they had expressed their willingness to enter with the international group into negotiations, looking to the revival of the active interest of the consortium in China.[39] Obviously they still preferred the principle of international control to that of independent action. They were more interested in the resuscitation of the consortium than in cooperating with Lee, Higginson and Company in straight loans which they said would simply irritate Japan.[40] Thus the combination or cooperation of the two rival banking groups failed to materialize.

It is to be remembered that the state department, while ready to encourage independent loans to China, was at that time not opposed to the idea of international participation in the proposed reorganization loan. Politically speaking, whatever loan could be used to counterbalance the threatened Japanese predominance in Chinese financial affairs was to be approved. The Wilson administration, repudiator of the consortium in the naive days of 1913, had come at last to realize that only through international concerted action could it keep Japan under restraint without resorting to force. This realization led gradually to a reversion to the consortium policy of the Taft administration.

While the American bankers were considering whether the reorganization loan was to be made independently or internationally, the Chinese government was nearing bankruptcy. For the resumption of specie payments, it direly needed an immediate loan of four or five million.[41] Both Wilson and the state department hoped that this loan would be made without delay. Lansing, therefore, made an appeal to representatives from the American group, Lee, Higginson and Company, and the American International Corporation.[42] Whereas the latter two banking houses failed to give formal replies, the American group subsequently made its stand clear in a long letter to the secretary of state. If the requested small loan was intended for administrative purposes and would be repaid from a larger reorganization loan, the group, bound not to conclude singly any loan in the scope of the reorganization loan of 1913, would have to offer participation to the other members of the consortium. If it was a separate venture, the group had to know what specific security would be offered, in what way it would be administered, *and how it would be collected in case of default.* On the whole the bankers of the American group were reluctant to take up the loan. They, however, concluded with the statement that if the American government desired them to undertake negotiations for this loan, they, although not hopeful of result, would be ready to do so.[43]

The state department which had refrained from serving as the collector of debts for American bankers in China was awkwardly embarrassed by the attitude of the American group. In reply Acting Secretary of State Polk said that while the American government "would be glad to see China receive the financial assistance which it requires, cannot place itself in the position of urging its citizens to engage in any particular enterprise." [44] Thus ended the attempt to interest the American group in an immediate small loan to China.

The destitute Chinese government turned to Lee, Higginson and Company and the Guaranty Trust Company for help. It offered a five-year loan of five million dollars at five per cent interest on the security of the Chinese mining tax.[45] The two American banking houses took this offer into consideration, but made no favorable decision. They backed down, because they, like the American group, were not sure that the American government would guarantee the repayment of the loan in case of default. Such a guaranty to private bankers was something that the Wilson administration could not bring itself to give.[46]

The failure of Messrs. Lee, Higginson and Company to advance the balance of $5,000,000 under a formal contract and to make any new loan greatly disappointed the Chinese government. The company itself had felt embarrassed and had on several ocasions offered to surrender its appointment as China's fiscal agent in the United States.[47] Under such circumstances the Chinese government decided to abrogate the fiscal agreement with that company, thus cancelling the latter's agency.[48]

To sum up: throughout the above-mentioned negotiations China's intention was merely to receive advances or smaller loans to be followed by a large reorganization loan. Her fiscal agents, Messrs. Lee, Higginson and Company, could not easily place Chinese loans on the American market without the co-operation of the old American group. But the latter, still bound by the six-power agreement, felt disinclined to make independent loans of an administrative nature in conjunction with other American bankers. The American government, eager as it was to see China receive financial assistance from American financiers, hesitated to urge them to engage in particular financial ventures. Without sufficient support or guaranty from their government the American banking houses would not take the risk of investing their money in administrative loans in China where conditions were so unsettled. The net result of China's efforts to seek such loans in the United States in 1916 was an advance of one million dollars made by Messrs. Lee, Higginson and Company under the guise of an industrial loan contract. This advance was later paid back by the Chinese government.

4.

Let us proceed to the category of industrial loans. As we have mentioned before, President Wilson, in proclaiming his economic policy toward China in 1913, expressed hope for the promotion of Sino-American trade relations and for the participation of American citizens in the opening of Chinese natural resources. This announcement seems to have encouraged at once some American bankers to enter into industrial loan negotiations with China. But since the Wilson administration did not intend to give special support to any particular enterprise, no such loans were actually contracted by American investors in 1913.

Soon after Wilson's first announcement of policy regarding China, H. B. Hollins and Company of New York showed readiness to relieve Chinese financial difficulties by placing loans on China's behalf in the United States.[49] Through the agency of that company, the Chinese government proposed to borrow from American bankers an amount not to exceed $10,000,000 gold. The interest thereon would be six per cent and the loan itself would be payable within five years. In order to benefit American commerce as well as Chinese industry, the Chinese government bound itself to purchase American goods to the extent of the amount of the loan.[50] Favorable as these proposed terms were, the Wilson administration did not want "to single out any individual firm or group of American investors for special commendation or to endorse the terms of any agreement entered into." [51] Lacking specific encouragement and guarantee from its government, H. B. Hollins and Company could not secure the support of enough bankers for the loan, and finally let the Chinese proposal drop.

At the same time the Chinese government was looking for a few other small loans that it could get anywhere in the United States. First, a representative of Vice-President Li Yüan-hung attempted to secure an American loan for the rebuilding of Hankow. Secondly, Sheng Hsüan-huai, the principal owner of the Ping-hsiang Colliery, the Ta-yeh Iron Mines, and the Hanyang Rolling Mills, was eager to raise a loan to pay off the indebtedness of these works to Japanese capitalists. [52] Thirdly, the Provinces of Hupeh and Hunan planned to receive a loan for the development of their mines. [53] Fourthly, negotiations had started between the Yunnan provincial government and an American capitalist for a loan of G$2,500,000 to be secured by the revenue from tin mines and to be used for railway building and mining. [54] Chiefly owing to the lack of sufficient security, none of these loans was actually negotiated.

During the period before the First World War, when the Kuomintang leader Sun Yat-sen cooperated with Yüan Shih-k'ai and served in the Peking government, he was interested in raising a big loan for the purpose of carrying out his plan for a national system of railways. Empowered earlier by Yüan Shih-k'ai, he had worked out a system of 10,000 miles of railroad for the furtherance of the economic and political welfare of China. In designing his scheme he had been careful not to conflict with rights already granted to foreign countries under treaties, agreements, or understandings. According to his estimates the construction of the entire projected system necessitated an expenditure of $500,000,000. He desired to enter into negotiations for the financing of his project with an international underwriting syndicate of American, British, French, and German financiers. The agreement to be reached should provide equal participation on an equitable commercial basis to the respective members of the syndicate. In the supply of materials each member should have a full share and should not be discriminated against. As a mark of his personal confidence in Americans he appointed an American expert George Bronson Rea as his technical secretary as well as his deputy with full powers to negotiate with foreign bankers.[55]

Wilson's encouragement of American enterprises in China, as expressed in March, 1913, was only a general announcement. Many people did not know whether he would support any further efforts of American citizens in the matter of constructing and developing Chinese railways. Even the American legation at Peking was at first not clear as to what attitude would be taken toward railway loans to China.[56] For this reason George Bronson Rea personally requested Wilson to give his specific views on the problem of independent American participation in the building of railways in China.[57]

To his disappointment Rea found that the Wilson administration then objected to any form of international monopolization in China and was therefore cool to Sun Yat-sen's proposal. Notwithstanding this he went ahead with the task entrusted to him and, in cooperation with the Chinese fiscal representative Ch'en Chin-t'ao, completed negotiations in Europe for the establishment of a Sino-International Construction Company which would include some British, French, and German firms and was open to American participation. It was provided that the Chinese government would have an interest of from ten to twenty per cent in that joint enterprise.

Reinsch saw the importance of the proposed railway construction organization and urged his government to bring about the entry of American bankers. His argument was that the realization of the Chinese railroad plan would mean the completion of economically and uniformly constructed railways throughout China and thus would check the tendency toward a subdivision of China into mutually exclusive spheres of influence favoring Japan and European countries.[58]

An American firm, J. G. White and Company, with which George Bronson Rea was associated, had entered into some negotiations with China concerning the formation of the Sino-International Construction Company and had already received an invitation to participate from Ch'en Chin-t'ao. With official encouragement from the American government it might have accepted the offer. But the state department took views diametrically opposite to those of Reinsch. According to E. T. Williams, chief of the division of Far Eastern affairs, to place all Chinese railway construction under the charge of an international company would mean to establish a monopoly in violation of the open door policy. Such an monopolistic enterprise was even more objectionable than the Six-Power Consortium and would hasten, not halt the disintegration of China. For this reason Williams believed that Reinsch should be instructed "to protest to the Chinese Government against the plan proposed as being a violation of treaty provisions and inimical to the best interests of China." [59]

Counselor Lansing concurred in the conclusions reached by Williams but opposed a protest to China. He preferred to remind the Chinese government of the proposed project as violating treaty obligations. Wilson accepted Lansing's suggestion, hoping that the attention of the Chinese government would be directed to the treaty violation "very earnestly." [60] As to the problem of the participation of J. G. White and Company in the Sino-International Construction Company the state department gave an explicitly unfavorable answer, holding to its position of offering no support to any enterprise which implied monopolization in the matter of building and equipping railways in any part of the world.[61]

Before the United States took any official action, Great Britain and France, for different reasons from those advanced by the state department, had raised objections to the Chinese plan. The British government took the position that any proposed railway traversing the Yangtze Valley or conflicting with the British control of the approaches to Hongkong would have to be constructed by the British participant in the company. The French government would not permit the participation of French bankers, should any projected line infringe on French rights in southern and western China.[62] Obviously both governments still had their spheres of influence in mind and would in no way have their preferred positions interferred with. Too timorous to overcome these obstacles, the Chinese government decided not to press the matter until a favorable opportunity arose.[63] The whole project as first planned by Sun Yat-sen and later supported by others was thus quietly dropped.

By vetoing American participation in the Sino-International Construction Company the Wilson administration was not indifferent to the development of China. It would not refrain from supporting such railway enterprises as were undertaken on the basis of free competition and did not aim at exclusive rights. To those railway interests already possessed by American citizens in China it continued its predecessor's policy of diplomatic protection. For instance, it never ignored the one-fourth share of the American group in the Hukuang railways in spite of the fact that a Hukuang loan had been previously provided for upon the security of Chinese provincial taxes—a fact it disapproved of on principle.

It is to be recalled in this connection that, according to the Hukuang loan agreement of May 20, 1911, the American group was to be in charge of building the trunk line from Ichang in Hupeh to Kweichowfu in Szechwan.[64] Later, on the basis of engineers' estimates, the funds provided for in that agreement would be insufficient to complete all the Hukuang lines under contemplation. Furthermore the situation in the financial markets of the world made it unlikely that additional funds could be raised to finish all these lines. Because of this the American group proposed to its British, French, and German associates that they negotiate with the Chinese government for the purpose of securing an agreement for the postponement of the Hupeh-Szechwan line and for the concentration of all expenditure on the Hankow-Canton line which was considered more capable of profitable operation. The other three groups did not accept this suggestion until after the outbreak of the European War when they were facing great financial strain at home.[65] Then the question came up of giving the American group an equal opportunity in the supply of equipment and materials for the construction of the Hankow-Canton line.[66] Only through persistent negotiation assisted by the state department and the American legation at Peking did the American group secure a satisfactory settlement of that problem. But owing to the World War not much construction work was actually accomplished.

American capitalists were interested in several other enterprises besides railways. First of all, the Standard Oil Company of New York intended to make investments in Chinese petroleum deposits which China decided to exploit. It concluded an agreement with the Chinese government on February 10, 1914, whereby competent American experts were to be sent to China to make a thorough investigation of the oil fields in the provinces of Shensi, Jehol and Chihli. All expenses involved in the investigation were to be divided between both contracting parties. An American-Chinese corporation was to be organized with both American and Chinese shareholders, if oil fields were found worth working.[67] Later, investigations were actually conducted and experimental boring operations were carried on at different places. But unfortunately no oil spring was found.

At the suggestion of the Standard Oil Company and with the consent of the Chinese government the Sino-American petroleum enterprise was discontinued and accordingly the agreement of February 10, 1914, was cancelled.[68]

The above-mentioned petroleum contract had been bitterly attacked by the Japanese press, which viewed every American enterprise as being directed against the interests of Japan.[69] Japanese newspapers took an even more antagonistic attitude toward the attempt of the Bethlehem Steel Company at a reaffirmation of a previous contract made with the Chinese government in 1911 for the construction of vessels as well as for the improvement of dockyards. In the winter of 1913-14 Archibald Johnston, a vice-president of the Bethlehem Steel Company, visited Peking on a mission to ascertain whether or not the Chinese republican government acknowledged the validity of the said contract. As the Chinese minister of marine had been dispatched to Fukien as acting military governor of that province, Johnston was asked to go there for personal conferences. In Fukien he gave some technical advice on the coastal defence of China, on the location and equipment of dockyards and naval bases and especially on the suitability of the Bay of Santuao as a naval base. His visit immediately gave rise to the fabrication of a contract for a loan of $30,000,000, supposed to have been concluded by the Bethlehem Steel Company and China for the construction of a naval base on the Fukien coast.[70] It was on the basis of this apocryphal document that the Japanese government formally made an inquiry at the state department in Washington.[71] The rumor was not squelched until Bryan officially denied the authenticity of the alleged contract and disclaimed any intention on the part of the United States to interfere with Japanese interests in Fukien. As a matter of fact the Chinese government, although reaffirming the validity of the Bethlehem contract of 1911, did not desire its immediate execution. The whole question of having vessels and materials furnished by the Bethlehem Steel Company was deferred until Chinese financial and political conditions should have improved.[72]

In 1914 the Huai River conservation project constituted a major topic for discussion between China and the United States. It was a plan previously inaugurated by the American Red Cross and approved by the Taft administration.[73] Aimed at river regulation, flood prevention, and land reclamation in the Huai Valley, it had been regarded as a humanitarian enterprise beyond personal, commercial, or political purposes. Chiefly for this reason it interested Wilson deeply and had his approval as well.[74]

It is to be recalled that in 1911 the American Red Cross, which had contributed a great deal to the relief of the famine of 1910-11 in the provinces of Anhui and Kiangsu, proposed to send to China an American engineer-expert to investigate the famine-stricken area with a view to the formulation of a project for the prevention of recurring floods. This proposal having been accepted by the Chinese government, the American Red Cross chose Charles Davis Jameson as an engineer for the task of investigation. After spending almost a year in the Huai Valley, he made a preliminary report in which the state department found some practicable suggestions.[75] Then the American government made representations to China to the effect that the Huai River conservation work should be conducted along the lines laid down by Jameson. As a result the Peking government, in December, 1913, offered to the American Red Cross an option for one year to raise funds and to make a contract for the execution of the conservancy plan.

By the nature of its activities the American Red Cross was not supposed to have a direct participation in an enterprise carried on for profit. For this reason it proposed that within the period of the option it would find a responsible American contractor who could in turn enter into business engagements with

China and make an arrangement with American bankers for the marketing of the Chinese bonds required to pay construction expenses.[76] To this proposal the Chinese government promptly consented.[77] Wilson was gratified by this arrangement between the Chinese government and the American Red Cross. He also made it clear "that the Government of the United States will give assurance of good offices and diplomatic support in behalf of the American contractor should he be able to agree with the Chinese Government on fair and equitable terms." [78]

The American bankers, before providing the contractors with funds, would like to have had definite assurances as to the value of the land to be reclaimed and improved, because the proposed conservancy loan was to be secured upon the taxes on the improved land as well as upon the proceeds from the sale of the reclaimed land. Such being the case, a supplementary survey of the Huai Valley was necessary.[79] This necessity led to the appointment of a board of engineers composed of Colonel William L. Sibert as chairman and Mr. Arthur P. Davis and Professor D. W. Mead.[80] These three eminent engineers were soon sent to China to re-examine the Huai River region. After a period of hard work there they wrote an extremely favorable report. As they discovered, the Huai River conservancy project was "so sound from a technical and financial point of view that it is good business." [81] Everything would turn out well if the American bankers could take positive steps to finance the plan.

In the autumn of 1914 an unusual flood again visited the provinces of Kiangsu and Anhui, bringing great calamity to the inhabitants. In order to furnish employment and relief for those starving people the Chinese government requested the American Red Cross to exercise its good offices toward the consummation of the Huai River loan and the immediate advance of $5,000,000 gold on that loan account. This advance was to be used at once in deepening the channels of the tributaries of the Huai and I rivers.[82]

At that time the world's disturbed financial situation resulting from the war made it most difficult to float loans for China in the United States. Having received no definite encouragement from the bankers, the American Red Cross found it impossible to complete the Huai River loan within a short time or to bring about an advance for the immediate use of relief work. The state department accepted this view and formally made it known to the Chinese government.[83]

In the meanwhile the optional agreement between the American Red Cross and the Chinese government was about to expire. Unable as the American Red Cross was to fulfill its promises within the time limit, its interest in the great humanitarian work was still unabated. Therefore it proposed to have the option renewed so that it might continue to exert efforts toward a realization of the Huai River engineering project. The Chinese government consented to this proposal, and by a presidential rescript Yüan Shih-k'ai extended the option for another year.[84]

Negotiations for the Huai River reclamation loan had made some progress during the year 1915 but did not come to a successful conclusion. Despite President Wilson's apparent willingness to give diplomatic support to this particular loan sponsored originally by the Red Cross, the American bankers hesitated because of the unsettled political situation in the Far East. Their apprehensions, according to Reinsch, were unwarranted, because no radical change had taken place such as to affect the security of American investment in China.[85]

When the expiration of the renewed option was drawing near, Reinsch arranged with the Chinese government for an extension of the option for four months from January 31, 1916, in order to give the American International Corporation the time necessary for an investigation as to the methods of improving and restoring the Grand Canal in the provinces of Kiangsu and Shantung. It is to be remembered here that this corporation was a banking firm designated by the American Red Cross and actively interested in the financing of the Huai River conservancy work of which the Grand Canal project was only a part. As it was mutually agreed, if the restoration of Grand Canal was actually taken up, the Chinese government, upon the completion of the work, should give that corporation the option of carrying out the larger plan for the drainage of the Huai River.[86]

The extension of the optional agreement having been granted, the American International Corporation entrusted the task of investigating the Grand Canal project and negotiating loan contracts to W. F. Carey and Ernest T. Gregory of the Siems-Carey Company, whom it had nominated as its representatives in the matter.[87] As a result they signed an agreement with the provincial government of Shantung on April 19, 1916, whereby the corporation was authorized to issue a loan of not more than $3,000,000 gold for improving the Shantung portion of the Grand Canal and reclaiming certain land areas.[88] On May thirteenth, T. J. N. Gatrell, on behalf of Ernest T. Gregory as representative of the corporation, signed another loan of not more than $3,000,000 gold with the Chinese government for the improvement of the Kiangsu section of the Grand Canal as a part of the Huai River conservancy scheme.[89]

Contrary to the judgment of its representatives at Peking, the American International Corporation approved the Shantung agreement only in principle and subjected it to an exchange of letters covering some details not specifically stipulated for. Furthermore it would not execute the Kiangsu agreement unless the loan was made an obligation of both the Peking government and the provincial government of Kiangsu.[90] Throughout the autumn of 1916 the corporation was engaged in negotiations with China about minor modifications to be inserted into this loan contract. Reinsch bitterly criticized the unwisdom of the policy of the corporation:

. . . the method of negotiation followed in this important matter is radically wrong, and will inevitably and at all times lead to endless trouble and the expenditure of fruitless efforts in China. If the original contract had been unconditionally accepted by the American International Corporation, it would have been just as easy subsequently to get the necessary administrative modifications and interpretations; but the whole enterprise is endangered when, after a general agreement has been arrived at, the contract is allowed to remain pending while minor modifications are being discussed. This method secures for such minor modifications an importance far beyond their real consequence. It is highly to be desired and absolutely essential that in the future American concerns attempting to do business in China should definitely make up their minds as to what they want and what they can grant before the main contract is finally signed. Nothing is more irritating to the Chinese than to have long and painful negotiations come to an end, supposedly definitive, and then to find that the negotiators on the other side continued to discover things which they would like to have put into the contract.[91]

Under the treaty of 1898 the Chinese government felt obliged to offer Germany participation in any loan for the improvement of the Grand Canal in Shantung Province. But in the midst of the war the German government did not desire to be involved in this project.[92] No formal treaty obligation in the matter had accrued in favor of Japan who, however, argued that the Chinese government should apply first to her for a loan touching upon rights in Shantung.[93] Under official promptings the Industrial Bank of Japan entered into direct negotiations with the American International Corporation for a participation in the Grand Canal enterprise. Taking care not to ignore Japanese influence in Chinese affairs, the American International Corporation accepted the proposed cooperation subject to the final approval of the Chinese government.[94] This was done without the previous consent of the state department through whose support the corporation had gained its contractual rights from China. The state department had noticed the exceptional character of the Grand Canal project in origin and desired the whole enterprise to be undertaken solely by Americans. Reinsch was particularly opposed to Japanese participation and for this reason was bitterly displeased with the deal made behind the back of the Chinese government.[95]

Long suspicious of Japanese intentions with respect to Shantung, China was greatly disturbed by the proposed Japanese cooperation. Some circles in China even interpreted the ill-considered action of the American International Corporation as a betrayal of faith.[96] But in the face of needing foreign loans for the restoration of the Grand Canal the Chinese government soon became reconciled to the idea of Japanese participation. In place of the Shantung agreement of April 19, 1916, it later concluded another agreement with the American International Corporation for a loan of $6,000,000 gold for improving the Grand Canal in both Shantung and Chihli. According to this new arrangement the Industrial Bank of Japan might participate in the flotation of the loan to the extent of $2,500,000 gold.[97] Up to that time no actual construction work had yet been started although negotiations had proceeded for years and loan contracts had been successively signed.

W. F. Carey of the Siems-Carey Company had played an active part in the above-mentioned loan negotiations. Through his efforts his company was designated as the contractor for the work of the restoration of the Grand Canal.[98] His interest, however, was not limited to the conservancy work, and the construction of railways in China attracted more of his attention. He and the Chinese government, on May 17, 1916, concluded an agreement by which the Siems-Carey Company obtained the right to build railroads in China to an aggregate of

1,500 miles.[99] Five railway lines making up this mileage were to be constructed between these points: (1) from Hengchowfu in Hunan to Nanning in Kwangsi, (2) from Fengcheng in Shansi to Ninghsia in Kansu, (3) from Ninghsia to Lanchowfu in Kansu, (4) from Chungchow in Kwangtung to Luhwei in Kwangtung, and (5) from Hangchow in Chekiang to Wenchow in Chekiang. Should obstacles come up to make the construction of any of these lines undesirable, an equal mileage between other points should be granted elsewhere.[100] In order to provide funds with which to build, equip, and operate these railroads the Chinese government was obligated to issue gold bonds in the sum of no less than $1,000,000 but no more than $10,000,000 per year during the life of the contract. The selling of these bonds should be undertaken by the partner of the Siems-Carey Company, the American International Corporation.[101] This contract contained two prominent features: first, the construction work was placed entirely under the charge of an expert American company; and second, that expert company was to have the control of the technical management, as well as a participating interest, in the operation of the railroads.[102]

The generous railway concessions made to the Siems-Carey Company soon revoked protests from Russia, France, and Great Britain. According to the Russian government the construction by an American company of the Fengcheng-Ninghsia Railway would violate an assurance made to Russia by the Chinese foreign office back in 1899.[103] The Peking government would not recognize the validity of the Russian argument.[104] Nor would the American government accede to the Russian claim to any exclusive rights in the region affected by the proposed railway.[105] But the American International Corporation was cautious and would not proceed to finance the railway unless the Russian objection was settled.[106] To the Russian ambassador in Washington it expressed its unwillingness to contemplate any enterprise in China "which would be unwelcome to the Russian

Government." In so doing it greatly embarrassed Reinsch who had been trying hard to oppose the Russian claim in Peking. To use his own words, "Never was the ground cut from under any one exerting himself to safeguard the interests of others as was done in this case." [107]

France objected to the track line across Kwangsi, because in a secret note of September 26, 1914, the Chinese foreign minister had promised to apply first to French capitalists if foreign capital was required for railway or mining enterprises in that province.[108] But the American government took the position that "a secret note covering privileges granted without a *quid pro quo* could not operate to defeat contractual rights obtained from the Chinese Government in due form." [109] When France denied the secret nature of the Chinese promise, the state department argued that, at any rate, France's pledge to adhere to the open door policy debarred her from any claim to exclusive rights to build railways in Kwangsi.[110]

Then Great Britain formally protested against the construction of railways in the provinces of Hupeh and Hunan on the ground that as early as 1905 Viceroy Chang Chih-tung had granted her preferential rights there.[111] The United States was definitely opposed to the British earmarking of the Yangtze region as a sphere of influence. By way of compromise the British government suggested the possibility of joint action in the proposed railway enterprise. The state department, without declining the suggestion, indicated that Great Britain had better cooperate in obtaining a stricter observance of the open door principle by the powers pledged thereto.[112]

As we have seen, the Wilson administration was both staunch and steadfast in its support of the Siems-Carey Company in the matter of railway construction in China. In the face of vehement protests from other powers it encouraged the company to proceed with engineering plans already decided upon. The company did survey a number of possible routes but actually constructed none of them.

In 1916 there was another American loan to China, which called forth protests from other powers. It was a loan of $5,000,000 gold concluded between the Chinese government and the Continental and Commercial Trust and Savings Bank of Chicago "for industrial purposes including the internal development of China, the strengthening of the reserves of the Bank of China and the Bank of Communications (both of which are official banks) and other similar purposes." Should the Chinese government decide to borrow an additional sum aggregating $25,000,000 gold in the United States, it promised the Chicago bank the first option on a corresponding loan.[113]

France immediately lodged a protest, because the Banque Industrielle de Chine, a French institution, had held a prior lien on the tobacco and wine taxes recently assigned by the Chinese government as security for the Chicago loan. The Allied members of the consortium unanimously raised objection on the ground that the loan was in conflict with Article XVII of the reorganization loan agreement of 1913. The Chinese government had offered the consortium members the option to raise a loan, but they had been unable to cooperate. So it considered itself free to offer the loan in question to any other party. Besides, the Chicago loan, by its industrial nature, would not come within the purview of the reorganization loan agreement.[114]

The American government also took a strong stand in coping with other powers' opposition to the Chicago loan. In its opinion the principle of equal commercial opportunity was being seriously threatened. Significantly Lansing instructed Reinsch to intimate to the diplomatic representatives of the consortium powers at Peking "that any strained construction of existing agreements between the Chinese Government and bankers, or any attempt to exclude our bankers from a fair participation in Chinese affairs, would meet with very decided resistance from this Government." [115] Fortunately enough, the consortium powers soon backed down. None of their representatives at Peking, upon inquiry from Reinsch, expressed any objection to the Chicago loan or to the free participation of American bankers in Chinese finance.[116] All obstacles having been removed, the Chicago bank actually advanced to China the sum of $5,000,000 gold as provided for in the loan contract. At the same time the Chinese government further secured the loan upon the goods tax receipts from the provinces of Honan, Anhui, Fukien, and Shensi.[117] This loan was paid back from the proceeds of another loan of $5,500,000 concluded on October 11, 1919, between the Chinese government and the Chicago bank.[118]

Before we conclude, a few more small loan matters are worthy of mention here. The Hankow Water Works and Electric Company, on December 4, 1915, had signed with an American firm, Andersen, Meyer and Company, a preliminary agreement for a loan of 2,500,000 taels for the purpose of paying its indebtedness to the Japanese bank and other creditors and providing funds for extensions and improvement of its property. After the completion of this agreement the American firm attempted to secure from the Chinese government the unconditional guarantee of the principal and interest of the loan. Negotiations went on for some time, but no definite arrangements could be reached. Besides, the American firm and the Hankow company soon entered into an insoluble dispute over the question of turning the loan into gold currency. In consequence the whole transaction failed.[119]

The provincial government of Heilungkiang, in 1916, requested of American bankers two loans for establishing industrial banks and developing timber industry. The state department transmitted the request to the Guaranty Trust Company, the American International Corporation, the American group, and Messrs. Lee, Higginson and Company. But none of these banking firms was interested in the matter.[120]

In order to strengthen the local Bank of China the provincial government of Kwangtung, in February, 1917, expressed the desire to secure a loan of $2,000,000 gold from Lee, Higginson and Company. The security offered was the provincial likin estimated at three million dollars a year. But the company found it impossible to consider the matter during that time. Thus another loan request from China came to nothing.[121]

5.

Viewed as a whole, the industrial loan transactions between China and American corporations, independently of any international consortium, were far from being successful and satisfactory. A series of long negotiations had been undertaken, but no large sums, with the exception of the Chicago loan, had been actually made over to the Chinese government. The industrial activities of American bankers in China from 1913 to 1917 seldom went beyond the state of negotiating contracts and making preliminary surveys—no large-scale construction work was actually set in motion. Neither side was solely to blame. The failure was due to many factors, the most important of which were: the generally disturbed financial markets of the world; the unsettled conditions in China; the obstructionist activities and protests of the consortium powers; the preoccupation of the United States with European loan matters; the over-cautiousness of some American bankers and their insistence upon the insertion of fine modifications and further securities into contracts already signed; and, most of all, the unwillingness of the government of the United States, under President Wilson's administration, to guarantee diplomatic protection for the execution of these proposed contracts, that is, to see to it that the Chinese government paid these loans which the department of state encouraged the American creditors to make.

Having finished our account of the various aspects of Wilson's China policy during his first administration, it is proper that we come to a conclusion by attempting, in the following chapter, an impartial evaluation of that policy.

NOTES:

1   A. A. Adee to certain American diplomatic officers, March 19, 1913, *For. Rels., 1913,* p. 171.

2   P. S. Reinsch, *An American Diplomat,* p. 63.

3. *Ibid.,* p. 64.

4   Willard Straight to Bryan, March 31, 1913, *For. Rels., 1913,* pp. 198-199. Under a Joint Resolution of Congress of May 25, 1908, the American government was to remit to China all her Boxer Indemnity payments in excess of the American legitimate claims growing out of the Boxer Rebellion of 1900. At the request of China this remitted portion of the indemnity was to be used for the education of young Chinese students in the United States. In order to prepare such students for coming to the United States, Tsinghua College was established in 1911 and was to a large extent supported by the funds remitted by the American government. All American claims were settled in 1914, and the total amount refunded to China under the Resolution of 1908 was $11,961,121.76. See Westel W. Willoughby, *Foreign Rights and Interests in China* (2 vols., Baltimore, 1927), II, 1012-1014. Hereafter cited as W. W. Willoughby, *Foreign Rights and Interests.* For Chinese indemnity payments for 1913 and 1914, see *For. Rels., 1913,* pp. 202-204, and *For. Rels., 1914,* pp. 69-80.

5   A. W. Fiedler to the acting chief of the division of Far Eastern affairs, August 27, 1913, *For. Rels., 1913,* p. 200.

6   *Ibid.,* p. 201.

7   E. T. Williams to Bryan, July 8, 1913, SD, 893.51/1446.

8   E. T. Williams to Bryan, July 11, 1913, *For. Rels., 1913,* p. 184.

9   E .T. Williams to Bryan, October 21, 1913, *ibid.,* pp. 189-191.

10   For the text of the agreement, see J. V. A. MacMurray, *Treaties and Agreements,* I, 841-849.

11   See *For. Rels., 1913,* pp. 196-198.

12 Reinsch to Bryan, February 6, 1914, *For. Rels., 1914,* p. 62.

13 Reinsch to Bryan, February 6, 1914, *ibid.,* pp. 62-63.

14 Reinsch to Bryan, February 6, 1914, *ibid.,* p. 63.

15 P. S. Reinsch, *An American Diplomat,* pp. 90-91.

16 *Ibid.,* pp. 101-102.

17 The American group to G. M. Gest, June 10, 1914, Wilson Papers, II, 57. Also see Memorandum for the President, July 24, 1914, *ibid.,* II, 58.

18 G. M. Gest to Wilson, July 1, 1914, *ibid.,* II, 57.

19 Lansing to J. V. A. MacMurray, August 5, 1914, SD, 893.00/2152.

20 Kai Fu Shah (Hsia Chieh-fu), Chinese minister to Washington, to G. M. Gest, March 24, 1915, *ibid.,* 893.51/1571. Upon an inquiry from G. M. Gest as to its attitude toward the loan, the state department expressed full approval and promised all proper diplomatic support. See G. M. Gest to Bryan, March 26, 1915; Bryan to G. M. Gest, March 27, 1915; and Lansing to G. M. Gest, July 1, 1915, *ibid.,* 893.51/1571.

21 W. W. Willoughby wrote to Frank J. Goodnow, inquiring about the possibility of placing the loan in the United States. Goodnow in turn asked B. H. Griswold, Jr., of Alexander Brown & Sons, Foreign and Domestic Bankers to undertake the necessary banking negotiations. See B. H. Griswold to Wilson, April 10, 1915, Wilson Papers, II, 79.

22 The Chinese ministry of finance to Messrs. Lee, Higginson and Company, October 29, 1915, SD, 893.51/1607. Reinsch to Lansing, November 13, 1915, *ibid.,* 893.51/1596.

23 Reinsch to Lansing, March 21, 1916, *ibid.,* 893.51/1610.

24 Reinsch to Lansing, March 20, 1916, *ibid.,* 893.51/1609. Reinsch to Lansing, April 7, 1916, *ibid.,* 893.51/1618. Also see P. S. Reinsch, *An American Diplomat,* p. 187.

25 Reinsch to Lansing, April 1, 1916, SD, 893.51/1614.

26 Liang Shih-yi to Reinsch, April 5, 1916, *For. Rels., 1916,* p. 134.

27 See Reinsch to Lansing, July 15, 1916, SD, 893.51/1667.

28 For the text of the loan contract between the Chinese government and Lee, Higginson and Company, see *For. Rels., 1916,* pp. 128-133.

29 Lansing to Reinsch, April 15, 1916, SD, 893.51/1629.

30 Reinsch to Lansing, April 27, 1916, *ibid.,* 893.00/2384.

31   Reinsch to Lansing, May 26, 1916, *ibid.,* 893.51/1642. Reinsch to Lansing, May 27, 1916, *ibid.,* 893.51/1644. Also see William Phillips to Frank Lyon Polk, July 12, 1916, Yale University Library, Frank Lyon Papers. Hereafter cited as Polk Papers.

32   Reinsch to Lansing, May 27, 1916, SD, 893.51/1644.

33   Reinsch to Lansing, June 15, 1916, *ibid.,* 893.51/1652.

34   William Phillips to Frank Lyon Polk, July 12, 1916, Polk Papers.

35   Lansing to Wilson, June 15, 1916, SD, 893.51/1652.

36   William Phillips to Frank Lyon Polk, July 12, 1916, Polk Papers.

37   Reinsch to Lansing, June 26, 1916, SD, 893.51/1657.

38   William Phillips to Frank Lyon Polk, July 12, 1916, Polk Papers.

39   Lansing to Reinsch, June 27, 1916, SD, 893.51/1652.

40   William Phillips to Frank Lyon Polk, July 12, 1916, Polk Papers.

41   Confidential memorandum from the office of the secretary to Frank Lyon Polk, July 3, 1916, *ibid.* See the same, SD, 893.51/1692½.

42   Frank Lyon Polk to Reinsch, August 5, 1916, *ibid.,* 893.51/1672.

43   The American group to Lansing, July 26, 1916, *For. Rels., 1916,* pp. 134-138.

44   Frank Lyon Polk to the American group, August 3, 1916, SD, 893.51/1670.

45   Reinsch to Lansing, August 9, 1916, *ibid.,* 893.51/1673.

46   Memorandum by E. T. Williams, August 19, 1916, *ibid.,* 893.51/1694.

47   Lee, Higginson and Company to Alvey A. Adee, September 6, 1916, *ibid.,* 893.51/1687.

48   Reinsch to Lansing, November 20, 1916, *ibid.,* 893.51/1708. Also see Frank Lyon Polk to Reinsch, December 6, 1916, *ibid.,* 893.51/1716.

49   New York *Times,* March 30, 1913.

50   H. B. Hollins and Company to Bryan, June 2, 1913, SD, 893.51/1451.

51   Bryan to H. B. Hollins and Company, June 4, 1913, *ibid.,* 893.51/1431.

52   E. T. Williams to Bryan, July 11, 1913, *For. Rels., 1913,* p. 184.

53   Roger Sherman Greene (American consul general at Hankow) to Bryan, November 20, 1913, SD, 893.51/1478.

54   E. T. Williams to Bryan, October 20, 1913, *ibid.,* 893.51/ 1476.

55   George Bronson Rea to Wilson, March 26, 1913, *ibid.,* 893.77/1263. Mr. Rea was editor of the *Far Eastern Review* of Shanghai and Manila and was well informed about Far Eastern affairs. See William C. Redfield to Bryan, June 11, 1914, Bryan Papers, box 38.

56   E. T. Williams to Bryan, July 11, 1913, *For. Rels., 1913,* p. 185.

57   George Bronson Rea to Wilson, March 26, 1913, SD, 893.77/1263.

58   Reinsch to Bryan, April 14, 1914, *ibid.,* 893.77/1366. Also see Reinsch to Bryan, April 20, 1914, *ibid.,* 893.77/1355.

59   Memorandum from E. T. Williams to Lansing, May 8, 1914, *ibid.,* 893.77/1366.

60   See the remarks made respectively by Lansing and Wilson at the end of the memorandum from E. T. Williams to Lansing, May 8, 1914, *ibid.,* 893.77/1366.

61   Lansing to Reinsch, May 20, 1914, *ibid.,* 893.77/1371.

62   George Bronson Rea to William C. Redfield, June 3, 1914, Bryan Papers, box 38.

63   Reinsch to Bryan, June 13, 1914, SD, 893.77/1389.

64   For the loan agreement, see J. V. A. MacMurray, *Treaties and Agreements,* I, 866-877. Also see W. W. Willoughby, *Foreign Rights and Interests,* II, 1071-1078.

65   The American group to Bryan, November 6, 1914, SD, 893.77/1424.

66   See *For. Rels., 1916,* pp. 150-168.

67   For the text of the agreement, see J. V. A. MacMurray, *Treaties and Agreements,* II, 1109-1111.

68   *Ibid.,* II, 1111-1113.

69   Reinsch to Bryan, March 16, 1914, SD, 893.00/2102.

70   Reinsch to Bryan, May 6, 1914, *ibid.,* 893.51/1511; Reinsch to Bryan, May 11, 1914, *ibid.,* 893.51/1579; and Reinsch to Bryan, May 26, 1914, *ibid.,* 893.51/1523. Also see P. S. Reinsch, *An*

American Diplomat, pp. 67, 84, 99-100; and J. V. A. MacMurray, *Treaties and Agreements,* II, 1236-1237.

71   Bryan to Reinsch, May 21, 1914, SD, 893.51/1514. Also see P. S. Reinsch, *An American Diplomat,* p. 99.

72   Reinsch to Bryan, May 26, 1914, SD, 893.51/1523.

73   Huntington Wilson to William H. Taft, October 25, 1912, Taft Papers, presidential series no. 2, box 33.

74   Wilson to Mabel T. Boardman, July 22, 1913, Wilson Papers, II, 37.

75   Mabel T. Boardman to Wilson, July 12, 1913, *ibid.,* II, 36. For extracts of the preliminary report of Charles Davis Jameson, see *For. Rels., 1914,* p. 97.

76   J. B. Moore to Wilson, January 26, 1914, Wilson Papers, II, 45.

77   See *For. Rels., 1914,* pp. 102-104.

78   Wilson to J. B. Moore, February 6, 1914, *ibid.,* p. 105.

79   E. T. Williams to the counselor, April 1, 1914, *ibid.,* p. 106.

80   Kai Fu Shah to Bryan, May 23, 1914, *ibid.,* p. 109. Colonel Sibert was an eminent ex-Panama Canal engineer and served in the corps of engineers of the American army. The Congress especially passed a joint resolution authorizing the President to grant leave of absence to an army engineer to take charge of the supplementary survey in the Huai River region. See Mabel T. Boardman to Wilson, April 4, 1914, Wilson Papers, VI, 227; P. S. Reinsch, *An American Diplomat,* p. 98. At the request of the American Red Cross, Wilson had exerted his personal influence with Congress for the passage of the bill. See Wilson to George E. Chamberlain, April 7, 1914, Wilson Papers, VI, 227. After the bill had been passed, Wilson appointed Colonel Sibert as chief of the above-mentioned engineering board.

81   Reinsch to Wilson, November 28, 1914, *ibid.,* VI, 473. In a letter to Mabel T. Boardman, Reinsch mentioned that according to the report of those expert engineers the execution of the conservancy plan, from the technical and financial points of view, "is even more attractive than had been anticipated." See Reinsch to Mabel T. Boardman, November 27, 1914, *ibid.,* VI, 473.

82   See *For. Rels., 1914,* pp. 111-114.

83   *Ibid.,* pp. 115-118.

84   *Ibid.,* pp. 115-118; and *For. Rels., 1915,* pp. 212-214.

85   Reinsch to Lansing, December 30, 1915, *ibid.,* pp. 215-216.

86   See *For. Rels., 1916,* pp. 103-106.

87   Reinsch to the Chinese minister of agriculture and commerce, January 14, 1916, *ibid.,* p. 104.

88   For the text of the agreement, see J. V. A. MacMurray, *Treaties and Agreements,* II, 1287-1291.

89   For the text of the agreement, see *ibid.,* II, 1304-1309.

90   See *For. Rels., 1916,* pp. 119-121.

91   Reinsch to Lansing, October 13, 1916, *ibid.,* p. 126.

92   Reinsch to Lansing, May 24, 1916, SD, 893.811/219.

93   Japan irrelevantly based her argument on the Sino-German treaty of 1898 and the Sino-Japanese convention of 1915. See the memorandum from the Japanese legation at Peking to the Chinese government, September 15, 1916, *For. Rels., 1916,* pp. 126-127.

94   For the agreement between the American International Corporation and the Industrial Bank of Japan for cooperation, see *For. Rels., 1917,* pp. 212-214.

95   See *ibid.,* pp. 207-216. Also see P. S. Reinsch, *An American Diplomat,* pp. 217-219.

96   Reinsch to Lansing, March 31, 1917, SD, 893.811/252. Also see Reinsch to Lansing, February 13, 1917, *For. Rels., 1917,* pp. 210-211.

97   The Chinese government concluded the new agreement with the American International Corporation on November 20, 1917. For the text of the agreement, see J. V. A. MacMurray, *Treaties and Agreements,* II, 1297-1302.

98   See *ibid.,* II, 1300.

99   Later the mileage was changed to 1,100 miles. See the supplementary agreement of September 29, 1916, *ibid.,* II, 1321.

100   According to this provision the Siems-Carey Company, in lieu of certain of these lines, was later granted the right to build the railway from Chuchow in Hunan to Chinchow in Kwangtung. *Ibid.,* II, 1313. Also see W. W. Willoughby, *Foreign Rights and Interests,* II, 1083.

101   *Ibid.,* II, 1084; and P. S. Reinsch, *An American Diplomat,* p. 219. The American International Corporation agreed to finance the railway project on condition that certain modifications were made in the contract. This was done in a supplementary agreement signed in September, 1916. See E. T. Williams' memorandum, October 20, 1916, SD, 893.77/1548.

102   *For. Rels., 1916,* pp. 179-187; J. V. A. MacMurray, *Treaties and Agreements,* II, 1313-1319; and W. W. Willoughby, *Foreign Rights and Interests,* II, 1083-1085.

103   The Russian minister at Peking to the Chinese vice-minister of foreign affairs, October, 1916, *For. Rels., 1916,* p. 208. For the Chinese assurance, see the Tsungli Yamen to the Russian legation at Peking, June 1, 1899, *ibid.,* p. 203.

104   The Chinese government contended that the Chinese assurance of 1899 referred only to railway lines connecting Peking with the Russian border and therefore had nothing to do with a line leading southwestward from Peking, away from Russian territory. See Reinsch to Lansing, October 19, 1916, *ibid.,* p. 190.

105   Lansing to Reinsch, November 2, 1916, *ibid.,* p. 205; and Frank L. Polk to Reinsch, December 7, 1916, *ibid.,* p. 209.

106   Willard Straight to Lansing, October 30, 1916, *ibid.,* p. 198.

107   P. S. Reinsch, *An American Diplomat,* p. 221.

108   See *For. Rels., 1917,* pp. 185-186.

109   Lansing to the French ambassador at Washington, May 1, 1917, *ibid.,* p. 188. Also see *ibid.,* pp. 183-184. Memorandum from the office of the solicitor to the Far Eastern division, April 5, 1917, SD, 893.77/1594. P. S. Reinsch, *An American Diplomat,* pp. 221-222.

110   The French minister to Lansing, May 27, 1917, *For. Rels., 1917,* pp. 189-190. Lansing to the French minister, August 24, 1917, *ibid.,* 192-194.

111   Chang Chih-tung to British Consul General Fraser, September 9, 1905, *ibid.,* pp. 206-207.

112   *Ibid.,* pp. 190-192 and 195-200.

113   J. V. A. MacMurray, *Treaties and Agreements,* II, 1337-1343. Also see *For. Rels., 1916,* pp. 138-143.

114   *Ibid.,* pp. 143-144 and 147-148.

115   Lansing to Reinsch, December 5, 1916, *ibid.,* p. 146.

116   Reinsch to Lansing, December 18, 1916, *ibid.,* pp. 148-149.

117   The Chicago loan was further secured according to a supplementary agreement reached on May 14, 1917 between the Chicago bank and the Chinese government. See J. V. A. MacMurray, *Treaties and Agreements,* II, 1343-1345.

118   C. F. Remer, *Foreign Investments,* pp. 296-297. Also see *For. Rels., 1919,* pp. 524-527. In connection with this new loan of

$5,500,000, only two payments of interest due May 1920 and May 1921 of U. S. $165,000 each had been met by the Chinese government until the close of 1934. See Chung-kuo Yin-hang Ching-chi Yen-chiu-shih (the Research Department of the Bank of China), *Chung-kuo Wai-chai Hui-pien, Chinese Government Foreign Loan Obligations* (both in Chinese and in English, Shanghai, 1935), p. 24.

119   Edwin S. Cunningham (American consul general at Hankow) to Lansing, December 14, 1915, SD, 893.51/1601. Also see Reinsch to Lansing, April 18, 1916, *ibid.*, 893.51/1637.

120   Charles K. Moser to Lansing, May 5, 1916, *ibid.*, 893.51/1633. Alvey A. Adee to Charles H. Sabin (vice-president of the Guaranty Trust Company), the American International Corporation, the American group, and Messrs. Lee, Higginson and Company respectively, May 6, 1916, *ibid.*, 893.51/1633. The American group and the Guaranty Trust Company respectively to the state department, May 10, 1916, *ibid.*, 893.51/1634. Lee, Higginson and Company to the state department, May 17, 1916, *ibid.*, 893.51/1639.

121   Reinsch to Lansing, February 15, 1917, *ibid.*, 893.51/1747; Alvey A. Adee to Lee, Higginson and Company, February 16, 1917, *ibid.*, 893.51/1747; Lee, Higginson and Company to the state department, February 20, 1917, *ibid.*, 893.51/1748; Frank L. Polk to Reinsch, February 26, 1917, *ibid.*, 893.51/1748.

CHAPTER SEVEN

Conclusion

As we have mentioned before, Woodrow Wilson, in his academic years, had acquired a knowledge, however inadequate, of China through reading or contact with American missionaries sent to that country. He had seen the significant part that Christianity was playing in the life of the Chinese people who had awakened from a state of slumber under the impact of Western culture. With an unflinching faith in Christian ideals and democratic tenets, he thought that America had an important mission to fulfill in the Far East. The principles of order, justice, character, liberty, and good government should all be taught to those politically undisciplined peoples in that region. American material or commercial interests were not to be neglected but should be subordinated to the higher interests of American morality and duty. The traditional open door policy had his full approval. The maintenance of China's administrative and territorial integrity, in his opinion, should be upheld whole-heartedly by all the powers concerned with Chinese affairs. In a word he had become predisposed to a benevolent policy toward China before he became President in 1913.

During Wilson's first administration China and the United States were on genuinely cordial and friendly terms. This was due to the altruistic nature of Wilson's policy on the one hand and to China's unswerving trust in the United States on the other. A treaty for the advancement of general peace was concluded between the two countries on September 15, 1914. It was one of the series of the conciliation treaties signed between the United States and other countries. Its purpose was to find a way of peaceful solution for any disputes between the two contracting parties which could not be settled through normal diplomatic proceedings.[1] As a matter of fact, Sino-American relations from 1913 to 1917 were so amicable that this treaty was never invoked. Nor has it ever been invoked since then.

At all times Wilson was alive to the awakening consciousness of the Chinese people and cherished a great hope for their progress and advancement along Christian and democratic lines. He realized that the task of Christianizing and democratizing China could be accomplished only through a long process of education and inculcation. He wanted always to stress Christian spiritual and American political ideals in the indoctrination of the Chinese people. To the success of this educational work American officials and missionaries in China could make a great contribution. Besides, the training of Chinese students in American schools was equally important. The more American-trained students there were, the more readily American thinking and ways of life could be introduced into China.

The significance of this matter was far-reaching beyond measure. Wilson came to realize this point as a result of his contact with Chinese students in his Princeton years. Within limits of law he never hesitated to facilitate the entrance of young Chinese students into the United States for advanced studies. Repeatedly he advised the American immigration authorities not to subject those people to unnecessary examination or mortifying treatment.[2]

Wilson's unselfish attitude and good intentions were heartily appreciated by the Chinese leaders of various occupational fields and different political affiliations, particularly those leading progressive intellectuals who always looked to the United States as to their friend and exemplar in the great tasks lying ahead of their nation. Even in their darkest hours they never lost faith in the noble principles as advocated and expounded by Wilson. American moral support for China, they thought, could not fail to be forthcoming in case of need. Insofar as China's confidence in the United States was inspired, Wilson's policy of moral encouragement was highly praiseworthy and remarkably successful.

As Wilson understood it, the weakness of China lay chiefly in her internal disunity. Civil strife which was prevalent throughout the country was the main obstacle to unification. The best remedy for this situation would be the establishment of a central government powerful enough to bring about domestic peace and stability. Only under peaceful circumstances could democratic ideals gradually but surely spread. For this reason Wilson, in considering Chinese political problems, always placed internal unity above the establishment of a democratic form of government. It was unnecessary that China, at the initial stage of her progress toward democracy, should adopt American political institutions without any modifications.

In the final analysis, what China urgently needed was such fundamental things as social justice, good order, political consciousness, a developed sense of responsibility, obedience to law, and the dictates of morality. According to Wilson, democracy was more a set of such basic principles than a form of government, and different democratic countries could have different forms of government. But it took time for China to master and put into practice these principles. In the long process of advancing toward the final goal of democracy, whatever Chinese central government could ensure internal peace should be encouraged. The United States should help to bring about conditions of internal peace under which democratic ideals could flourish rather than inopportunely to impose American political institutions which might not work well in the China of the present. This was the key to the understanding of Wilson's support of Yüan Shih-k'ai as the head of the Peking government.

After the establishment of the Chinese Republic, Yüan Shih-k'ai, an astute and iron-handed statesman of the old school, promised to organize a central government capable of reuniting a country which had disintegrated with the collapse of the Manchu Dynasty. As a symbol of a new and unified China he appeared to be worthy of support from friendly nations. Thus he had the full approval of the United States which, in 1913, took the lead among the powers in according recognition to his new regime.

The American action of recognition was justified in the sense that the Peking government was thus greatly strengthened. Before long Yüan easily crushed a Kuomintang revolt in the South, and his influence and prestige increased by leaps and bounds. All dissidents being forced to hide behind the scene, he seemed to have politically unified his country. But as a matter of fact the unification was only superficial. The opposition elements were suppressed but not eradicated. Wherever the climate proved favorable, they sowed the seeds of revolution. They lost no time particularly in attempting to court the favor of the United States. To their disappointment Wilson, sympathetic to their democratic ideals as he was, always turned a deaf ear to their appeals. The famous Kuomintang leader, Sun Yat-sen, seemed to Wilson merely the head of a rebellious party to be discouraged. Any revolution aiming at the overthrow of the newly stabilized central government at Peking was injurious to the Chinese nation. Wilson's support of Yüan was really as positive as his disapproval of the Kuomintang revolutionists.

Without doubt Yüan Shih-k'ai was a capable administrator. As he had won his reputation and power as a military commander, he possessed such qualities of a good soldier as efficiency, strict discipline, perseverance, strong will, and power of quick decision. After many years of active service both in the capital and in the provinces, he had acquired an intimate knowledge of Chinese politics. Through enduring patience, keen perception, and adroit maneuvers, he outwitted and defeated his political contestants and finally seized the reins of government. At one time he wielded so much power that he struck terror into the hearts of his enemies and commanded respect among his followers, particularly the military captains. But he had his weaknesses, too. Obsessed with imperial inclinations and personal ambitions, he did not care about democratic principles of government. What he desired to do was to centralize authority in his hands. It seemed to him that the Parliament could only stand in the way of the realization of his administrative programs.

Essentially Yüan's government was just as despotic as the imperial government of the Manchus. Old imperialism simply gave way to his personal dictatorship. As time went on, he resorted to tyrannical measures more and more. He dissolved both the national legislature and the provincial assemblies. He ordered not only the dissolution of the Kuomintang but also the arrest of its leaders. In order to perpetuate the rule of his family he soon embarked upon a restoration of the monarchy with himself as Emperor.

The monarchical movement of Yüan Shih-k'ai was not unacceptable to the American government. In fact Wilson was ready to recognize the new imperial government as soon as its establishment could be formally announced. Although personally reluctant to see the return of monarchism in China, Wilson still resolutely gave support to Yüan in this new political adventure. For he feared that in case the central authority at Peking should break down the whole of China would be thrown back into general chaos and exposed to the aggression of the imperialist powers, notably Japan. It was his belief that China's internal stability was of greater importance than her form of government.

But things happened contrary to expectations. Everywhere in China banners of revolt were raised against monarchism. Yüan's power daily weakened, and new developments were beyond his control. Despair, embarrassment, overwork, and illness combined to put an end to his life in the midst of confusion and upheaval. With his death also ended the monarchical movement which had enjoyed Wilson's unwavering support.

The successor of Yüan Shih-k'ai, President Li Yüan-hung, was not capable, nor did he command much respect among the militarists. Moreover, his discord with Premier Tuan Ch'i-jui, the leader of the Anfu Clique, further weakened his personal influence. In spite of this, the government that he was heading still promised to unify and stabilize China and therefore had the full support of Woodrow Wilson. For the latter always considered problems of China in terms of her internal stability and danger from abroad. The problem of China's severance of diplomatic relations with Germany could serve best to illustrate this point.

When the United States broke off diplomatic relations with the German government early in February, 1917, Woodrow Wilson formally invited all neutral countries to take similar action. His was a blanket invitation designed to win universal approval of America's dispute with Germany rather than to fit the exact conditions in any single country. But Minister Reinsch, upon receipt of instructions from the state department to transmit Wilson's circular telegram to Peking, took the initiative to persuade the Chinese government to follow the lead of the United States. Before giving formal consent, the Peking authorities asked such guarantees as American financial assistance, full membership in the future peace conference, and exclusive control of their own arsenals and military forces. Acting on his own authority Reinsch made some definite assurances to China in order to bring about her break with Germany speedily.

208

Soon the state department repudiated Reinsch's action. It specifically cautioned him against making any unwarranted promises or assurances. In its opinion China should take no isolated action and should seriously consider "the willingness of any other important neutral to follow American example." [3] According to Woodrow Wilson, China, handicapped by her troubles at home and with Japan, ought not to associate with the United States in a rupture of relations with the German government.[4] Appreciative of China's disposition as he was, he did not want her to be so involved in the World War as to be internally weakened by disagreement among political leaders and externally exposed to further aggression.

Regardless of the cautious warning of the American government, China, eager to obtain a place at the future peace conference, protested the German policy of submarine warfare first and then decided to break off relations with Germany as Reinsch urged and wished. The breach was officially effected on March 14, 1917, ten days after the second administration of Woodrow Wilson was inaugurated.[5] Wilson accepted this fact reluctantly. Then he began to warn China against taking any further action of declaration of war in case of hostilities between Germany and the United States. As events developed, his advice was not heeded; that is, China later joined the war on the side of the Allies.

Then, let us turn our attention from the problem of China's internal stability to that of Japanese aggression, which equally occupied the mind of Woodrow Wilson and was indeed his principal reason for desiring a strong and competent government, even a monarchy, for China. His benevolently developing China policy, resting on the good will of an academic environment and Christian missionary impulses, collided with the hard-fisted realities of imperialism: first with the imperialism of European powers at equipoise in the Far East as represented by their governmentally sponsored private bankers, and next with the aggressive imperialism of Japan so favored by the breakdown of the balance of power in Asia upon the outbreak of the First World War. President Wilson, essentially a teacher and a preacher of peace and good will, had to confront this threat to China's integrity, and to the traditional Far Eastern policy of the United States, with only "peaceful means," and that at a time when the United States was steadily becoming more and more involved in the menacing European situation.

Before the First World War broke out in 1914, there existed an international equilibrium in China. No power could individually secure exclusive privileges without incurring the opposition of others. But this equilibrium soon broke down with the extension of the war into the Far East. A golden opportunity being thus offered, Japan lost no time in launching an unprecedented large-scale program for eliminating the influence of other powers in China and placing the whole of China under her own control. Her declaration of war upon Germany, her seizure of Tsingtao and some other parts of Shantung, her presentation of the Twenty-One Demands, and her provocation of the Chengchiatun Affair in Manchuria[6] could all be viewed in this light. The European powers were so entangled in their own war problems that they could not give sufficient attention to the changing international situation in China. Great Britain, Japan's ally, whose interests in the Yangtze Valley surpassed those of any other power, was fully aware of the seriousness of the situation but could do little about it. The only power whose hands were not similarly tied was the United States.

The growing predominance of Japan in Chinese affairs worried Woodrow Wilson. He was by no means unwilling to hold the Japanese aggression in check. But the American military unpreparedness, the manifest unwillingness of the American people to go to war for China, and the increasing gravity of disputes with the European belligerents over neutral rights kept him from taking too strong an action. All he could do was to give moral support and at the same time register diplomatic caveats or protests with the Japanese government. That was all he did during the Japanese occupation of Shantung and the Sino-Japanese discussions of the Twenty-One Demands. Except regarding the Fukien question, Wilson did not give much actual help to China, because nothing short of warlike action could have effectively stopped Japanese actions. It was simply out of the question to fight Japan while the United States itself was stepping into war on the side of the Allies. There was little that Wilson could do to stem the tide of Japanese expansion in China. In this sense his policy of maintaining China's integrity was largely a failure.

Woodrow Wilson's economic policy toward China during his first administration was one of independent action. It was a repudiation of the so-called "dollar diplomacy," a reversal of international concert in the matter of financial, commercial, and industrial activities. The withdrawal of the American group from the international banking consortium was the first concrete and summary expression of Wilson's views on the future course of American enterprise in China. His political philosophy, social idealism, and deep sympathy for the weak nations all played a part in his refusal to join with other powers in economic exploitation of the young republic of the Far East. American entrepreneurs, instead of being bound up with investors and traders of other countries, should help independently to develop China's natural resources on the basis of fair play and mutual advantage. The United States as the foremost democracy of the world should set an example of justice and helpfulness in its economic dealings with China. Wilson's statement of policy regarding the consortium was morally faultless. For the time at least, he won the heartfelt gratitude of the Chinese people.

However well-intentioned Wilson's policy of independent action was, it in fact resulted from a precipitate decision and an imperfect knowledge of the Chinese situation. In remaining outside of the consortium, the United States could no longer exercise a great restraining influence on European and Japanese imperialism. After American retreat from the consortium, other powers tightened rather than loosened their control over Chinese financial affairs, until the First World War distracted the policy of the European powers and threatened a free hand for Japan. In the long run it was China who suffered the consequences of Wilson's apparently wise and morally unblemished action.

Furthermore Wilson's encouragement of American enterprise was merely a generalized principle. In practice he always refrained from giving sufficient and specific diplomatic support to those American individuals really interested in investments in China. All investors had to enter into engagements upon their own initiative and were left to their own devices in securing their loans. The American government, according to Wilson, was in no way responsible for collecting debts in case of default. Lacking any reliable guarantee or support from their own government, few bankers would run risks for their clients and depositors, making loans to a country in a state of recurring unrest and confusion. It was the absence of adequate official support, rather than the absence of interest on the part of investors, that caused the stagnation of American economic and fiscal efforts in China.

Wilson's economic policy toward China was as impractical as it was morally praiseworthy. The net results of American economic activities in China during his first administration were merely the conclusion of one small educational loan, an advance of one million dollars by Lee, Higginson and Company, the contract for the Chicago loan of five million dollars, and a few loan contracts in connection with the Huai River conservancy and the Grand Canal restoration project. As we have mentioned before, these loans were later repaid by the Chinese government.

The inactivity of American enterprise in China was in sharp contrast to Japanese economic expansion in that country. After

European powers turned their attention away from the Far
East in the midst of war, Japanese influence penetrated throughout that region. Mainly for the sake of restraining Japan,
Woodrow Wilson later reverted to the old policy of concerted
action and started to organize a new international consortium.
This marked the utter failure of the policy of independent
action.

By the beginning of 1917 China, despite American warning,
was on the brink of war with Germany. Her internal dissension
was still recurrent. High democratic principles, as defined by
Wilson, were yet to take root in Chinese soil. Japan, in alliance
with Great Britain and Russia, was marching triumphantly and
irresistibly on the road to hegemony at China's expense. The
position of the United States in China was daily becoming un-
tenable. Under such circumstances Wilson needed a drastic
revision of his whole China policy. This revision he effected
later by concluding the Lansing-Ishii Agreement and by organizing the new consortium. But this is a topic beyond the scope of
the present volume.

NOTES:

1 For the text of the treaty, see *For. Rels., 1915,* pp. 41-43.
2 See Wilson to William B. Wilson, September 30, 1914; William B. Wilson to Wilson, October 7, 1914; and Wilson to William
B. Wilson, October 8, 1914, Wilson Papers, VI, 227. Also see
J. B. Densmore to Wilson, October 3, 1914, *ibid.,* II, 64.
3 Lansing to Reinsch, February 10, 1917, *For. Rels., 1917,
Supplement 1,* p. 408.
4 R. S. Baker, *Wilson,* VI, 467.
5 For China's severance of relations with Germany, see *For.
Rels., 1917, Supplement 1,* pp. 400-421; T. E. LaFargue, *China and
World War,* pp. 86-99; A. W. Griswold, *Far Eastern Policy,* pp.
199-203.
6 For an account of the Chengchiatun Affair, see Wang Yün-
sheng, *China and Japan,* VII, 45-71.

Bibliography

I. BIBLIOGRAPHICAL AIDS

A. STATE PAPERS

D. P. Myers, *Manual of Collections of Treaties and of Collections Relating to Treaties* (Cambridge, 1922).

An indispensable bibliography of collections of treaties.

Hunter Miller, "Bibliography of United States Treaty Collections," in his *Treaties and Other International Acts of the United States of America* (8 vols., Washington, 1931-1948), I, 39-54.

A useful annotated bibliography.

Winifred Gregory, ed., *List of the Serial Publications of Foreign Governments, 1815-1931* (New York, 1932).

Includes a list of the publications of the Chinese government.

The Department of State, the Division of Communications and Records, *The Classification of Correspondence* (4th ed., Washington, 1939).

Is indispensable for scholars using the state department archives classified under the decimal filing system.

Laurence F. Schmeckebier, *Government Publications and Their Use* (2nd and rev. ed., Washington, 1939).

A handy guide to the use of the publications of the United States government.

Philip M. Hamer and others, *Guide to the Records in the National Archives* (Washington, 1948).

Supersedes the *Guide to the Material in the National Archives* published in 1940. Provides a clear general description of records deposited in the National Archives.

B. NEWSPAPERS AND PERIODICALS

N. W. Ayer and Son, *Directory of Newspapers and Periodicals,* 1880-1949 annually (Philadelphia, 1880-1949).

This annual contains a very carefully prepared catalogue of American newspapers and periodicals. The title varies. I used only the issues for the years 1912-1917 under the title of *American Newspaper Annual and Directory.*

The H. W. Wilson Company, *Readers' Guide to Periodical Literature,* 1900-1949 (Minneapolis and New York, 1905-1949).

Is a very useful guide and contains many articles having some bearing upon this study. I used Vols. III and IV for the years 1910-1918 (New York, 1915-1919).

The London Times, *The Official Index to the Times,* 1912-1917 (London, 1912-1917).

A systematically prepared index to the *London Times.* The two annual volumes for 1912 and 1913 are entitled *The Annual Index to the Times.*

The New York Times, *The New York Times Index,* 1913-1917 (New York, 1913-1917).

An excellent index issued quarterly. I used Vols. I-V for the years 1913-1917.

C. DOCTORAL DISSERTATIONS

The Library of Congress, *A List of American Doctoral Dissertations Printed in 1912-1938* annually (Washington, 1913-1940).

An annual list of American doctoral dissertations printed in the years from 1912 through 1938. Altogether 27 volumes.

Carnegie Institution of Washington, the Department of Historical Research, *List of Doctoral Dissertations in History Now in Progress at Universities in the United States and the Dominion of Canada, with an Appendix of Other Research Projects in History now in Progress in the United States and in Canada,* 1913-1940 annually (Washington, 1914-1941).

The title varies. The lists for the years 1913-1935 are entitled *List of Doctoral Dissertations in History Now in Progress at the Chief American Universities.* The lists for the years 1936-1938 are entitled *List of Doctoral Dissertations in History Now in Progress at American Universities.* No list was published from 1941 to 1946. In 1947 the American Historical Association revived this work by publishing a list under the title *List of Doctoral Dissertations in History Now in Progress at Universities in the United States.* The association published a new list under that title in September, 1949.

The Association of Research Libraries, *Doctoral Dissertations Accepted by American Universities,* 1933-1948 annually (New York, 1934-1949).

An annual list. Altogether 15 volumes.

D. GENERAL AND DIPLOMATIC HISTORY

Grace Gardner Griffin, *Writings on American History,* 1906-1940 annually (New York, New Haven, and Washington, 1908-1949).

A complete annual bibliography which includes many contents and descriptive notes and refers to critical reviews.

George M. Dutcher and others, eds., *A Guide to Historical Literature* (New York, 1931).

A standard guide containing a section of critical bibliography of books on China.

W. L. Langer and H. F. Armstrong, *Foreign Affairs Bibliography; A Selected and Annotated List of Books on International Relations, 1919-1932* (New York, 1933).

A very valuable work based in part on bibliographies appearing in *Foreign Affairs.*

P'sing Hsin, *Sheng-huo Ch'üan-kuo Tsung-shu-mu, A Classified Catalogue of Current Chinese Books with Complete Index Translation* (in Chinese, Shanghai, 1935).

A complete catalogue of about twenty thousand current Chinese books including books on history. Contains no dates of publication of the books catalogued.

Samuel Flagg Bemis and Grace Gardner Griffin, *Guide to the Diplomatic History of the United States, 1775-1921* (Washington, 1935).

An indispensable guide for the student of the diplomatic history of the United States. Is divided into two main parts: Part I, "Bibliography"; and Part II, "Remarks on the Sources."

Robert G. Woolbert, *Foreign Affairs Bibliography; A Selected and Annotated List of Books on International Relations, 1932-1942* (New York and London, 1945).

The sequel to the bibliography prepared by W. L. Langer and H. F. Armstrong under the same title for the years 1919-1932.

E. CHINESE AND JAPANESE STUDIES

Kenneth Scott Latourette, "Chinese Historical Studies during the Past Seven Years," *American Historical Review,* XXVI (1921), 703-716.

A brief critical review of Chinese studies during 1914-1921.

Raymond Leslie Buell, "Problems of the Pacific," *International Conciliation,* No. 218 (March, 1926), pp. 147-171.

An annotated list of representative books on the Pacific.

Arthur Probsthain, *Encyclopaedia of books on China* (London, 1927).

A fairly complete annotated catalogue.

Kenneth Scott Latourette, "Chinese Historical Studies during the Past Nine Years," *American Historical Review,* XXXV (1930), 778-797.

A brief summary of the progress of Chinese historical studies during 1921-1930.

Harold S. Quigley, *An Introductory Syllabus on Far Eastern Diplomacy* (Chicago, 1931).

Contains a number of short reading lists under its various topics.

Charles S. Gardner, *A Union List of Selected Western Books on China in American Libraries* (Washington, 1932).

A very brief list.

K'ai-ming Ch'iu (Ch'iu K'ai-ming), *Mei-kuo Ha-fo Ta-hsüeh Yen-ching Hsüeh-she Han-Ho T'u-shu-kuan Han-chi Fen-lei Mu-lu, A Classified Catalogue of Chinese Books in the Chinese-Japanese Library of the Harvard-Yenching Institute at Harvard University* (2 vols., in Chinese, Peiping, 1938-1940).

Books relating to the subject of my study can be found from the second volume.

Hoh To-Yuen (Ho-To-yüan), *Chung-wen Ts'an-k'ao-shu Chih-Nan, Guide to Chinese Reference Books* (rev. ed., in Chinese, Shanghai, 1939).

A very valuable annotated guide in Chinese.

Robert J. Kerner, *Northeastern Asia: A Selected Bibliography* (2 vols., Berkeley, 1939).

A comprehensive, though uneven, bibliography. Was of great use for my study.

Hugh Borton, Serge Elisséeff, and Edwin O. Reischauer, *A Selected List of Books and Articles on Japan in English, French and German* (Washington, 1940).

Contains 842 numbered items in the subject list.

John King Fairbank and Kwang-ching Liu (Liu Kwang-ching), *Modern China: A Bibliographical Guide to Chinese Works 1898-1937* (Cambridge, 1950).

Lists all works, with a few exceptions, in the Chinese-Japanese Library maintained at Harvard by the Harvard-Yenching Institute.

F. BIOGRAPHICAL AIDS

Allen Johnson and Dumas Malone, eds., *Dictionary of American Biography* (New ed., 22 vols., New York, 1946).

The short bibliography at the end of each biography is useful.

Laura Shearer Turnbull, *Woodrow Wilson: A Selected Bibliography of His Published Writings, Addresses and Public Papers* (Princeton, 1948).

A very useful working tool for the student using Woodrow Wilson's published writings, addresses and public papers. Also contains a selected list of books in the Woodrow Wilson field, prepared by Katharine E. Brand.

II. MANUSCRIPT SOURCES

A. PRIVATE PAPERS

Gordon Auchincloss, the Sterling Memorial Library, Yale University.

This collection includes correspondence, papers, and diary assembled by Gordon Auchincloss, assistant to the counselor of the state department in 1917 and secretary to Colonel E. M. House at the Interallied Conference in 1917 and during the Paris Peace Conference of 1919. It reveals much of House's part in the foreign affairs of the Wilson administration.

Ray Stannard Baker, the Division of Manuscripts, the Library of Congress.

Series IA of this collection contains 17 boxes of papers including letters to and from Woodrow Wilson. All of these papers were assembled by Ray Stannard Baker during his fifteen years of work on the biography of Woodrow Wilson. They were useful for my subject of study.

Tasker H. Bliss, the Division of Manuscripts, the Library of Congress.

These papers are divided into two periods: the early period ending with March, 1917, and the period from 1917 to 1930. The World War and Peace Conference files of the second period are invaluable for a study of American participation in the First World War and the peace negotiations which followed. But I found little pertaining to this study.

William Jennings Bryan, the Division of Manuscripts, the Library of Congress.

This collection is extremely miscellaneous and by no means complete. However it throws much light on many phases of William Jennings Bryan's career. His correspondence with President Wilson, fellow cabinet members, and members of the Senate and the House is important. Typewritten copies of part of the Bryan-Wilson Correspondence 1913-1915 have been bound into two notebooks. But the copies are so inaccurate that reference to the original letters or carbon copies is necessary in every case. Unfortunately not all the originals and carbons remain in this collection. So in many cases I had to consult the original Bryan-Wilson Correspondence 1913-1915 in the National Archives. This correspondence reveals the attitude of the Wilson administration toward the Twenty-One Demands.

Josephus Daniels, the Division of Manuscripts, the Library of Congress.

These papers numbering about 500,000 pieces, are grouped for the most part under five main headings: Early Period, Navy Period, Interim Period, Mexico Period, and

Late Period. The papers classified under the Navy Period, 1913-1921, were useful to my study. From the Diary, 1913-1921, which is temporarily outside the above-mentioned arrangement, I found quite a few entries concerning the policy of the Wilson Administration toward the old consortium and the problem of recognizing the Chinese Republic.

Edward M. House, the Sterling Memorial Library, Yale University.

This well-indexed collection is of great value. The Wilson-House Correspondence, the Diary and other papers reveal House's pro-Japanese leanings and his personal interest in Far Eastern affairs. There can be found a great deal of material regarding China.

Gilbert M. Hitchcock, the Division of Manuscripts, the Library of Congress.

This small collection of papers of Gilbert M. Hitchcock, senator from Nebraska, 1911-1923, helps to illuminate the relations between Woodrow Wilson and Congress. But I found little of direct use to this study.

Philander C. Knox, the Division of Manuscripts, the Library of Congress.

This collection contains much material concerning the policy of the Taft administration toward China and the consortium. It also reveals Knox's distrust of the China policy of the Wilson administration.

Robert Lansing, the Division of Manuscripts, the Library of Congress.

The papers of Robert Lansing concern chiefly his service as counselor for the state department from March 20, 1914 to June 23, 1915 and as secretary of state from June 23, 1915 to February 13, 1920. In no sense do these papers constitute a full record of his activities in the state department. They, however, do supplement most of his official papers which remained in the state department files and now in the National Archives. Much material concerning China can be found in his correspondence and diaries. In the *Private Memoranda of Robert Lansing* previously referred to as the *Private Diaries of Robert Lansing,* I found a number of memoranda concerning the Shantung problem, the Siberian intervention and the Sino-Japanese dispute at the Paris Peace Conference, but little concerning American policy toward China before 1917.

Breckinridge Long, the Division of Manuscripts, the Library of Congress.

This collection does not cover all the papers of Breckinridge Long. It covers mainly the period from 1917 to 1922. Very useful as it is for the study of the China policy of the second Wilson administration, there is not much material of direct use for my present study.

Frank L. Polk, the Sterling Memorial Library, Yale University.

These papers deal with matters of the state department and the American Peace Commission. They were assembled by Frank L. Polk, counselor for the state department from 1915 to 1919, under-secretary of state from 1919 to 1920, and head of the American Peace Commission from July to December in 1919. I found this collection of much use.

William Howard Taft, the Division of Manuscripts, the Library of Congress.

This extensive collection covers the whole lifetime of William Howard Taft. The Presidential File throws much light upon Taft's China policy, especially American participation in the consortium.

William A. White, the Division of Manuscripts, the Library of Congress.

This collection concerns partly William A. White's activities during the First World War. A considerable part of it was assembled in connection with his books on Woodrow Wilson and others. I found little of direct use for this study.

Woodrow Wilson, the Division of Manuscripts, the Library of Congress.

This enormous collection contains 1,183 boxes of papers classified under nine series:

(I)	Miscellaneous items, 1569-1921.
(II)	Personal series, 1761-1921. Most valuable for this study.
(III)	Notes and manuscripts, proofs, and papers relating to academic lectures, 1877-1924.
(IV)	Correspondence between Woodrow Wilson and Ellen Axson Wilson, 1883-1913.

(V)   New Jersey series, 1912-1913.

(VI)   Official file kept at the executive offices during the Wilson administration, 1913-1921. This series contains 630 boxes of papers and is the largest of all.

(VII)   Letterpress books, 1913-1921.

(VIII) Paris Peace Conference series, 1918-1919.

(IX)   Correspondence file kept by John Randolph Bolling after Wilson's retirement, 1921-1924.

This collection is invaluable for a study of Woodrow Wilson's China policy, and this study is based to a large extent upon it.

B. OFFICIAL PAPERS

State Department Files, the National Archives, Washington, D. C.

In these files there can be found an enormous amount of material which is left out in the *Papers Relating to the Foreign Relations of the United States.* I consulted all the files relevant to my subject of study and found a great deal of invaluable information which gave me an insight into the formulation of the China policy of the Wilson administration. This study is based mainly upon these papers. Individual documents out of these voluminous files are cited in the footnotes accompanying this essay, by their particular archival numbers.

III. PRINTED SOURCES

A. PRINTED OFFICIAL AND PRIVATE PAPERS

China

The Chino-Japanese Negotiations: Chinese Official Statement with Documents and Treaties with Annexures (Peking, 1915).

A Chinese version of the Sino-Japanese negotiations of 1915.

The Browbeating of China and the Analysis of the Japanese Demands Together with the Documents Exchanged between Japan and China, Including the Treaties Signed by the Two Powers (Shanghai, 1915).

Reprinted from the *Far Eastern Review,* pp. 467-486, May 1915.

Wai-chiao-pu, The Ministry of Foreign Affairs, *Wai-chiao Wen-tu: Ts'anchan An, Diplomatic Documents: Participation in the War* (in Chinese, Peking, 1921).

In 1921 the Chinese ministry of foreign affairs produced a red-covered series of diplomatic documents, some of the documents going back as far as 1912. *The Participation in the War* is a collection of documents concerning various aspects of China's entrance into the First World War in 1917.

Wunsz King, ed., *V. K. Wellington Koo's Foreign Policy: Some Selected Documents* (Shanghai, 1931).

An incomplete collection of documents in English, concerning Koo's foreign policy. A Chinese translation of the documents is attached at the end.

Wang Yün-sheng, *Liu-shih-nien-lai Chung-kuo yü Jih-pen, China and Japan during the Last Sixty Years* (7 vols., in Chinese, Tientsin, 1932-1934).

Imperfect as it is, it is the best available collection of documents relevant to Sino-Japanese relations during the period covered. The sixth and seventh volumes were of great value for this study.

Chung-kuo Yin-hang Ching-chi Yen-chiu-shih (the Research Department of the Bank of China), *Chung-kuo Wai-chai Hui-pien, Chinese Government Foreign Loan Obligations* (Shanghai, 1935).

A compilation both in Chinese and English, dealing with the position of the Chinese government loan issues and obligations in 1935. All loan agreements concerned are appended at the end.

Pai Chiao, *Yüan Shih-k'ai yü Chung-kuo, Yüan Shih-k'ai and China* (in Chinese, Shanghai, 1936).

Mainly a collection of documents with interpretations decrying Yüan Shih-k'ai's dictatorial and imperialistic policies, particularly his restoration of the monarchy.

France

Ministère des Affaires Étrangères, *Documents diplomatiques français,* 1871-1914 (3 series, 33 vols., Paris, 1929-1948).

I used chiefly the third series, 1911-1914. Many documents concerning the old consortium were found.

Germany

Johannes Lepsius, Albrecht Mendelssohn Bartholdy, and Friedrich Thimme, eds., *Die grosse Politik der europäischen Kabinette,* 1871-1914 (40 vols., Berlin, 1922-1927).

Vol. 32 entitled *Die Mächte und Ostasien, 1909-1914* contains much information about the attitude of the powers toward the old consortium and the problem of recognizing the Chinese Republic.

Great Britain

British Parliamentary Papers, 1914-1916, XLV, *Correspondence Respecting Military Operations against German Possessions in the Western Pacific* (London, 1915).

Throws light on British attitude toward war against Germany in the Western Pacific.

G. P. Gooch and Harold Temperley, eds., *British Documents on the Origins of the World War, 1898-1914* (11 vols., London, 1926-1938).

Vol. VIII entitled *Arbitration, Neutrality and Security* (London, 1932) contains a number of documents concerning the international situation in China prior to the First World War.

Russia

B. de Siebert, trans., and George Abel Schreiner, ed., *Entente Diplomacy and the World: Matrix of the History of Europe, 1909-14* (New York and London, 1921).

Is translated from the original texts in his possession by B. de Siebert, late secretary of the imperial Russian embassy at London. Contains many documents relating to the powers' railway and other rivalries in Manchuria, Mongolia, and other parts of China. There are also a few documents concerning the old consortium and its loans to China.

B. von Siebert, ed., *Graf Benckendorffs diplomatischer Schriftwechsel* (3 vols., Berlin and Leipzig, 1928).

The greater part of the diplomatic correspondence contained in this collection was written or received by Aleksandr Konstantinovich Benckendorff, Russian ambassador in London, 1903-1916. This collection contains some documents about the consortium and the powers' rivalries in China.

Otto Hoetzsch, ed., *Die internationalen Beziehungen im Zeitalter des Imperialismus; Dokumente aus der Archiven der zarischen und der provisorischen Regierung* (8 vols., Berlin, 1931-1936).

This collection contains a great number of documents relating to Chinese problems during the period which this study covers. Very informative.

The United States

The Department of State, *Papers Relating to the Foreign Relations of the United States,* 1909-1917, including *Supplements* (Washington, 1914-1932).

Most of the important state department papers relating to Sino-American relations are included in this publication. I used both the regular annual volumes and the supplementary volumes and found them invaluable.

Congressional Record, 1912-1917 (Washington, 1912-1917).

It contains the proceedings and debates of the United States Congress from the 62nd Congress to the 65th Congress.

Edgar E. Robinson and Victor J. West, *The Foreign Policy of Woodrow Wilson, 1913-1917* (New York, 1918).

It presents a brief account of Woodrow Wilson's foreign policy in the period covered and provides the important statements of the President and his secretary of state announcing and carrying forward that policy.

James Brown Scott, ed., *President Wilson's Foreign Policy* (New York, 1918).

A collection of messages, addresses, and papers with an introduction and notes.

Ray Stannard Baker and William E. Dodd, eds., *The Public Papers of Woodrow Wilson* (6 vols., New York and London, 1925-1927).

The authorized collection of the addresses, messages, and other writings of Woodrow Wilson.

Charles Seymour, ed., *Intimate Papers of Colonel House* (4 vols., New York, 1926-1928).

This collection contains valuable sources concerning many aspects of Woodrow Wilson's foreign policy, but little information about China for the period this study covers.

John Randolph Bolling and others, *Chronology of Woodrow Wilson* (New York, 1927).

A short chronology with direct quotations from Woodrow Wilson's addresses, messages, letters, etc.

Wilson L. Godshall, ed., *American Foreign Policy: Formulation and Practice* (Ann Arbor, 1937).

A useful collection of documentary materials illustrative of the evolution of the principles of American foreign policy, including American policy toward the Far East.

The Department of State, *Papers Relating to the Foreign Relations of the United States, the Lansing Papers 1914-1920* (2 vols., Washington, 1939-1940).

This collection contains a number of documents relating to American attitude toward the Shantung question, the Twenty-One Demands, and Japanese actions in China.

Paul H. Clyde, ed., *United States Policy toward China: Diplomatic and Public Documents, 1839-1939* (Durham, North Carolina, 1940).

A collection of selected documents relating to American relations with China from 1839 to 1939.

Saul K. Padover, ed., *Wilson's Ideals* (Washington, 1942).

Highlights of Woodrow Wilson's writings and speeches arranged in logical sequence and showing his thoughts on America, democracy, business, foreign policy, America's responsibilities, etc.

General

The Maritime Customs, *Treaties, Conventions, etc., between China and Foreign States* (2 vols., 2nd ed., Shanghai, 1917).

This excellent collection contains the full texts of all those treaties entered into by China from 1689 to the date of publication. English or French translations of some treaties are provided in cases in which the originals are in neither of those languages.

John V. A. MacMurray, ed., *Treaties and Agreements with or concerning China, 1894-1919* (2 vols., New York, 1921).

This collection provides, for the period covered, the

most valuable of all the treaty compilations relating to China. It contains valuable notes and an excellent index. In all cases the English text or translation is given.

Carnegie Endowment for International Peace, Division of International Law, *The Sino-Japanese Negotiations of 1915: Japanese and Chinese Documents and Chinese Official Statement* (Washington, 1921).

A handy collection of documents relating to the Sino-Japanese discussions of the Twenty-One Demands.

——————, *Shantung: Treaties and Agreements* (Washington, 1921).

A useful collection of documents relating to Shantung.

Treaties, Conventions, International Acts, Protocols and Agreements between the United States and Other Powers, Vol. III, 1910-1923, Senate Document No. 348, 67th Congress, 4th Session (Washington, 1923).

A very useful collection compiled under resolution of the Senate of August 19, 1921. This volume continues Vols. I and II under the same title, 1776-1909, compiled by William M. Malloy (Washington, 1910).

Harley Farnsworth MacNair, ed., *Modern Chinese History: Selected Readings* (Shanghai, 1923).

A collection of extracts from various sources chosen to illustrate some of the chief phases of China's international relations during the past hundred years.

B. PRINTED LETTERS AND MEMOIRS

William Jennings Bryan, *Letters to a Chinese Official* (New York, 1906).

It contains the author's views on the spread of Christian ideals in China.

Woodrow Wilson, letter to ex-Mayor of San Francisco, in *Independent,* LXXIII (1912), p. 863. Extract.

Written in support of the exclusion of Chinese and Japanese.

Joseph P. Tumulty, *Woodrow Wilson as I Know Him* (Garden City, N. Y., 1921).

Written by Wilson's admirer, supporter, and secretary to correct current misapprehensions about the President. Too sympathetic in tone.

Paul S. Reinsch, *An American Diplomat in China* (Garden City, N. Y., and Toronto, 1922).

A personal account of China's political conditions and her relations with the United States during the author's stay in China, based on first-hand knowledge. Invaluable for my subject of study.

William C. Redfield, *With Congress and Cabinet* (Garden City, N. Y., 1924).

Only casually and insignificantly touches upon China.

Edward Grey, *Twenty-Five Years, 1892-1916* (2 vols., New York, 1925).

Reveals British attitude toward Japan's entrance into the First World War.

William Jennings Bryan and Mary Baird Bryan, *The Memoirs of William Jennings Bryan* (Chicago, Philadelphia and Toronto, 1925).

Memoirs first taken up by Mr. Bryan himself and then finished by his wife. Little information about American policy toward China except a dictated statement about the six-power loan and a short paragraph about the American recognition of the Chinese Republic.

Thomas Riley Marshall, *Recollections of Thomas R. Marshall: a Hoosier Salad* (Indianapolis, 1925).

Contains a few insignificant remarks about Japan, but nothing about American policy toward China.

David F. Houston, *Eight Years with Wilson's Cabinet, 1913 to 1920* (2 vols., Garden City, N. Y., 1926).

A dependable and analytical record of Wilson's conduct of the American government at home, together with a personal estimate of the President, by one of Wilson's closest associates in the cabinet. Contains some valuable information about Wilson's attitude toward the six-power loan and the problem of recognizing the Chinese Republic.

William G. McAdoo, *Crowded Years: the Reminiscences of William G. McAdoo* (Boston and New York, 1931).

Personal recollections chiefly concerned with the financial affairs of the Wilson administration. The last chapter gives a favorable description or analysis of Wilson's personality.

229

David Lloyd George, *War Memoirs of David Lloyd George* (6 vols., Boston, 1933-1936).

Memoirs covering the years 1914-1918. Contains some remarks about the problem of Japan's control of the German Pacific islands and Kiaochow.

Robert Lansing, *War Memoirs of Robert Lansing* (Indianapolis and New York, 1935).

The author originally intended to review the foreign affairs of the United States during the period from June 23, 1915 to February 13, 1920 when he was secretary of state. At the time of his death (October 30, 1928) the work was still incomplete. Events dealt with ended with the year 1917. Chapter XX, "The Far East and the War— Lansing-Ishii Agreement," contains much information about American policy toward China and Japan during the First World War. Must be supplemented by the *Lansing Papers* (see above).

William R. Langdon, trans. and ed., *Diplomatic Commentaries* (Baltimore, 1936).

An English version of the third edition of *Gaiko Yoroku* by Viscount Ishii. It throws much light on Japan's diplomacy regarding China during the First World War. It is written purely from the Japanese point of view.

Edith Bolling Wilson, *My Memoir* (Indianapolis and New York, 1939).

Mrs. Wilson's personal account of her experience in the White House, during the First World War, and at the Paris Peace Conference. Lack of information about China.

Josephus Daniels, *The Wilson Era: Years of Peace—1910-1917* (Chapel Hill, 1944).

The third volume of the author's memoirs. Contains some information about the six-power loan and the American recognition of the Chinese Republic. Strongly sympathetic to Wilson's reversal of Taft's China policy.

F. M. Huntington Wilson, *Memoirs of an Ex-Diplomat* (Boston and Toronto, 1945).

Contains one chapter on the China consortium and another on the resignation of the author from the state department. Bitterly criticizes Wilson's policy and strongly defends the dollar diplomacy.

IV. SPECIAL WORKS

A. MONOGRAPHS

The Far Eastern Policy of the United States

Thomas F. Millard, *Our Eastern Question: America's Contact with the Orient and the Trend of Relations with China and Japan* (New York, 1916).

Contains much information about Japan's seizure of Shantung and her presentation of the Twenty-One Demands. Journalistic and pro-Chinese.

Henry Chung, *The Oriental Policy of the United States* (New York, Chicago, London and Edinburgh, 1919).

A brief history of the development of American Far Eastern policy, written by a Korean and based upon both American and Oriental sources.

En Tsung Yen (Yen En-tsung), *The Open Door Policy* (Boston, 1923).

Based on some printed sources easily accessible in English.

Mingchien Joshua Bau (Pao Ming-ch'ien), *The Open Door Doctrine in Relation to China* (New York, 1923).

Tells the origin, history, meaning and application of the **open door** policy. Criticizes the policy of independent action of Woodrow Wilson. No use of Wilson's papers or the state department archives for the Wilson period.

Payson J. Treat, *Japan and the United States, 1853-1921, Revised and Continued to 1928* (Stanford, 1928).

A brief sketch.

T'ang Ch'ing-tseng, *Chung-Mei Wai-chiao Shih, History of Chinese-American Relations* (In Chinese, Shanghai, 1928).

A sketchy work poorly written and undocumented.

F. R. Dulles, *America in the Pacific: A Century of Expansion* (Boston and New York, 1932).

An account of the emergence of the United States as a Pacific power.

David N. Rowe, *A Comparative Analysis of the Historical Background of the Monroe Doctrine and the Open Door Policy in the Far East* (a dissertation, the University of Chicago, 1935).

A well-written dissertation part of which was printed in 1938 by the University of Chicago.

Woodrow Wilson's China Policy

Wen Hwan Ma (Ma Wen-huan), *American Policy toward China as Revealed in the Debates of Congress* (Shanghai, 1936).

Based almost exclusively on Congressional records.

F. R. Dulles, *Forty Years of American-Japanese Relations* (New York, 1937).

A readable account based on secondary works.

Stephen C. Y. Pan (P'an Ch'ao-ying), "An Analytical Study of Principles of American Diplomacy with an Emphasis on Their Application in China," *Chinese Social and Political Science Review,* XXII (1938), 10-27; 111-126.

Explains the fair and benevolent nature of American policy particularly in China.

A. Whitney Griswold, *The Far Eastern Policy of the United States* (New York, 1938).

An excellent realistic analysis of the advances of American Far Eastern policy after the occupation of the Philippines. The most authoritative work on the subject for the period covered. Much information about the China policy of the Wilson administration.

Tyler Dennett, *Americans in Eastern Asia: A Critical Study of the Policy of the United States with reference to China, Japan and Korea in the 19th Century* (reprint ed., New York, 1941).

First published in 1922. Still the most authoritative work on American policy in China, Korea and Japan during the nineteenth century.

F. R. Dulles, *China and America: The Story of Their Relations since 1784* (Princeton, 1946).

Readable but not scholarly.

Kenneth Scott Latourette, *The United States Moves across the Pacific; The A. B. C.'s of the American Problem in the Western Pacific and the Far East* (New York and London, 1946).

A short treatment. Touches upon President Wilson's policy in China.

*Ideals and Policies of Woodrow Wilson
and His Associates*

Woodrow Wilson, "Democracy and Efficiency," *Atlantic Monthly,* LXXXVII (1901), 289-299.

Reveals Professor Woodrow Wilson's thoughts on American duty in the Far East.

George Creel, *Wilson and the Issues* (New York, 1916).
Briefly deals with such issues as Mexico, Belgium, the Lusitania, etc.

Harris Henry Wilson, *President Wilson, His Problems and His Policy* (New York, 1917).
Represents an English view.

William W. Hollingsworth, *Woodrow Wilson's Political Ideals as Interpreted from His Works* (Princeton, 1918).
A thesis showing the connection between the principles of Woodrow Wilson's political philosophy and his statesmanship and leadership.

Charles Seymour, *Woodrow Wilson and the World War: A Chronicle of Our Own Times* (New Haven, 1921).
A scholarly account containing some remarks about China.

Ernest W. Young, *The Wilson Administration and the Great War* (Boston, 1922).
Contains little information about the Far East.

Samuel F. Bemis, ed., *The American Secretaries of State and Their Diplomacy,* Vol. X (10 vols., New York, 1927-1929).
Volume X includes a study of the diplomacy of William Jennings Bryan by an anonymous author, and a study of the diplomatic career of Robert Lansing by J. W. Pratt. Both studies are carefully written and touch upon American policy toward China.

Merle E. Curti, "Bryan and World Peace," *Smith College Studies in History,* Vol. 16 (Northampton, 1931).
Refers to Wilson's comparison of Japan to Germany.

Charles Seymour, *American Diplomacy during the World War* (Baltimore, 1934).
One of the best works on the diplomacy of the Wilson administration during the First World War.

Frederic L. Paxson, *American Diplomacy and the World War: Pre-War Years, 1913-1917* (Boston, 1936).
A general account. Little information about the Far East.

Harley Notter, *The Origins of the Foreign Policy of Woodrow Wilson* (Baltimore, 1937).

A thorough study of the origins of Wilson's individual foreign policies as developed and enunciated chronologically during his Presidency. Throws much light on the origin of Wilson's China policy.

Willaim Diamond, *The Economic Thought of Woodrow Wilson* (Baltimore, 1943).

A doctoral dissertation attempting at an objective exposition of Wilson's economic thought. Touches upon Wilson's foreign policy.

Daniel J. Gage, *Paul S. Reinsch and Sino-American Relations* (an unpublished dissertation, Stanford University, 1939).

A careful treatment based to a large extent on the *Papers Relating to the Foreign Relations of the United States.*

Francis C. Prescott, *The Lansing-Ishii Agreement* (an unpublished dissertation, Yale University, 1949).

A thorough study. Chapter II gives a lucid account of Japanese attempts to gain predominance in China in the years 1915-1917.

Philip H. Lowry, *The Mexican Policy of Woodrow Wilson* (an unpublished dissertation, Yale University, 1949).

Only indirectly helps this study.

*China, Japan, the United States,
and the First World War*

Thomas F. Millard, *The Great War in the Far East* (Shanghai, 1915).

A journalistic account with special emphasis on the rights and interests of China and the United States.

M. T. Z. Tyau (Tiao Min-ch'ien), "Diplomatic Relations between China and the Powers since and concerning the European War," *Chinese Social and Political Science Review,* II (1917), 6-67.

A topical summary.

Payson J. Treat, "Japan, America, and the Great War," *League of Nations,* I (1918), 417-442.

A sympathetic explanation of Japan's entry into the war.

W. R. Wheeler, *China and the World War* (New York, 1919).

A fair and clear contemporary account.

Kenneth S. Latourette, "China, the United States and the War," *League of Nations,* II, Special Number (1919), 167-191.

A summary which stresses American efforts to preserve China's independence and integrity.

Thomas F. Millard, *Democracy and the Eastern Question* (New York, 1919).

Journalistic and informative.

Nagao Ariga, *La Chine et la Grande Guerre Européenne au point de vue du droit international d'après les documents officiels du gouvernement chinois* (Paris, 1920).

A concise and readable account by a legal adviser to the President of China.

Liu Yen, *Ou-chan Ch'i-chien Chung-Jih Chiao-she Shih, A History of the Sino-Japanese Negotiations during the European War* (in Chinese, Shanghai, 1921).

Describes the Japanese occupation of Shantung in 1914 and the relations of Yüan Shih-k'ai and various warlords with the Japanese through 1920. Fairly useful.

C. N. Spinks, "Japan's Entrance into the World War," *Pacific Historical Review,* V (1936). 297-311

A scholarly treatment of Japan's decision to enter the war in 1914.

Thomas E. La Fargue, *China and the World War* (Stanford and London, 1937).

One of the most authoritative works on China and the First World War.

*The Chinese Revolution of 1911
and the Chinese Republic before 1917*

Arthur J. Brown, *The Chinese Revolution* (New York, 1912).

A brief account of the Chinese Revolution and its immediate result.

J. O. P. Bland, *Recent Events and Present Policies in China* (London, 1912).

A general survey. Chapter XI deals with American policy in China.

Frederick McCormick, *The Flowery Republic* (New York, 1913).

A journalistic account of the Chinese Revolution.

Putnam Weale (B. L. Simpson), *The Fight for the Republic of China* (New York, 1917).

A lucid account of the Chinese Republic from 1911 to 1917. Informative about Yüan Shih-k'ai, the Twenty-One Demands, and the monarchical movement.

F. A. Coleman, *The Far East Unveiled: An Inner History of Events in Japan and China in the Year 1916* (London and New York, 1918).

Informative about what happened in China and Japan in 1916.

Ma Chen-tung, *Yüan-shih Tang-kuo Shih, A History of Yüan Shih-k'ai's Rule* (in Chinese, Shanghai, 1930).

A detailed account.

John G. Reid, *The Manchu Abdication and the Powers, 1908-1912: An Episode in Pre-War Diplomacy; A Study of the Role of Foreign Diplomacy during the Reign of Hsüan-T'ung* (Berkeley, 1935).

A scholarly work dealing in part with American attitude toward the Manchu abdication.

Economic Relations between China and the Powers

Wang Ching-chun (Wang Ching-ch'un), "The Hankow-Szechuan Railway Loan," *American Journal of International Law,* V (1911), 653-664.

Shows that in contrast to suspicion and jealousy among other powers there was goodwill between China and the United States throughout the negotiations for that railway loan.

Willard Straight, "China's Loan Negotiations," in George H. Blakeslee, ed., *Recent Developments in China* (New York, 1913), pp. 119-161.

An address given by Willard Straight, sometime the representative of the American banking group in China. Explains the significance of Chinese loans, the importance of securing and retaining American interest therein, and the difficulties encountered in the reorganization loan negotiations. Strongly defends President Taft's dollar diplomacy.

Herman Rosenthal, "America and the Chinese Loan," *American Review of Reviews* XLVII (1913), 726-728.

Strongly supports Woodrow Wilson's policy of withdrawing the American group from the consortium and protecting American business interests in China.

Rowland R. Gibson, *Forces Mining and Undermining China* (New York, 1914).

Chapter 8 tells the story of the reorganization loan.

Mongton Chih Hsu, "Railway Problems in China," in the Faculty of Political Science of Columbia University, ed., *Studies in History, Economics, and Public Law,* Vol. LXVI, No. 2, Whole No. 159 (New York, 1915), pp. 229-412.

An interpretative analysis of the important economic and political problems of railway development in China from the very beginning down to the First World War. Deals with all the railway loan agreements reached between China and foreign countries in that period.

Ching Wen-sze, "The Treaty Relations between China and the United States Relating to Commerce," *Chinese Social and Political Science Review,* II (1917), 38-57.

A summary analysis.

Theodore W. Overlach, *Foreign Financial Control in China* (New York, 1919).

Contains a separate chapter on American financial relations with China. Overemphasizes the American consistent attitude of unselfishness.

Feng-hua Huang (Huang Feng-hua), "Public Debts in China," in the Faculty of Political Science of Columbia University, ed., *Studies in History, Economics, and Public Law,* Vol. LXXXV, No. 2, Whole No. 197 (New York, 1919), pp. 347-451.

A study of China's loan negotiations and agreements up to 1918.

George A. Finch, "American Diplomacy and the Financing of China," *American Journal of International Law,* XVI (1922), 25-42.

A brief treatment of the American financing of China from 1909 to 1921.

S. Nearing and J. Freeman, *Dollar Diplomacy: A Study in American Imperialism* (New York, 1925).

A careless study making uncritical use of source materials.

C. F. Remer, *The Foreign Trade of China* (Shanghai, 1926).
Begins with the early trade at Canton and ends with China's trade relations in 1921. A careful study.

Tan Shao-hua (T'an Shao-hua), "The Diplomacy of American Investments in China," in the University of Chicago, *Abstracts of Theses, Humanistic Studies,* VI (1929), 165-171.
Based on state papers and records supplied by the American Chamber of Commerce and J. P. Morgan and Co.

Arthur G. Coons, *The Foreign Public Debt of China* (Philadelphia and London, 1930).
A clear outline of the history of all the contracted obligations of the successive recognized Chinese governments.

P. H. Clyde, "Railway Politics and the Open Door in China, 1916-1917," *American Journal of International Law,* XXV (1931), 642-657.
A study based chiefly on the *Papers Relating to the Foreign Relations of the United States.*

Frederick V. Field, *American Participation in the China Consortiums* (Chicago, 1931).
So far the only detailed account of the old and new consortiums in relation to the United States. Based exclusively on American sources of information.

C. F. Remer, *Foreign Investments in China* (New York, 1933).
A scholarly work resulting from several years of investigation of the powers' investments in China. Contains a separate chapter on American investments in China.

Kao Ping-shu, "Foreign Loans to China," *Sino-International Economic Pamphlets,* No. 2 (New York, 1946).
Chapter I gives a brief account of foreign loans to China previous to the Second World War.

American Recognition Policy
and the Recognition of the Chinese Republic

Louis Livingston Seaman, "A Plea for Fair Play and the Recognition of the Chinese Republic," in George H. Balkeslee, ed., *Recent Developments in China* (New York, 1913), pp. 50-65.
Enumerates the reasons why China deserved recognition. Is an address given by Louis Livingston Seaman, president of the China Society of America.

Wang Ching-chun (Wang Ching-ch'un), "A plea for the Recognition of the Chinese Republic," *Atlantic Monthly*, CXI (1913), 42-45.

Points out why the Chinese Republic should be recognized without delay.

Julius Goebel, Jr., "The Recognition Policy of the United States," in the Faculty of Political Science of Columbia University, ed., *Studies in History, Economics and Public Law*, Vol. LXVI, No. 1, Whole No. 158 (1915), pp. 1-228.

A scholarly historical treatment.

Taylor Cole, *The Recognition Policy of the United States since 1901* (Baton Rouge, 1928).

A fairly well written dissertation which helps to understand American recognition policy since 1901.

J. L. McMahon, *Recent Changes in the Recognition Policy of the United States* (Washington, 1933).

Contains a brief survey of American recognition policy before 1920.

M. E. Cameron, "American Recognition Policy toward the Republic of China, 1912-1913," *Pacific Historical Review*, II (1933), 214-230.

Rests on printed sources. Points out the difference between Taft's policy of international cooperation and Wilson's policy of independent action.

The Shantung Question

Otto Franke, *Deutschland und China vor, in und nach dem Kriege* (Hamburg, 1915).

Too sketchy to be of much use.

Jefferson Jones, *The Fall of Tsingtau, with a Study of Japan's Ambitions in China* (Boston and New York, 1915).

A journalistic account of the fall of the German leasehold in Shantung in 1914.

Charles Burke Elliott, "The Shantung Question," *American Journal of International Law*, XIII (1919), 687-737.

Traces the development of the Shantung question and discusses the Shantung provisions of the Versailles Treaty. Sympathetic to China's claims.

Ge-Zay Wood, *The Shantung Question: A Study in Diplomacy and World Politics* (New York, Chicago, London, and Edinburgh, 1922).

An account of the Shantung question from the German occupation of Kiaochow Bay down to the new Shantung settlement at the Washington Conference. Sets forth the Chinese attitude.

Wilson L. Godshall, *The International Aspects of the Shantung Question* (Philadelphia, 1923).

A dissertation giving a historical and analytical account of the Shantung question.

——————, *Tsingtau under Three Flags* (Shanghai, 1929).

An extensive survey of the international and administrative status of Tsingtao and the Kiaochow leased territory. Also a historical account of the Shantung question.

T'an T'ien-k'ai, *Shan-tung Wen-t'i Shih-mo, A Complete Account of the Shantung Question* (in Chinese, Shanghai, 1935).

A serious study of the Shantung question from 1898 to 1922.

Feng Djen Djang (Chang Feng-chen), *The Diplomatic Relations between China and Germany Since 1898.* (Shanghai, 1936).

Much information about the Shantung problem.

The Twenty-One Demands

The Chinese Students' Union, *The Truth about the Sino-Japanese "Conversations"* (London, 1915).

A pamphlet in defense of China.

S. N. D. North, "The Negotiations between Japan and China in 1915," *American Journal of International Law,* X (1916), 222-237.

A brief account and analysis of the Twenty-One Demands and the Sino-Japanese negotiations in 1915. Uses documents available up to 1916.

Ge-Zay Wood, *The Twenty-One Demands: Japan versus China* (New York and Chicago, 1921).

An analysis of the demands, together with an account of the immediate circumstances leading to the presentation of the demands and of the manner in which the Sino-Japanese negotiations were conducted.

——————, *The Chino-Japanese Treaties of May 25, 1915* (New York and Chicago, 1921).

A study of the validity of the treaties of 1915. A plea for the abrogation of them at the Washington Conference.

Paul S. Reinsch, "Secret Diplomacy and the Twenty-One Demands," *Asia*, XXI (1921), 937-943; 972; 974.

Practically the same as Chapter XII of *An American Diplomat in China* by Paul S. Reinsch.

Shu-hsi Hsü (Hsü Shu-hsi), "The Treaties and Notes of 1915," *Chinese Social and Political Science Review*, XVI (1932), 43-66.

A discussion of the validity of the treaties of 1915. Argues that the Chinese National Assembly had the right to declare those treaties null and void.

Manchuria and Mongolia

Shu-hsi Hsü (Hsü Shu-hsi), *China and Her Political Entity* (New York, 1926).

An account of the policy of China and other powers in Manchuria, with sections on Mongolia and Korea. Makes extensive use of materials in Chinese.

P. H. Clyde, *International Rivalries in Manchuria, 1689-1922* (2nd and rev. ed., Columbus, Ohio, 1928).

A clear historical account of the Manchurian problem.

C. Walter Young, *The International Relations of Manchuria: A Digest and Analysis of Treaties, Agreements, and Negotiations concerning the Three Eastern Provinces of China, Prepared for the 1929 Conference of the Institute of Pacific Relations in Kyoto, Japan* (Chicago, 1929).

An informative and analytical summary.

Masamichi Royama, *Japan's Position in Manchuria* (Tokyo, 1929).

A paper prepared for the third biennial conference of the Institute of Pacific Relations in Kyoto in 1929. Presents a Japanese view of Japan's special position in Manchuria.

P. H. Clyde, "An Episode in American-Japanese Relations; The Manchurian Freight-Rate Controversy 1914-1916," *Far Eastern Review*, XXVI (1930), 410-412; 480-483.

A short article based almost exclusively on the *Papers Relating to the Foreign Relations of the United States* for the years 1914-1916. Both American and Japanese views regarding the freight-rate problem are well presented to the reader.

C. Walter Young, *Japan's Special Position in Manchuria: Its Assertion, Legal Interpretation and Present Meaning* (Baltimore and London, 1931).

An analytical narrative of Japan's special position in Manchuria. Thoughtful but not definitive.

Ernest B. Price, *The Russo-Japanese Treaties of 1907-1916 concerning Manchuria and Mongolia* (Baltimore, 1933).

Is of some value in helping to understand Russo-Japanese relations relating to Manchuria and Mongolia.

Owen Lattimore, *Manchuria: Cradle of Conflict* (rev. ed., New York, 1935).

One of the best works on the various aspects of Manchuria as a geographical region. Founded on a large amount of source material in Chinese as well as on the author's experience gained during about nine months of travel and residence in Manchuria in 1929-1930.

Other Problems

M. T. Z. Tyau (Tiao Min-ch'ien), *The Legal Obligations Arising out of Treaty Relations between China and Other States* (Shanghai, 1917).

A very scholarly interpretation. A thesis of the University of London.

Ching-lin Hsia (Hsia Chin-Lin), *Studies in Chinese Diplomatic History* (Shanghai, 1924).

Deals with foreign encroachments on Chinese sovereignty. Uses only English sources.

Chang Chung-fu, *The Anglo-Japanese Alliance* (Baltimore, 1931).

A well documented thesis giving a historical treatment of the alliance.

Kikujiro Ishii, *The Permanent Bases of Japanese Foreign Policy* (New York, 1933).

A pamphlet from *Foreign Affairs* for January 1933. Emphasizes Japanese vital interests in China.

Alfred L. P. Dennis, "The Anglo-Japanese Alliance," in David P. Barrows, Edwin Landon, and Frank M. Russell, eds.,

University of California Publications in International Relations, Vol. I, 1923-1929 (Berkeley, 1934), pp. 1-111.

A brief historical survey of the origin and development of the alliance. This monograph was first published in 1923 by the University of California Press, Berkeley.

B. BIOGRAPHIES

Woodrow Wilson

Henry J. Ford, *Woodrow Wilson, the Man and His Work: A Biographical Study* (New York and London, 1916).

A favorable account of Wilson's career and principles.

Eugene C. Brooks, *Woodrow Wilson as President* (Chicago and New York, 1916).

A sympathetic account of President Wilson's work during the years 1913-1916.

Africanus, *President Wilson: New Statesman* (London, 1919).

A brief interpretation of President Wilson and the principles of his policy. Africanus is the pseudonym of a British author.

George Creel, *The War, the World and Wilson* (New York and London, 1920).

Written in defense of Wilson and as a plea for the ratification of the peace treaty.

Josephus Daniels, The Life of Woodrow Wilson, 1856-1924 (Chicago, Philadelphia and Toronto, 1924).

An eulogistic biography written by one of Woodrow Wilson's loyal associates.

David Lawrence, *The True Story of Woodrow Wilson* (New York, 1924).

A thoughtful narrative by a correspondent who represented the Associated Press with Wilson at the White House from 1913 to 1915.

Robert Edwards Annin, *Woodrow Wilson: A Character Study* (New York, 1924).

A critical account of incidents throwing light on Woodrow Wilson's character and mentality.

William Allen White, *Woodrow Wilson: The Man, His Times and His Task* (Boston and New York, 1924).

A general brief biographical study.

James Kerney, *The Political Education of Woodrow Wilson* (New York and London, 1926).

A critical but friendly appreciation of Wilson's political career. Contains some information about the question of selecting an American minister to China.

Ray Stannard Baker, *Woodrow Wilson: Life and Letters* (8 vols., Garden City, N. Y., 1927-1939).

A monumental and authorized biography of Woodrow Wilson, based upon Wilson's private papers and a large amount of material made available by Wilson's friends, associates and relatives. Invariably sympathetic in tone. Contains some information about Wilson's China policy. Very useful for this study.

William Edward Dodd, *Woodrow Wilson and His Work* (new and rev. ed., New York, 1932).

Written with a view to a just estimate of President Wilson and his work. Touches upon Chinese problems.

John K. Winkler, *Woodrow Wilson: The Man Who Lives On* (New York, 1933).

Eulogistic, journalistic and undocumented. Chapter XI touches upon American withdrawal from the consortium and Wilson's recognition of the Chinese Republic.

Edith G. Reid, *Woodrow Wilson: The Caricature, the Myth and the Man* (London, New York and Toronto, 1934).

A portrait of Wilson with special emphasis on his ideas, purposes and motives. Gains its authority from the authoress' long and close friendship with Wilson. Contains some remarks about the six-power loan to China.

Jennings C. Wise, *Woodrow Wilson, Disciple of Revolution* (New York, 1938).

A well-documented biographical study of Wilson, resulting from careful research work.

Thomas A. Bailey, *Woodrow Wilson and the Lost Peace* (New York, 1944).

Deals chiefly with the work of the Paris Peace Conference and the reactions of American opinion to it. Contains a brief summary of Wilson's policy during the war years.

——————————, *Woodrow Wilson and the Great Betrayal* (New York, 1945).

Follows the last work. A study of events in the United States from Wilson's return from Paris to the death of Warren Harding. Of little use for this study.

H. C. F. Bell, *Woodrow Wilson and the People* (Garden City, N. Y., 1945).

Shows Wilson's sustained effort to establish and maintain contact with the people. No use of new material.

Ruth Cranston, *The Story of Woodrow Wilson: Twenty-Eighth President of the United States, Pioneer of World Democracy* (New York, 1945).

A favorable account of Wilson's life and achievements, based on a large amount of source material. Contains some information about Chinese problems.

Harold Garnet Black, *The True Woodrow Wilson, Crusader* (New York, London and Edinburgh, 1946).

A concise personal and political account. Uses no new material and leans heavily to the side of admiration.

Arthur S. Link, *Wilson: The Road to the White House* (Princeton, 1947).

The first volume in a series which, upon completion, will carry the story to the end of Wilson's life. A critical, scholarly and exhaustive study.

E. M. Hugh-Jones, *Woodrow Wilson and American Liberalism* (New York, 1948).

A careful study. Contains some information about Wilson's attitude toward China.

Others

Herbert Croly, *Willard Straight* (New York, 1924).

A reliable biography based upon a large amount of source material. Valuable for studying international loans to China.

G. F. Herrick and J. O. Herrick, *The Life of William Jennings Bryan* (Chicago, c 1925).

Ardently admires Bryan. Uncritical and journalistic.

Paul Linebarger, *Sun Yat-sen and the Chinese Republic* (New York and London, 1925).

Sympathetic to Sun Yat-sen as against militarists at Peking.

245

Burton J. Hendrick, *The Life and Letters of Walter H. Page* (3 vols., Garden City, N. Y., 1925-1926).

Invaluable for studying Wilson's foreign policy in general. Little information about China.

Ito Masanori, *Kato Takaaki* (in Japanese, 2 vols., Tokyo, 1929).

Reveals Japanese intentions in China during the First World War.

Morris R. Werner, *Bryan* (New York, 1929).

Is a readable account of Bryan's career but adds little that is new.

Allan Nevins, *Henry White: Thirty Years of American Diplomacy* (New York and London, 1930).

Contains some information about the Chinese problem at the Paris Peace Conference. Of little help to this study.

Henry James, *Charles W. Eliot: President of Harvard University, 1869-1909* (2 vols., Boston and New York, 1930).

Contains some factual errors. The information about the suggested appointment of Charles W. Eliot to the Japanese post instead of to the Chinese post is inaccurate.

Henry Bond Restarick, *Sun Yat-sen, Liberator of China* (New Haven and London, 1931).

A readable account of Sun Yat-sen's life, with a preface by Prof. K. S. Latourette.

Thomas W. Lamont, *Henry P. Davison: The Record of a Useful Life* (New York and London, 1933).

A sympathetic account by Henry P. Davison's friend and partner. Chapter VIII records Davison's relations with the old and new consortiums. Unfavorably criticizes Wilson's consortium policy.

Basil Mathews, *John R. Mott: World Citizen* (New York and London, 1934).

An illuminating biographical sketch with information about Woodrow Wilson's offer to appoint John R. Mott as American minister to China.

L. Sharman, *Sun Yat-sen, His Life and Its Meaning: A Critical Biography* (New York, 1934).

The best critical biographical study of Sun Yat-sen.

Henry F. Pringle, *The Life and Times of William Howard Taft* (2 vols., New York and Toronto, 1939).

A thorough study of Taft's life and career. But throws little light on Taft's policy toward the consortium and the problem of recognizing the Chinese Republic.

V. GENERAL WORKS

A. CHINA

John Stuart Thomson, *China Revolutionized* (Indianapolis, 1913).

Contains one chapter on the history of the Chinese Revolution of 1911.

Sih-gung Cheng, *Modern China: A Political Study* (London, New York and Toronto, 1919).

A brief account of the political situation of modern China. Also touches upon American and Japanese policies in China.

Mingchien Joshua Bau (Pao Ming-ch'ien), *The Foreign Relations of China: A History and a Survey* (New York, Chicago, London and Edinburgh, 1921).

A general sketch of China's relations with the powers. Lacks historical insight.

Min-ch'ien T. Z. Tyau (Tiao Min-ch'ien), *China Awakened* (New York, 1922).

Deals with the various aspects of Chinese national life during the First World War. Also touches upon China's foreign relations. Chapter XVI, "Rupture with the Central Powers," is of some use for this study.

Mingchien Joshua Bau (Pao Ming-ch'ien), *Modern Democracy in China* (Shanghai, 1923).

A readable history of modern constitutional government in China.

Westel W. Willoughby, *Foreign Rights and Interests in China* (2 vols., Baltimore, 1927).

Provides a very informative statement of the rights of foreigners and the interests of foreign states in China. Is of great help to this study.

Henry K. Norton, *China and the Powers* (New York, 1927).

Sets forth the various aspects of the Chinese Revolution,

each in its relation to the others. Contains some first-hand knowledge of conditions in the Far East.

P. T. Etherton, *The Crisis in China* (Boston, 1927).

Contains one chapter on the conflict between Yüan Shih-k'ai and the Kuomintang.

Edward T. Williams, *A Short History of China* (New York and London, 1928).

A well-written history containing one chapter on Yüan Shih-k'ai's administration and another chapter on China in the First World War.

Kenneth Scott Latourette, *A History of Christian Missions in China* (New York, 1929; reissued in 1932).

A scholarly and thorough historical treatment of the work and influence of Christian missions in China from before the Mongols to the close of 1926. Excellently documented and annotated.

T'ang Leang-li (T'ang Liang-Li), *The Inner History of the Chinese Revolution* (New York, 1930).

Covers the period from the genesis of the National Revolution to 1930. Represents the views of the Wang Ching-wei faction of the Kuomintang.

S. T. King (Chin Chao-tzu), *Hsien-tai Chung-kuo Wai-chiao Shih, The Diplomatic History of Modern China* (in Chinese, Shanghai, 1930).

Written in clear Chinese, but undocumented.

Chia I-chün, *Chung-hua Min-kuo Shih, History of the Chinese Republic* (in Chinese, Peiping, 1930).

A readable general account.

Li Chien-nung, *Tsui-chin San-shih-nien Chung-kuo Cheng-chih Shih, A Political History of China during the Past Thirty Years* (in Chinese, 2nd ed., Shanghai, 1930).

Contains much information about Chinese political affairs during the administration of Yüan-Shih-k'ai. Carefully presented but undocumented.

Liu Yen, *Ti-kuo-chu-i Ya-p'o Chung-kuo Shih, A History of Imperialist Oppressions in China* (in Chinese, 13th ed., 2 vols., Shanghai, 1932).

Volume II deals in detail with the foreign relations of the Chinese Republic. Informative but undocumented.

Bibliography

Harold Archer Van Dorn, *Twenty Years of the Chinese Republic: Two Decades of Progress* (New York, 1932).

Chapter I, "Political Progress," includes a political history of China from 1911 to 1917.

Edward T. Williams, *China Yesterday and Today* (5th ed. rev., New York, 1932).

Includes brief accounts of the Chinese Revolution of 1911, the reorganization loan, the recognition of the Chinese Republic, the Shantung question and the Twenty-One Demands.

Robert Thomas Pollard, *China's Foreign Relations, 1917-1931* (New York, 1933).

Deals mainly with the post-war foreign relations of China.

Ch'en Kung-lu, *Chung-kuo Chin-tai Shih, A History of Modern China* (Shanghai, 1935).

Is the most comprehensive account of its kind in spite of its shortcomings. Contains chapters on the Chinese Revolution of 1911 and the domestic and foreign affairs of the Chinese Republic.

Chang Chung-fu, Chung-hua Min-kuo Wai-chiao Shih, A Diplomatic History of the Chinese Republic, Volume I (in Chinese, Peiping, 1936; reissued in Chungking in 1943).

The best book of its kind by a Chinese scholar of diplomatic history. Clearly presented and fairly well documented. This volume carries the story to the Washington Conference, and the second volume is to be completed.

John T. Pratt, *War and Politics in China* (London, 1943).

An attempt at a new interpretation of the principal events in China's relations with the modern world. Deals largely with British policy in China during the past two hundred years. Also touches upon American and Japanese policies in China.

Ch'en Ju-hsüan, *Tseng-ting Chung-kuo Hsien-fa Shih, A Constitutional History of China* (in Chinese, rev. ed., Shanghai, 1947).

The first seven chapters deal with the government of Yüan Shih-k'ai. Fairly informative.

B. JAPAN

Kiyoshi Karl Kawakami, *Japan in World Politics* (New York, 1917).

Most of the chapters were originally published as separate articles in periodicals. Discusses Sino-Japanese and Japanese-American relations. Attempts to justify Japan in China.

————, *Japan and World Peace* (New York, 1919).

Touches upon China's entrance into the war and the Sino-Japanese controversy. States that China was utterly incapable of managing her own affairs.

Andrew M. Pooley, *Japan's Foreign Policies* (New York, 1920).

Records the rapid imperialistic developments in Japan and her policy in China before and during the First World War.

Kiyoshi Karl Kawakami, *Japan's Pacific Policy, Especially in Relation to China, the Far East, and the Washington Conference* (New York, 1922).

Gives an analysis of the part taken by Japan in the Washington Conference and of the Pacific problem.

Arthur M. Young, *Japan in Recent Times, 1912-1916* (New York, 1929).

Written by the editor of the Japan Chronicle. Represents the gist of many editorials by the author. Japanese course in China is discussed.

Sterling Tatsuji Takeuchi, *War and Diplomacy in the Japanese Empire* (Chicago, 1935).

A scholarly work with separate chapters on Japan's entrance into the First World War and the Sino-Japanese negotiations of 1915.

Albert E. Hindmarsh, *The Basis of Japanese Foreign Policy* (Cambridge, 1936).

Deals mainly with the relation between Japanese internal pressures and Japanese foreign policy.

C. THE UNITED STATES

Woodrow Wilson, *A History of the American People* (5 vols., New York and London, 1901).

Reveals Professor Woodrow Wilson's view of history and his conception of China and American Far Eastern policy.

John Bassett Moore, *The Principles of American Diplomacy* (New York and London, 1918).

A well-written work by a famous scholar of international law and diplomacy who served as President Wilson's counselor of the state department from April 1913 to March 1914. It substantially incorporates the entire text of the volume published by the author in 1905 under the title of *American Diplomacy: Its Spirit and Achievements.* Mentions American policy in China.

Charles A. Beard with the collaboration of G. H. E. Smith, *The Idea of National Interest: An Analytical Study in American Foreign Policy* (New York, 1934).

A careful study of the growth of the doctrine of national interest in America and its application to problems of territorial and commercial expansion. Devotes one section of a chapter to the American diplomacy of national interest in China 1914-21.

Samuel Flagg Bemis, *A Diplomatic History of the United States* (rev. ed., New York, 1942).

A standard work containing a scholarly and proportionate treatment of the relations between the United States and the Far East. Concisely records American policy in China during the Wilson administration.

Thomas A. Bailey, *A Diplomatic History of the American People* (3rd ed., 11th printing, New York, 1947).

A good general account the main emphasis of which is upon American public opinion. Touches upon Woodrow Wilson's policy in China.

D. THE FAR EAST

Paul S. Reinsch, *Intellectual and Political Currents in the Far East* (Boston and New York, 1911).

A readable account which reveals Professor Paul S. Reinsch's sympathetic understanding of China.

Stanley K. Hornbeck, *Contemporary Politics in the Far East* (New York and London, 1916).

A realistic and critical analysis. Contains a historical sketch of the relations between China, Japan and the United States.

Guy H. Scholefield, *The Pacific, Its Past and Future, and the Policy of the Great Powers from the Eighteenth Century* (London, 1919).

Mainly a short history of British foreign policy in the Pacific.

Hosea Ballou Morse and Harley Farnsworth MacNair, *Far Eastern International Relations* (Boston, New York, Chicago, Dallas, Atlanta and San Francisco, 1931).

An excellent comprehensive account containing much information about China's relations with other powers.

Payson J. Treat, *The Far East: A Political and Diplomatic History* (rev. ed., New York and London, 1935).

A clarifying summary of recent history and politics in the Far East. Apologetic for Japanese policy.

Taraknath Das, *Foreign Policy in the Far East* (New York and Toronto, 1936).

Presents a picture of the trend of Far Eastern nationalist movements and gives a popular interpretation of foreign policies in the Orient. Anti-imperialistic in tone.

G. Nye Steiger, *A History of the Far East* (Boston, New York, etc., 1936).

A clear and readable general account with a good selected bibliography at the end.

Paul H. Clyde, *A History of the Modern and Contemporary Far East; A Survey of Western Contacts with Eastern Asia during the Nineteenth and Twentieth Centuries* (New York, 1937).

Concerned primarily with the impact of imperialism upon the Far East in the nineteenth century and with the rise of Japan to the position of a world power in the twentieth century.

P. H. B. Kent, *The Twentieth Century in the Far East: A Perspective of Events, Cultural Influences and Policies* (London, 1937).

A historical account of Eastern Asia from the Boxer Rebellion to the Sian Coup in 1936. The author has some intimate knowledge of China.

Harold M. Vinacke, *A History of the Far East in Modern Times* (4th ed., 12th printing, New York, 1945).

A standard textbook of its kind.

Kenneth Scott Latourette, *A Short History of the Far East* (New York, 1946).

An objective treatment of the peoples, cultures and current problems of the Far East. Devotes much space to the relations between the United States and Far Eastern peoples.

E. EUROPE AND THE WORLD

Sidney B. Fay, *The Origins of the World War* (2nd ed. rev., 2 vols. in one, New York, 1930).

An authoritative work on the causes of the First World War. Touches upon European diplomacy relating to China before the First World War.

Herbert Feis, *Europe: The World's Banker, 1870-1914* (New Haven, 1930).

A scholarly study. Contains some information about the financing of China by the powers through the consortium.

Eugene Staley, *War and the Private Investor: A Study in the Relations of International Politics and International Private Investment* (Garden City, N. Y., 1935).

An objective and scientific inquiry into the relation between war and private investors. Touches upon the consortium and foreign investments in China.

VI. CHRONOLOGIES, ANNUALS, PERIODICALS, AND NEWSPAPERS

A. CHRONOLOGIES

Pan-su, *Chung-shan Ch'u-shih hou Chung-kuo Liu-shih-nien Ta-shih-chi, Important Chinese Events in the Sixty Years after the Birth of Sun Yat-sen* (in Chinese, rev. ed., Shanghai, 1929).

Informative and useful.

Liu Yen, *Chung-hua Min-kuo Erh-shih-nien-lai Ta-shih-chi, Important Events in the Twenty Years of the Chinese Republic* (in Chinese, 2 vols., Shanghai, 1932).

A daily record. Detailed and informative.

B. ANNUALS

H. T. Montague Bell and H. G. W. Woodhead, eds., *The China Year Book,* 1912-1914 annually (3 vols., London and New York, 1912-1914).

A useful yearbook.

Francis G. Wickware, ed., *The American Year Book: A Record of Events and Progress,* 1912-1917 annually (6 vols., New York and London, 1913-1918).

The chapters on international relations and foreign affairs are useful.

Chung-kuo Wai-chiao-pu T'ung-chi-k'o (the Statistical Department of the Chinese Ministry of Foreign Affairs), *Min-kuo Chiu-nien-fen Wai-chiao Nien-chien,* Foreign Relations *Yearbook, 1920* (in Chinese, 2 vols., Peking, 1921).

Includes data for the period from 1912 to 1920.

Juan Hsiang and others, eds., *Ti-i-hui Chung-kuo Nien-chien, The China Year Book, No. I* (in Chinese, Shanghai, 1924).

Contains a useful chapter on foreign affairs.

C. PERIODICALS

American Historical Review (New York and London).
American Journal of International Law (New York).
American Review of Reviews (New York).
Asia, Journal of the American Asiatic Association (New York).
Asiatic Review (London).
Atlantic Monthly (Boston).
China Weekly Review (Shanghai).
Chinese Recorder (Shanghai).
Chinese Social and Political Science Review (Peking).
Current Opinion (New York).
Far Eastern Review (Shanghai).
Foreign Affairs (New York).
Harper's Monthly Magazine (New York).
Harper's Weekly (New York).
Independent (New York).
International Conciliation (New York).
Literary Digest (New York).
North China Herald and Supreme Court and Consular Gazette (Shanghai).
Outlook (New York).

Pacific Historical Review (Glendale, Calif.).
Pacific Review (Seattle).

D. NEWSPAPERS
Chicago Tribune (Chicago).
China Press (Shanghai).
London Times (London).
New York Times (New York).
New York Tribune (New York).
North China Daily News (Shanghai).
Hua-pei Jih-pao (in Chinese, Peking).
Shen Pao (in Chinese, Shanghai).
Sun (New York).
Ta-kung Pao (in Chinese, Tientsin).
Wall Street Journal (New York).
Washington Post (Washington, D. C.).

APPENDIX A

*Chinese People's Names Used in the Text and the Notes
and Their Corresponding Chinese Characters*

1. Chang Chih-tung 張之洞
2. Chang Chung-fu 張紱忠
3. Chao Wei-hsi 趙惟煕自
4. Chou Tzu-ch'i 周自齊
5. Chu Jui 朱瑞
6. Ch'en Chin-t'ao 陳錦濤
7. Feng Kuo-chang 馮國璋
8. Hsiung Hsi-ling 熊希齡
9. Hsü Shih-ch'ang 徐世昌
10. Huang Hsing 黃興
11. V. K. Wellington Koo (Ku Wei-chün) 顧維鈞
12. Li Lieh-chün 李烈鈞
13. Li Yüan-hung 黎元洪
14. Liang Shih-yi 梁士詒
15. Liang Tun-yen 梁敦彥
16. Lu Tseng-tsiang (Lu Cheng-hsiang) 陸徵祥
17. Lu Tsung-yü 陸宗輿
18. Wen Hwan Ma (Ma Wen-huan) 馬文煥
19. Kai Fu Shah (Hsia Chieh-fu) 夏偕復
20. Sheng Hsüan-huai 盛宣懷
21. Sun Yat-sen (Sun I-hsien) 孫逸仙
    (Also called Sun Wen or Sun Chung-shan) (孫文，孫中山)
22. Sung Chiao-jen 宋教仁
23. T'ang Shao-yi 唐紹儀
24. Ts'ao Ju-lin 曹汝霖
25. Tuan Ch'i-jui 段祺瑞
26. Wang Cheng-t'ing 王正廷
27. Wang Ch'ung-hui 王寵惠
28. Wang Yün-sheng 王芸生
29. Wu T'ing-fang 伍廷芳
30. Yang Tu 楊度
31. Yen Hsi-shan 閻錫山
32. Yüan K'o-ting 袁克定
33. Yüan Shih-k'ai 袁世凱

APPENDIX B

*Chinese Authors, Books and Newspapers Used in the Notes
and the Bibliography and Their Corresponding
Chinese Characters*

1. Chang Chung-fu 張忠紱 , *Chung-hua Min-kuo Wai-chiao Shih* 中華民國外交史
2. Ch'en Kung-lu 陳恭祿, *Chung-kuo Chin-tai Shih* 中國近代史
3. Ch'en Ju-hsüan 陳茹玄, *Tseng-ting Chung-kuo Hsien-fa Shih* 增訂中國憲法史
4. Chia I-chün 賈逸君 , *Chung-hua Min-kuo Shih* 中華民國史
5. K'ai-ming Ch'iu (Ch'iu K'ai-ming) 裘開明, *Mei-kuo Ha-fo Ta-hsüeh Yen-ching Hsüeh-she Han-Ho T'u-shu-kuan Han-chi Fen-lei Mu-lu* 美國哈佛大學燕京學社漢和圖書館漢籍分類目錄
6. Chung-kuo Wai-chiao-pu T'ung-chi-k'o 中國外交部統計科 *Min-kuo Chiu-nien-fen Wai-chiao Nien-chien* 民國九年份外交年鑑
7. Chung-kuo Yin-hang Ching-chi Yen-chiu-shih 中國銀行經濟研究室 *Chung-kuo Wai-chai Hui-pien* 中國外債彙編
8. Hoh To-yuen (Ho To-yüan) 何多源 , *Chung-wen Ts'an-k'ao-shu Chih-nan* 中文參考書指南
9. *Hua-pei Jih-pao* 華北日報
10. Juan Hsiang and others 阮湘等 , *Ti-i-hui Chung-kuo Nien-chien* 第一回中國年鑑
11. S. T. King (Chin Chao-tzu) 金兆梓 , *Hsien-tai Chung-kuo Wai-chiao Shih* 現代中國外交史
12. Li Chien-nung, 李劍農 , *Tsui-chin San-shih-nien Chung-kuo Cheng-chih Shih* 最近三十年中國政治史
13. Liu Yen 劉衍 , *Chung-hua Min-kuo Erh-shih-nien-lai Ta-shih-chi* 中華民國二十年來大事記
14. Liu Yen 劉彥 , *Ou-chan Ch'i-chien Chung-Jih Chiao-she Shih* 歐戰期間中日交涉史
15. Liu Yen 劉彥, *Ti-kuo-chu-i Ya-p'o Chung-kuo Shih* 帝國主義壓迫中國史
16. Ma Chen-tung 馬震東 , *Yüan-shih Tang-kuo Shih* 袁氏當國史
17. Pai Chiao 白蕉 , *Yüan Shih-k'ai yü Chung-kuo* 袁世凱與中國

18. Pan-su　牟粟, *Chung-shan Ch'u-shih hou Chung-kuo Liu-shih-nien Ta-shih-chi*　中山出世後中國六十年大事記
19. P'ing Hsin　平心, *Sheng-huo Ch'üan-kuo Tsung-shu-mu* 生活全國總書目
20. *Shen Pao*　申報
21. *Ta-kung Pao*　大公報
22. T'an T'ien-k'ai 譚天凱, *Shan-tung Wen-t'i Shih-mo*　山東問題始末
23. T'ang Ch'ing-tseng　唐慶增, *Chung-Mei Wai-chiao Shih* 中美外交史
24. Wai-chiao-pu　外交部, *Wai-chiao Wen-tu: Ts'an-chan An* 外交文牘：參戰案
25. Wang Yün-sheng　王芸生, *Liu-shih-nien-lai Chung-kuo yü Jih-pen*　六十年來中國與日本

Index

Cape Horn, 95
Carey, W. F., 187, 189
Carnegie, Andrew, loan by, 166
Caveat to Japan, 125-128
Chamber of Commerce of t h e United States, 69
Chang Chih-tung, 191
Changing Chinese, The, by Ross, 83
Chaochou, 104
Chefoo, 81, 102
Chekiang, 78, 167, 170, 190
Ch'en Chin-t'ao, 179, 180
Chengchiatun Affair, 210
Chicago loan, 192-193, 194, 212; opposition to, 192-193
Chicago, *News,* 43; *R e c o r d - Herald,* 43; *Tribune,* 68
Chihli, 78, 182, 189
China Revolutionized, by Thomson, 68
China Society of America, 60, 68
Chinda, Ambassador, 118, 119
Chinese-Anglo-American Friendship Association, 79
Chinese Parliament, 128
Chinese Republic, 39, 42, 48, 57-68, 76, 80-82, 84, 126, 139-141, 148, 206. *See also* Republic of China
Chou Tzu-ch'i, 27
Christianity in C h i n a , 5, 203, 204; *see also* Missionaries
Ch'un, Prince, 24
Chungchow, 190
Civil War, 140, 141
Clark University movement for recognition, 68
Coaling station on Samsah Bay, 116-118
Coalition government, 63
Coastal defence, 183
Commerce. *See* Trade
Concert of the powers, 64-66, 69, 74, 80, 81

Concessions, economic, 24; foreign settlements, 92; oil, 168-169; to foreign powers, 116-120
Congress, 62, 66, 67, 69
Conservation project, Huai River, 184-189
Consortiums, banking, 5, 19, 23-55; Five-Power, 47, 166, 168; Four-Power, loans by, 24-28; policy, reversion to, 175; Six-Power, 6, 28, 163, 169, 173, 174, 180; withdrawal of the United States, 23-55, 211-212; withdrawal, Chinese views on, 45, 46; withdrawal, newspaper and foreign opinions of, 43-45
Constitution, Nanking, 158
Constitution, Provisional, 142
Consular Body of Shanghai, 141
Continental a n d Commercial Trust and Savings Bank, 192, 194
Cooperation, international, 5
Council, National, 63
Council of State, 149, 153
Crane, Charles R., 83
Crisp, G. Birch and Company, loan agreement by, 29-30
Cuba, 74
Culture, Western and Eastern, 12
Currency, depreciation of, 167; reform, 25, 27, 167-168, 170; reform loan agreement, 168

Dairen, 103
Davis, Arthur P., 185
Davison, Henry P., 32, 33, 35, 36, 40
Debts. *See* Consortiums; Loans
Defence, coastal, 183
Demands by Japan. *See* Twenty-One Demands
Democracy, 5, 6, 205